Books by Stephen Davis

Reggae Bloodlines (1977)
Reggae International (1982)
  (both with Peter Simon)
Bob Marley (1983)
Hammer of the Gods (1985)
Say Kids! What Time Is It? (1987)

Say Kids!
WHAT TIME IS IT?

Buffalo Bob Smith and Howdy Doody circa 1950. (EDDIE KEAN COLLECTION)

Say Kids!
WHAT TIME IS IT?
Notes from the Peanut Gallery

BY
STEPHEN DAVIS

LITTLE, BROWN AND COMPANY
Boston   Toronto

"It's Howdy Doody Time" by John Crosby
from the *New York Herald Tribune* (1951), © I.H.T. Corporation.
Reprinted by permission.

Howdy Doody and all related characters © 1987
National Broadcasting Company, Inc. All rights reserved.
Howdy Doody is a trademark of NBC, Inc.

Library of Congress Cataloging-in-Publication Data

Davis, Stephen, 1947–
  Say Kids! What time is it?

  1. Howdy Doody Show (Television program)
I. Title.
PN1992.77.H663D38 1987   791.45'72   87-3256
ISBN 0-316-17662-1

RRD VA

*Published simultaneously in Canada
by Little, Brown & Company (Canada) Limited*

PRINTED IN THE UNITED STATES OF AMERICA

Dedicated with love
to my father,
Howard Lawrence Davis

Here a knave in a fool's coat,
with a trumpet sounding or a drum
beating invites you to see his
puppets. Here a rogue like a wild
woodman, or in an antic shape like an
incubus, desires your company to
view his motion.
—*Bartholomew Fair*

Contents

Part One

1947–1952

It is some years now, since we first conceived a strong veneration for Clowns, and an intense anxiety to know what they did with themselves out of pantomime time, and off the stage. As a child, we were accustomed to pester our relations and friends with questions out of number concerning these gentry; — whether their appetite for sauşages and such like wares was always the same, and if so, at whose expense they were maintained; whether they were ever taken up for pilfering other people's goods, or were forgiven by everybody because it was always done in fun; how it was they got such beautiful complexions, and where they lived; and whether they were born Clowns, or gradually turned into Clowns as they grew up. On these and a thousand other points our curiosity was insatiable. Nor were our speculations confined to clowns alone: they were extended to Harlequins, Pantaloons, and Columbines, all of whom we believed to be real and veritable personages, existing in the same forms and characters all the year round. How often have we wished that Pantaloon were our god-father! And how often thought that to marry a Columbine would be to attain the highest pitch of all human felicity.

— "Boz" (Charles Dickens),
Memoirs of Joseph Grimaldi

Judy Tyler as Princess Summerfall Winterspring, 1950. (COURTESY LORELEI HESS)

One

The Dream

ARE YOU OLD ENOUGH to remember Princess Summerfall Winterspring? I'm only asking because she came to me in a dream the other night. It was one of those very clear dreams in the astral-travel style. Everything was in compatible color and Dolby stereo, one of those predawn excursions in which You Are There.

It was a shocker to see the Princess again. I hadn't seen her in the flesh in thirty-five years. She'd been dead almost as long.

In this dream, I was a child again, barefoot on a forest carpet of pine needles, like at my old summer camp. Suddenly Princess Summerfall Winterspring stepped from behind a big spruce and startled me. I could hear wind rushing through the boughs and water flowing down a brook. The scent of honeysuckle was in the air. The Princess looked right at me, appearing exactly as she had to millions of children every day in the early 1950s on the old *Howdy Doody* show: seventeen years old and elegantly coltish, with bombshell dark eyes and jet-black braids, buckskin shirt and leggings, topped by a sky-blue crown decorated with symbols of the four seasons that were her mystical dominion.

In the old days, when I was a kid backstage in Studio 3A at NBC, Princess Summerfall Winterspring would have bubbled with sparky enthusiasm and might have given me a little hug. But in my dream she only looked at me rather gravely and said, "Come and find me." That was all. Then I woke up.

"Come and find me." They were haunting words because Princess Summerfall Winterspring, Howdy Doody's vividly imagined princess of the Tinka Tonka tribe, is truly a lost soul, a faint glow in the collective imagination of the now-grown children of postwar America — the so-called Baby Boom. Once she was one of the biggest stars in America. Today she's remembered, if at all, as the embod-

4

iment of the innocence and security experienced by many of us who grew up in the prosperous and safe America of the 1950s. Now she was calling to me in dreamtime, commanding me to find her. Where had she gone? What could be gained by searching for her, other than an elusive memory? It all happened so long ago. I had to ask myself if there was anything I could even remember about the Princess. In fact, I was amazed that my life had progressed to the point where it was possible for me to remember back three decades and more.

Thinking about the Princess and my childhood as a Baby Boomer, my mind kept returning to an incident in 1952, when I was five years old and deeply in love with both Princess Summerfall Winterspring and the teenage actress who played her, Judy Tyler. Like all the other kids on my street (and in the country) in those days, I tuned in to *Howdy Doody* every weeknight at five-thirty to see what was happening in Doodyville. There was Buffalo Bob and his boy-puppet friend, Howdy, trying to prevent the Doodyville Circus from falling into the clutches of the elderly capitalist, Mr. Phineas T. Bluster, and his unwitting stooge Dilly Dally. At the same time, Howdy was running for reelection as President of the Kids of America, trying for a repeat of his stunning landslide of 1948. And there were other problems. Chief Thunderthud was outraged because that maniac of the seltzer bottle, Clarabell the clown, was seeking admittance into the Chief's sacred tribe, the Ooragnak. The Flubadub, a bizarre marionette composed of portions of various animals, was in a state because another puppet, Inspector John J. Fadoozle, the World's Number One (sound effect: *BOINNGG!)* Private Eye, had made off with Flub's favorite food, a plate of meatballs and spaghetti. There was always lots of light conflict, rivalry, and manipulation on *Howdy Doody;* basically it was a soap opera for kids. But all the slapstick stopped when they brought out Princess Summerfall Winterspring. When the Princess toed her mark in front of a big Image Orthikon camera in the NBC studio in New York and sang Howdy's campaign theme — "I'm for Howdy Doody" — the children of America just died for love. So did many of their fathers, who had started watching *Howdy* after the irrepressibly sexy Judy Tyler got the part. So did *Howdy*'s aggressive sponsors — Wonder Bread, Hostess Twinkies, Poll Parrot shoes, Ovaltine, Kellogg's — who kept the show's advertising time sold out during its thirteen-year run, from 1947 through 1960. And so did I, entranced by the little Princess who cavorted in black-and-white on the ten-inch screen of my father's blond console television in the living room of our house on Long Island.

In those days I thought I was pretty special, because I was a fairly regular member of the Peanut Gallery, that itching and squirming kid-filled bleacher that overlooked Doodyville. This despite the fact that the Peanut Gallery was the hottest ticket in the country, at least for the under-ten set and their parents. But I became a true Peanut in 1952 when my father, Howard Davis, an NBC staff director since 1948, was hired to direct the show, which he did for two years before he became Howdy's chief writer and script supervisor in 1954. The reflected glory of my family situation stood me well in the schoolyard. The boys all wanted to know if Buffalo Bob was a nice guy and how did TV work anyway? The girls wanted the inside scoop on the Princess. I couldn't tell them much, but my best friends got tickets to the show. Once in second grade a boy who definitely would never get a coveted spot in the Peanut Gallery called me Doody-brain, and I was embarrassed, but mostly, like all the people connected to the show in one way or another, I've dined out on Howdy ever since.

But now I'm almost forty years old, and Princess Summerfall Winterspring has started calling to me in my sleep. And yet, unprodded until recently by photographs, my memories of her were pretty dim, even though she was the luscious young goddess of my early life. I could remember almost peeing with joy when I met Judy Tyler in costume for the first time and she knelt and put her vivid white face close to mine to greet me. And that was about it, as far as my conscious memory went. Think back to your own childhood and see how much you can remember from age five.

So I did now what I would have done back then. I called my mother, who remembers the Princess quite well. She reminded me that Judy Tyler came to a big party at our house in 1952 and scandalized the neighborhood's young mothers with her exaggerated show-biz manners and salty backstage mouth. This jogged my own memories of that party, which was an important event on our quiet suburban street, since most of *Howdy Doody*'s cast was there, as well as other NBC luminaries. The party swam into focus as a big cooked turkey wrapped in yellow cellophane, a red-jacketed bartender, lots of laughter and clinking cocktail glasses and cigarette smoke. I also had the following unexpected memory for the first time in decades. Having been put to bed after the eagerly awaited arrival of Judy Tyler, I snuck downstairs about an hour later. Since I wasn't allowed to be at the party, I peeked into my parents' room. Coats were piled high on the bed, and I could hear low, muffled voices. When I stuck my head through the door I saw Judy Tyler — my Princess Summerfall Winterspring — passionately embracing a man whose face I couldn't see. Mortified, I closed the door and climbed back up to my room. As I trudged up the staircase, my ears felt hot, and it occurred to me that the man Judy was kissing didn't look like the man who had brought her to the party.

This stolen image of Judy Tyler is much stronger in my mind than any I have of the Princess, but reflecting on it I was ashamed to say that I couldn't be sure the scene had really happened. For several days after talking with my mother I thought I might have dreamed this incident as well, since dreams and memories often meld when viewing childhood from the mid-peak promontory of middle age. So I called my mother again and told her of this memory and asked her if what I remembered were possible. Would Judy Tyler have kissed somebody in the coatroom? Absolutely, said my mother. My father, who knew the princess much better since he had worked with her for two years, said he wasn't certain but would think about it.

Then I decided I had to respond to Princess Summerfall Winterspring's dreamy summons and try to find her. My quest, as it turned out, would involve more than a year of searching out and interviewing dozens of *Howdy Doody* veterans, including most of the show's surviving cast and crew, all now retired or nearing retirement in late middle age. I tracked the millionaire television pioneer Buffalo Bob Smith to his lakeside camp in the remote forests of northern Maine and asked him about the Princess. He told me some stories but only went so far, sensibly commenting that he wouldn't want to take a chance on wrecking any long-term marriages still in progress. Then I found the three Clarabells; one of them didn't want to talk about the Princess. Chief Thunderthud did, but I had to stop him. I even visited the retired Howdy Doody. Like me, he was born in 1947, but his career really ended when he was only thirteen. Today, unfortunately, he is institutionalized in Washington, D.C. On the subject of his old friend Princess Summerfall Winterspring, he was mute.

When I finally found the elusive Princess — forever young, enshrined in stone and celluloid — all I could do was wipe the tears from my face and marvel. Princess Summerfall Winterspring is still my personal goddess, nearly two score years down the road.

In the process, I learned the true history of *The Howdy Doody Show*. I uncovered the nearly forgotten earliest days of television in New York and met some of its founding technocrats. I recovered dusty sixteen-millimeter kinescope recordings (henceforth referred to as kines, pronounced "kinnies") from damp cellars of former *Howdy* crew members. And I rediscovered television as that notorious slayer of the minds of children, including my own.

The best part of my quest was talking to my own generation, which for the purposes of Howdy Doody proved to be almost anyone born in America between 1943 and 1955. Everyone born during the Baby Boom has memories of Howdy's show (not all of them pleasant), as if the show had left an indelible brand upon my generation. The inhabitants of Doodyville, both wooden and human, colonized the consciousness of postwar American children and made as strong an impression as the atomic air-raid drills and polio shots with which we all grew up.

And then there was my own somewhat confused childhood, with its uncertain memories shifting like glass shards in a kaleidoscope. At the root of everything, I wanted to know: what was a real memory and what was a dream? So I began to ask the people who had been there, people I had known in childhood. Here is what I found out.

When the earliest experimental Howdy Doody program was shown on NBC's fledgling three-station network late in 1947 under its original title, *Puppet Playhouse,* it marked the first time that the ancient juvenile theater arts of clowning, puppetry, mime, and song had ever been broadcast to a mass audience of children. In this sense, Howdy Doody has his roots in the millennia of human theatrical activity. But in the modern age Howdy's family tree can be traced as far back as the first years of the twentieth century, the era of flamboyant showmen like Buffalo Bill Cody and P. T. Barnum and of visionary inventors like Thomas Edison and Guglielmo Marconi. Although he practically invented television, Howdy Doody was actually born on the radio.

Radio itself is considered to have been born, for practical purposes, when Signore Marconi sent the coded letter *S* across the Atlantic ocean using "wireless" radio waves in 1901. Cut to New York in April 1912. A nervous rumor scurries through the city rooms of

Gotham's aggressively competitive press: the New York office of the White Star Line has lost radio contact with its heavily publicized "unsinkable" luxury liner, the *Titanic*. There are fears that the great ship has gone down, with much loss of glamorous life, but the press has no way of verifying the story. So they besiege the office of the Marconi Wireless Company as the first day's fateful messages beam in from the rescue ships on the scene. The tragedy makes a national figure of a young Russian immigrant named David Sarnoff, who tirelessly mans the radio shack above the Marconi office in the days after the *Titanic* is lost. The loss of the ship is the first important news story to come off the wireless and establishes the radio as a vital planetary communications system.

In 1920, the first commercial radio station, KDKA, went on the air in Pittsburgh, with evening-only broadcasts paid for by equipment manufacturers RCA and Westinghouse. The following year the newly formed Radio Corporation of America (RCA) gobbled up Marconi Wireless; the general manager of the new company was former Marconi employee David Sarnoff. In 1922 the first advertising time was sold in New York when a Queens entrepreneur advertised his apartments on WEAF, a local station owned and operated by AT&T. The apartments sold out immediately, and soon the great department stores — Wanamakers, Altman's, Saks — wanted to buy time to sell products. In early 1923, RCA linked six of its stations in different cities into a radio network via telephone cable, and the network broadcast Calvin Coolidge's State of the Union address live from the Capitol. The age of radio had begun.

Even early on, there was a big problem with the commercials. At the dawn of the radio age in the early twenties, Secretary of Commerce Herbert Hoover declared it "inconceivable that we should allow so great a possibility for service [as radio] to be drowned in advertising chatter." Hoover and others supported a British-style government-owned broadcasting system, strictly regulated and supported by taxes and subscriptions. Radio receivers would have been heavily taxed under this system, which was defeated after David Sarnoff told a congressional committee that "the air belongs to the people. Its main highways should be maintained for the main travel. To collect a tax from the radio audience would be a reversion to the days of toll roads and bridges; to the days when schools were not public and free and when public libraries were unknown."

Yet, in the early days, when radio receivers were expensive and mainly the playthings of the well-to-do, many companies considered that direct advertising — "the pitch" — was vulgar and unscientific. Instead, the advertising agencies decided that their clients should "sponsor" popular programs so that radio listeners would buy their products in gratitude. Thus, in 1925, the National Carbon Company hired RCA's network of fourteen stations to broadcast *The Ever-Ready Hour* to present its musical artists "in original radio creations." From then on, advertisers would produce (and control) network broadcasting in America, using studios and facilities owned by the stations themselves.

Until 1926 the Radio Corporation of America was controlled by a consortium that included General Electric and Bell Telephone, but that year an antitrust decision forced the telephone company out of commercial broadcasting. RCA established the first permanent radio network, the National Broadcasting Company (NBC), to connect its flagship station, WEAF, acquired from Bell Telephone, to other "affiliate" stations around the country. The service was launched (as far as Kansas City) with a gala concert by the new NBC Orchestra, conducted by Walter Damrosch. And in November 1926, the first coast-to-coast broadcast featured that annual pageant of the American elite, the Harvard-Yale Game.

In its first years, NBC charged its local affiliates about ninety dollars an hour for its network programming. The stations hated this system, whereby they had to pay for programs. The stations wanted the networks as advertisers — *clients* — not suppliers. In 1928 many big affiliates switched to a new network in New York, the Columbia Broadcasting System, because CBS offered its stations unsponsored programs for free, in return for an option on the station's advertising time if the network could sell it. This way, CBS's time salesmen could offer guaranteed network coverage for a sponsor's show. NBC was forced in turn to adopt this system on what would evolve into its two chains of stations, the Red and Blue networks.

This is how advertising created the centrally controlled New York broadcasting networks. The advertisers produced the programming and bought a half hour on a network of stations around the country. The cost of the advertising time included the use of network studios, and was much less than what the advertisers would have had to spend on the stations individually. Companies didn't sponsor shows, their products did, so it was important that a product never be sullied by questionable editorial content. Even when the network actually produced the programming, the advertiser (as buyer and client) exercised final control. It wasn't really a joke at all that radio's greatest wit and comedian, Fred Allen, joked ruefully for years about "the man from the sponsor" who wouldn't let him do gags about booze and girls on the air.

Meanwhile, television was already on the scene, at least in the laboratories of the big equipment manufacturers — RCA, General Electric, Westinghouse. The idea of "seeing by telegraph" had intrigued inventors since the early 1870s, when it was discovered that the electrical conductivity of the "magical" element selenium varied when the element was exposed to light. Within ten years a German scientist had patented a device for sending pictures by wire. But nothing really came of it until another Russian emigré, Dr. Vladimir Kosma Zworykin, patented a couple of his inventions in 1923 and 1924.

Zworykin, the true father of the tube, earned his degree in electrical engineering from the Saint Petersburg Institute of Technology in 1912. At S.P.I.T. they were trying to perfect the cumbersome mechanical system of whirling perforated disks that dominated the early, ill-fated experiments with television; but Zworykin believed that the future of the medium lay instead in the direction of the new cathode-ray tube. Zworykin came to America after World War I, and joined Westinghouse in 1920. In 1923 he patented the Iconoscope camera tube; the following year he patented the Kinescope picture tube. Together, these formed the first electronic television system. The first demonstration of the new system was held in Pittsburgh in 1924 for an audience of executives of the Westinghouse Electric and Manufacturing Company. A few days later, Dr. Zworykin was informed that the demonstration had been interesting, but that his time might be better spent on something a little more useful.

Parallel developments in television technology abounded throughout the 1920s. In 1927 Herbert Hoover appeared in a mechanical television transmission, over wires from Washington to New York, that dimly displayed the future president's silhouette via a light-and-spinning-disk system. A similar device was used the following year to telecast a play at General Electric's headquarters in Schenectady, New York.

In 1929 Vladimir Zworykin held another demonstration for his employers at Westinghouse. His refined Iconoscope, which vastly reduced the amount of light needed to capture a viable image, would become the heart of the first practical television camera. But Westinghouse was still not impressed, so Zworykin took his machine to David Sarnoff at RCA. How much, Sarnoff asked, would Zworykin need to perfect his system? "About a hundred thousand dollars," his fellow Russian replied. Years later, General David Sarnoff would enjoy telling people that RCA had spent nearly fifty million dollars before it ever got a penny back from television. The same year Zworykin joined RCA, he obtained his first patent for color television.

During the 1930s, the most interesting developments in television technology took place outside the United States. By 1930 an Englishman named J. L. Baird was selling television receivers for £130. These received video signals that Baird broadcast from the BBC after the radio station had signed off for the night. Six years later, engineers at Electrical and Mechanical Industries (EMI) developed an improved version of the Iconoscope and called it the Emitron; it was adapted by the BBC and used to televise the coronation of King George VI in 1937. But the first television broadcast of any real power was achieved when Adolf Hitler opened the 1936 Olympic Games in Germany. (Some scientists believe that this electromagnetic image of Hitler is still cascading through outer space and will be the first television image of life on Earth to be picked up by any monitoring extraterrestrial intelligence.)

In 1939 New York hosted the greatest World's Fair in history at a site on Flushing Meadows in Queens. Symbolized by large geometrical constructions called the Perisphere and the Trylon, the 1939 World's Fair provided a tantalizing glimpse of what technology and engineering would offer the world someday, despite the obviously perilous times that were to follow. The biggest sensation of the '39 Fair was the RCA Exhibition Hall, in which overflowing and incredulous crowds witnessed the first public wireless television broadcasts in America. All they saw were talking heads, but that was enough — it was a miracle right out of Jules Verne or H. G. Wells! RCA held an FCC license for these experimental broadcasts; their revised system — 441 electronic "lines" on the TV camera and screen — preceded the more precise 525-line system that would come into use in 1946. RCA television receivers sold for $625, a small fortune in those days. In 1940, RCA took its television exhibit on a national tour of universities, which proved to be very influential. Even though Europe was on fire and its lights were going out, those who marveled at RCA's brilliant new toy realized that there might be a future after all.

What was on TV in those days? Not much: news, boxing, talking heads. But then America went off to World War II, and the scientists and engineers were forced to drop fun gadgets like TV and turn to more serious items like radar and atoms. NBC's executive in charge of television, Warren Wade, left to command the Army Signal Corps Photo Center at D. W. Griffith's old Astoria studio in Queens, where Wade made propaganda films (and, in the bargain, assembled some of the future technocrats of the *Howdy Doody* show). Yet television development continued at RCA on a small scale despite the war. It wasn't so much that the technology advanced, but that the language and imagery of television began to be invented. In 1944, for instance, NBC broadcast one-hour versions of the operas *Carmen* and *La Bohème*. The director, Dr. Herbert Graf, devised techniques for these shows that were basically shorthand versions of cinematic methods. Thus, in movielike sequence during a musical prelude, Graf introduced a scene from *La Bohème* with titles, lettered in nineteenth-century type, to indicate the period; turned pages of an enlarged volume of Murger's *La Vie de Bohème* for expository description; used a three-dimensional model of snowy Paris rooftops to establish locale. A camera shot through high studio windows caught a full-scale detail of gables and made the transition into Rodolfo's attic in a matter of seconds; the camera then dollied away to include first the poet at his desk, then the cold, fireless, cracked-plaster atelier. Television's earliest artists were already learning that a TV studio, unlike a stage set, is never seen in its entirety, and that the roving eye of the Iconoscope required careful set dressing. Three or more cameras were directed toward a single small acting area under broiling hot lights. Suggestive props had to be relied on to set a scene: a quill pen replaced a Tudor arch; the table laid for dinner, rather than the complete room, revealed the economic status of the family group. These were the small-scale experiments that sustained the growth of television during the dark years of the war.

In 1945 the United States emerged the victor from World War II. Despite great hopes for the future, the country was still caught up in the psychology of the Depression years, which had been reinforced by the austerity and rationing measures of the war. Television receivers were available but prohibitively expensive, rich men's toys. Radio was still king. When, in 1945, the FCC announced that any qualified company could be awarded up to five local television licenses in the VHF band, nobody really cared. CBS took only one of the licenses available to it. Nobody really thought that television would ever . . . *catch on.* Who cared about those fuzzy little five-inch TV pictures when you could go out to the movies and be riveted by giant images of Humphrey Bogart and Lauren Bacall? TV was an overpriced piece of hardware for which no software was available, even when regular programming began in 1946. Later, of course, CBS would be forced to buy back its discarded licenses for tens of millions of dollars. New York radio magnates would thank God that Doc Zworykin hadn't taken his spurned invention to Hollywood. (If he had, then the movies, not radio, would have controlled television.) But in 1946, hardly anyone even wanted to *be* on television. It was a real problem. TV couldn't get arrested! The great radio stars — Fred Allen, Eddie Cantor, Jimmy Durante, Kate Smith — weren't interested.

What was needed was a new generation of young radio performers with the vision to see that, in midcentury, a new era was about to commence, and that radio would be this era's victim rather than its herald.

The first of this new generation was already in place at NBC by August 1946. The previous month, a press release from NBC's New York radio outlet, WEAF, had announced: "Bob Smith, one of radio's top-rated daytime personalities, moves to New York and WEAF for new morning program."

Enter Buffalo Bob.

The press release went on to say that its new drive-time jock was being given six and a quarter hours of air time per week, the largest time segment ever granted by WEAF to a single personality. "He is Bob Smith, who within a short time on [Buffalo's] WBEN built that city's most popular daytime programs through his style of presenting piano music, songs, recordings, light commentary, news headlines, time signals and weather reports." The release went on to note that expectations for Smith's success were so high that his show's advertising time had been sold out even before Smith went on the air; sponsors included the *Saturday Evening Post,* Eastern Air Lines, Colgate Dental Cream, *Colliers* magazine, Steero Jellied Consommé, Halo, Supersuds, and the *New York Herald Tribune.*

At the age of twenty-eight, Bob Smith had been raised to the pinnacle of local radio broadcasting in the United States. But it was only a logical step in a career steeped in both music and radio, one that began almost as soon as Bob Smith learned to walk.

Buffalo Bob Smith, television father-figure to an entire generation of Baby Boomers, was born in Buffalo, New York, in 1917, the fourth and youngest child of a second-generation German-American carpenter named Emil Schmidt and his wife, Emma, the daughter of Gottholt Kuehn, a Lutheran pastor. The German-American communities of western New York State had a rich musical tradition, and Robert Schmidt showed talent early; at four he could recreate any melody on the piano with two fingers. His father, a master carpenter and frustrated trombone player, made Robert practice every night, telling the boy to play *"von hertz"* — from the heart.

One day at work, in the mid-1920s, Emil Schmidt was hit in the head by a slab of wet concrete and lost his sight in one eye. Since he had to stop working, he amused himself by becoming an avid radio listener. Emil's hobby was "DX-ing," tuning in remote stations on a three-dial radio. He kept a radio scrapbook, and the whole Schmidt family, like every other family in America, was glued to the receiver for major shows like *The Shadow* and *The Atwater Kent Auditions*. Every Saturday the man from the radio store came to the house, removed the radio's spent battery, and replaced it with a recharged cell. Almost everyone who grew up in that era, including Buffalo Bob, ultimately preferred radio to television. Radio let people think and conjure up images and ideas in their minds. People back then could actually *see* Amos driving his cab down the street in *Amos & Andy*. When Fibber McGee opened his closet door to see who was hiding there, the entire nation *knew* what that old door looked like. Bob Smith grew up in an era when he could walk to church on Tuesday evenings for his Boys' Club meeting listening to *Amos & Andy* during the whole half-hour trek, because the entire neighborhood and town had the radio on and windows open to catch the evening breeze.

Bob Smith first went on the air in 1928, when he was just eleven years old. He and his dad always listened to a show called *Boys Club of the Air* on WGR in Buffalo. One day Emil Schmidt told his talented son to try to get on that show. So young Robert went down to WGR for an audition and was hired — *allowed,* actually — to play piano for the station's youth orchestra. On other nights Bob played piano for a string trio or sang with a boys' glee club.

In 1933, his last year in high school, Robert Schmidt formed a vocal trio with two other boys, which they called the High Hatters. It was the year of Repeal (of Prohibition), and the boys were fortunate when Simon Beer, one of the largest breweries in Buffalo, started a radio program on WBEN, a station owned by the Buffalo *Evening News.* The High Hatters auditioned for the *Simon Supper Club of the Air,* sang the then-current pop hit "Smooth Sailin'," and got the job at twenty-five dollars per show, three shows a week — very respectable wages in the depths of the Depression.

Elated at his good luck, Bob Schmidt ran home to tell his father the amazing news. When he got to the house he saw his mother standing at the top of the stairs. She told Robert to run for the doctor, who came right over and pronounced Emil Schmidt dead of a heart attack. Fifty years later, with tears in his eyes, Bob Smith remembers how his father used to love to hear the High Hatters floating their harmonies in practice, how Emil used to make popcorn for the boys . . .

The High Hatters performed on the *Simon Supper Club of the Air* for just over a year. Then in 1934 the patriotic pop singer Kate Smith came to Buffalo to hold auditions for her top-rated CBS show, sponsored by Hudson Terraplane automobiles. The High Hatters beat 950 other contestants and went to New York City with Kate Smith. There the trio was discovered by an announcer named Tom Kennedy, who paired them with his wife in a vaudeville act — Micki and her Boyfriends — that played around New York and Long Island for six months until Robert Schmidt got homesick for the coziness of family, church, and neighborhood back in Buffalo.

So by 1935, at the age of eighteen, Robert Schmidt was a seasoned entertainer, piano player, and on-air personality. Back in Buffalo, he formed a vocal duo called Jack & Gill for WGR, where he landed a job as staff pianist. The station sold the boys to Personal Finance and sent Jack & Gill out over the CBS network every Saturday at one-fifteen in the afternoon. Bob also did local shows on WGR as Smilin' Bob Smith. But the "Bob Smith" radio personality didn't really appear until 1937, when Bob Schmidt emceed and wrote comedy sketches for a morning show on the Mutual Network (WGR was a Mutual affiliate) from eleven to eleven-thirty, *The Cheer Up Gang.* The show featured plenty of music and dialect humor for Buffalo's huge immigrant audiences. Bob did the voices: a dumb Polish character named Lukie (Buffalo's population was fifty percent Polish by that time); a Jewish character, Yitzie Goldfinger; an *Amos & Andy*–style takeoff on the Ink Spots that Bob called the Pink Spots. As a musician, Bob Smith was famous for and proud of his perfect pitch. His good ear carried over into accents, voices, and characters as well. In many ways, Yitzie the Yid and Lukie the Polack were ancestors of the characters that emerged on *Howdy Doody* ten years later.

In 1940, Robert Schmidt married his childhood sweetheart, Mildred Metz, and changed his name to Bob Smith so he could more easily cash checks made out to his *nom de radio*. The BBD&O ad agency hired him to write and emcee a show for Corning Glass using talent recruited from Corning's nine thousand employees (whose normal occupations involved making Pyrex and bomb sights). Smith did *The Corning Glass Works Family Hour* for three years, broadcasting from Ithaca and Elmira and earning $350 a week, again princely wages. He also continued to do his other shows at WGR.

But Bob Smith's big break in Buffalo radio came in 1942, when WGR's popular morning disc jockey Clint Buehlman defected to NBC affiliate WBEN and Smith was hired to replace him. Emceeing a big Series E war-bond rally in downtown Buffalo's Lafayette Square on an hour-long broadcast for WGR, Smith got his chance: the rally's star attraction, singer Wee Bonny Baker, didn't want to perform her big hit of the day, "Oh Johnny," because she didn't have any musicians to back her. Bob Smith saved the day; the expert pianist told Bonny he would comp for her on his upright. Then he teased the crowd and his radio audience until they pledged fifteen thousand dollars to hear Wee Bonny do "Oh Johnny." It was a sales record for a bond rally in Buffalo, which made the news and impressed local sponsors.

Soon Bob got a call from WBEN. The most popular morning show on network radio at the time was CBS's *Breakfast Club,* broadcast from Chicago from 9:00 to 10:00 A.M. and hosted by Don McNeil. McNeil always had big ratings in New York and grabbed WBEN's audience after the 9:00–9:15 NBC news. So WBEN hired Bob Smith and put him on at 9:15 against Don McNeil.

Bob's show was called *Early Date at Hengerer's.* It was on every morning from 9:15 to 10:00 A.M., broadcast from the Tea Room of Hengerer's department store. The show was designed to hold the western New York audience between the NBC morning news and NBC's first network broadcast at 10:00 A.M. To accomplish this, Bob would perform songs and skits and play records for a hundred gals from, say, the ladies' auxiliary of the Lackawanna Fire Department. While the ladies ate breakfast, Bob would run nutty contests — the heaviest handbag, the oldest grandchild, "Stump Bob Smith" by trying to name a tune he couldn't play on the piano.

Within six months, Bob Smith buried Don McNeil in Buffalo. In that time, the ratings for *Early Date at Hengerer's* skyrocketed.

At NBC's headquarters, a majestic gray granite skyscraper at 30 Rockefeller Plaza in New York City, the big radio boys soon started to hear about this show in Buffalo that was out-McNeiling Don McNeil. So they sent a scout out to Buffalo, who cut an acetate recording of Bob's show and took it back to New York. Meanwhile, Bob started a solo lunchtime show from twelve to one, playing records and his ever-present piano, keeping track of exactly what key the records were in so that, for instance, when Dinah Shore's monster hit "Buttons and Bows" came on, he could sing along with her. They loved this in Buffalo, and soon Bob's lunch show was also top-rated. Best of all, the Men from the Sponsor loved him too. Bob talked their language, and the advertising time on his shows was always sold out. He was making very good money.

After the war ended in the spring of 1945, millions of American warriors came home, got married, started families, and resumed their rudely interrupted lives. Radio and the movies were still the country's entertainment, and in New York, NBC still had a problem. Their morning lineup on their flagship New York station, WEAF, was a hodgepodge of jingles and news emceed by Robert Q. Lewis. Mornings over at CBS featured a seemingly unbeatable radio institution, Arthur Godfrey. Also ahead of NBC in the ratings was the legendary John Gambling on Mutual's WOR. NBC needed an early-morning drivetime personality, so they sent another man out to Buffalo to look at Bob Smith and to put another hour of Bob's act on acetate.

In the spring of 1946 New York called, and Smith went to talk to NBC. For Bob Smith, this was it. New York was the Big Time, the Varsity! Years later he told a reporter, "I could've jumped up and kissed the moon!" But not before he did a little negotiating. The network told him that the powerful New York musicians' union, Local 802, wouldn't let him play the piano on the air until he had completed a six-month residency requirement. Smith shocked NBC by telling them to forget it. After all, the upright piano was Bob Smith's prop — his very *act*. So in May 1946 NBC leaned on the union and got an OK for their new morning man's piano. Bob and his wife, Mil, flew to New York, signed the contracts, and bought a big Tudor-style house at 195 Paine Avenue in suburban New Rochelle, in what had been Revolutionary writer Thomas Paine's old cherry orchard.

In August 1946, Bob Smith took over as WEAF's morning disc jockey. His workday began at 5:30 A.M., and he went on the air at 7:05. He didn't exactly out-Godfrey Arthur Godfrey at first, but he held his own. Buffalo Bob's career had begun in earnest.

Howdy Doody was born the following year.

Frank Paris's original Howdy Doody, 1948. (PHOTO: ELLEN LORD. COURTESY ALAN COOK, INTERNATIONAL PUPPETRY MUSEUM PHOTO ARCHIVES)

Two

Puppet Playhouse

HOWDY DOODY AND I were both born late in 1947. Howdy is slightly older. His voice (if not his actual body) was born in a midtown radio studio in the spring of that year, the creation of Bob Smith in his role as host of a kid's radio quizzer called *Triple B Ranch*. I came along in September, arriving at a private maternity hospital on Park Avenue at the corner of East Eighty-third Street. My father, Howard Davis, was a young NBC employee who had been a major in the Army Air Corps in England, where he met and married my mother, Hana Fischer, an Austrian-born refugee. My parents had settled on Long Island earlier in the year and, like millions of families at the end of the war, set about having children — the Baby Boom.

It was an interesting year to come alive. America was still reeling from the deprivations and heartbreak of the war years. Rationing was still in partial effect, and people lived with Eggless Thursdays and Meatless Mondays. A film about the difficulties faced by returning combat veterans, *The Best Years of Our Lives,* won the Academy Award. And it was a year of grief and funerals, as thousands of American bodies were shipped home from all over the world. President Harry Truman ordered General Marshall, the Army chief of staff, to oversee an immense plan to rebuild the industrial world at American expense. America the Victorious was beginning to flex her muscles over her new empire.

Other headlines: the United Nations partitioned Palestine. An English princess named Elizabeth married Philip Mountbatten. Al Capone died, and Bugsy Siegel was machine-gunned. Boss Petrillo of the Musicians' Union banned all recordings as unfair to musicians. General Eisenhower was named president of Columbia University and became the dark-horse presidential candidate of the Republicans. In a widely publicized battle of the bandleaders, Tommy Dorsey punched out the King of Swing, Benny Goodman. Jackie Robinson broke the color barrier in major-league baseball and reached the World Series despite a vicious campaign of spikings and beanballs and the threat of a National League players' strike. Babe Ruth's farewell at Yankee Stadium choked up millions of Americans who listened to the Sultan of Swat say goodbye on the radio. New Yorkers were stunned by Mayor Paul O'Dwyer's request for an eight-cent transit fare, as well as the news that Loew's State theater on Broadway was dropping vaudeville and would just show movies!

Those who lived through it remember 1947 as a time of great excitement and innovation. There was a sense that the immediate postwar years marked the end of an old era, and that America, as it approached the midcentury, would lead the world with good intentions and technological expertise. Emblematic of this new technology was television.

Most televisions in use in 1947 were only five inches wide and made their subjects look — according to Fred Allen's famous derisory remark — like a collection of passport photos. But this was the year that television changed from chalk talks and boxing matches to entertainment and news, entering the mainstream of American culture through its saloons. In the four eastern cities where network television service was available — New York, Philadelphia, Washington, and Schenectady (home of General Electric) — there were television screens in every bar. These receivers were usually switched on at seven o'clock in the evening, when network programming began, and bar owners generally reported that business subsequently improved. There still wasn't much to watch, but in some neighborhoods men brought their families into local taverns for the first time to see 1947's historic television firsts, such as the opening of the Eightieth Congress in January and President Truman's speech from the White House that spring. But television service, the bar owners complained in their trade journals, was still a chancy business draw. On some nights there was literally nothing on. CBS didn't even broadcast every night, and at one point even announced it was shutting down its New York studios because the network's proposal for a mechanical, nonelectronic color TV system had been rejected by the FCC.

Yet by mid-1947 there were ten stations on the air around the country and fifteen thousand TV sets in use along NBC's northeast network. Gradually new programs like *Meet the Press* and *Kraft Television Theater* began to attract an audience. These had to compete with the greatest radio talents and programs in America —

Eddie Cantor, Jimmy Durante's variety show, and Fred Allen's *Allen's Alley*, with its household-word cast of characters like Senator Claghorn, blustering and pompous, and the fabled Mrs. Nussbaum. Television countered with shows like *Tex & Jinx* (in which New York publicist Tex McCrary and his wife Jinx Falkenburg invented the TV chat show) and *Author Meets the Critics*, a literary free-for-all produced by *Howdy Doody*'s future patron Martin Stone (and occasionally directed by my father in his capacity as a staff director at WNBT, then the call letters of NBC's New York TV station). *Author Meets the Critics*, hosted by John K. M. McCaffrey, was very primitive and immensely popular: perspiring writers and their critical nemeses harangued each other under the inhumanly hot white lights needed to candle-power an image into the electronic lines of the Iconoscope cameras. Under the brutal, interrogating studio lights, tempers would flare, and McCaffrey would lose control. There were several shoving and jostling incidents between overheated litterateurs. There was that lost early television feeling that *anything* could happen. Once the studio grew so warm that Eugene O'Neill passed out drunk, on camera. General Sarnoff worried that celebrities mopping their brows was bad for television. It was a hothouse. Conditions behind the camera were primitive as well. Martin Stone remembers that early shows were budgeted at around $150 apiece.

From early 1947, there were a few shows for children on television. The first of these was *The Small Fry Club,* which was shown from 7:00 to 8:00 P.M. on Tuesdays on the DuMont Network, which originated from Channel 5 in New York. (DuMont had been founded by a scientist, Dr. Allen DuMont, who came up with an early all-electronic TV set. He was marketing fourteen-inch versions of these as early as 1948 and, like NBC, had a four-station network in 1947.) *The Small Fry Club* was hosted by Big Brother Bob Emory, a genial disc jockey who narrated old silent films, displayed children's drawings, and later formed the first television "club" for children. A few months after *Small Fry Club* went on the air in March 1947, DuMont debuted another kids' show, *Birthday Party,* on Thursday nights at seven-thirty, hosted by a young New York deejay named Ted Brown. Around the same time, NBC aired *its* first kids' show, *Juvenile Jury,* a problem-solving panel show hosted by Jack Barry that became the first commercially sponsored network series.

The first puppets came to television that summer, although marionettes handled by puppeteer Bernard H. Paul had appeared on experimental station W3XK in Wheaton, Maryland, as early as 1931.

Chicago puppeteer Burr Tillstrom had also put his hand puppets through their paces on an NBC broadcast at the New York World's Fair in 1939. But in 1947 ventriloquists and their dummies were among the biggest stars in American mass entertainment. The most famous was radio's Edgar Bergen and his dummies Charlie McCarthy and Mortimer Snerd. Also on the scene was the younger and more hep Paul Winchell, who took his dummy Jerry Mahoney onto the DuMont network in June 1947 in a thirteen-week summer replacement for DuMont's biggest show, *Captain Video* on Saturday night. *Winchell & Mahoney* was a hit for DuMont. Over at NBC, General David Sarnoff made a note of it.

It wasn't until later in 1947 that television transcended its image as small and stuffy. Two events helped push television into more American homes. The first was the World Series in October. This savagely fought subway series between the upstart Brooklyn Dodgers and the mighty New York Yankees featured two of the most famous men in American life, the majestic Yankee Clipper Joe DiMaggio and the catlike Dodger hero Jackie Robinson. Every television set in America, many viewed by hundreds of men in saloons, was tuned to NBC the day Cookie Lavagetto broke up Bill Bevens's ninth-inning no-hitter with a double in Ebbets Field. A few days later the same audience gasped with delight and amazement and hubris as they *witnessed* Al Gionfriddo's heroic catch and robbery of a DiMaggio home-run ball in the stands at Yankee Stadium. When people saw this, they had to have a television of their own at home.

Another televised sports event in December 1947 gave television a further push. This was the heavyweight championship fight in which Joe Louis, the Brown Bomber, successfully defended his title after being knocked down twice by Jersey Joe Walcott. Again, every television in the country was tuned to this dramatic fight. Pro wrestling was also popular on television, and not only in the bars. In those days the legendary Italian maestro Arturo Toscanini was living in New York's Riverdale section while he was conducting the NBC Symphony Orchestra. Often, when Toscanini's wife returned to Europe for family visits, the maestro, home alone, would invite musicians and colleagues in for dinner. These guests, many of them distinguished, would suppose they were destined for a semimystical evening of European culture and intimate memories of Puccini and other composers. Alas, after dinner the great Toscanini would almost invariably herd his guests into the library and turn on the wrestling matches on his new seven-inch RCA television. As his guests gaped at each other, the maestro would shout approval of a Gorgeous George eye-doink or an Antonino Rocca flying dropkick! Such was television's inherent power that it could turn great artists into morons at the flick of a switch.

Somewhere around mid-1947, Warren Wade at NBC had two new ideas. Wade had run NBC television in the early forties, and when he came back to NBC after the war he brought with him some of the best young technical talent from his command at the Army Signal Corps Photo Center. Wade was famous around NBC for his weekly military-style staff meetings and the bold, imposing physical presence of a full colonel returned to the inconveniences of civilian life. Warren Wade announced in his blustering manner at one of his staff meetings that NBC needed some kind of puppet show for kids. Not another talking dummy like Bergen and Winchell had, mind you, but some kind of marionette, which Wade felt would be better suited to the purposes of the small TV screen. Several NBC staffers of that era remember that Warren Wade was looking for "a Charlie McCarthy on strings." This in itself wasn't such a big deal, and Wade's staff was told to think about it. His other concept was much more radical: he wanted to put the puppet show on in the daytime. No one had done anything like that before. NBC president Niles Trammel told Warren Wade that NBC would consider it.

The creative seeds of *Howdy Doody* were, however, already being sown elsewhere.

In March 1947, WEAF's station management informed their morning jock Bob Smith that they were going to block out the entire Saturday-morning radio schedule for kids' programs. Frank Luther, a children's recording star of the day, was being given the 9:00 A.M. show, and Smith was asked if *he* would come up with something else for kids. With visions of another four hundred dollars a week dancing in his head, Smith said, Sure. So Bob Smith huddled with his writer, Vic Campbell, who had been an announcer with Bob at WGR in Buffalo and had run General MacArthur's radio command in the Pacific during the war. Campbell had been writing Bob's morning show since the previous autumn, and now came up with a quiz show for Saturday-morning radio called *Triple B Ranch*. Four kids from one school would compete with four from another. The *Triple B* was for "Big Brother Bob," and the *Ranch* part suggested a Western theme, so each team of four kids was perched on a wooden hobbyhorse and answered questions posed by a cowboy-suited Bob

Smith. If a child answered a question wrong, he was off the horse. NBC bought the concept.

Triple B Ranch went on in late March 1947 and was an immediate hit for NBC Radio. Bob Smith wrote a theme jingle — "*I wanna be-be-be at the Triple B Ranch every Saturday morning*" — and played his omnipresent piano for the commercials. The studio was packed with kids for every show. Eventually Vic Campbell asked Bob to try some comedy sketches. So Bob did Lukie the Polack and Yitzie the Yid and Vic said, No, Bob, like a *Western* voice.

As it happened, Bob Smith did have another voice.

Elmer.

The Original Howdy Doody.

Elmer came from Buffalo. In his local radio days there, Bob had sometimes talked over the air to the engineer of his afternoon show, whose name was Eddie. In his relaxed way Smith might say something like, "Eddie, we gotta find another way to sell these soap flakes today." And of course Smith's listeners would write in: "Who's Eddie?" So Smith would explain that Eddie was the engineer in the control room, who actually played the records they were hearing over the radio. The people out there in radioland wrote back: "Why can't we hear Eddie?" So one day Smith introduced Eddie to the listeners. "Well, friends, you wanted to meet the man who gets the news for you and shares my lunch every day? Here's Eddie! Eddie, I want you to say hello to all our friends."

And Eddie turned a bright shade of crimson and stammered out a horrible yokel laugh: *Hyuh Hyuh Hyuh Hyuh Hyuh Hyuh Hyuh Hyuh!* Eddie was an engineer, but he couldn't speak on the radio! He was struck totally *dumb*. Nothing but that stupid laugh. It was the laugh of the oaf, the rube, the idiot. And it was hilarious. It was even funnier than Mortimer Snerd, Edgar Bergen's bumpkin-dummy.

So when Vic Campbell asked if Bob had a Western voice, Bob thought of Eddie the engineer and did the laugh: "Aawwrrgh — gosh, Mr. Smith ... *Hyuh Hyuh Hyuh Hyuh.*" It was so dumb that Vic Campbell fell over laughing. "That's a *dumb* character," Vic said. "Let's give him a dumb name. How about Elmer?"

Let's put on an old acetate of a *Triple B Ranch* program. Bob Smith is saying, "Say, kids, I want you to meet my ranch hand here at the Triple B Ranch — here's Elmer. C'mon in, Elmer." And he'd say, "Ho *Ho* Mr. Smith and boys and girls, well *howdy doody*. Hyuh Hyuh Hyuh Hyuh Hyuh Hoo!" And Big Brother Bob and his Elmer voice would do some corny hee-haw gags.

Now, the kids laughed hard at this *howdy doody* bit. The children, especially the under-nine set, thought this *howdy doody* stuff was a scream. *Howdy* they could relate to, and *doody* was right there, bringing it all back home. The kids knew all about doody firsthand! At the end of the bit, Big Brother Bob said so long to Elmer and again deployed the unbelievably dumb voice: "Well *Howdy Doody,* boys and girls! *Hyuh Hyuh Hyuh!*"

The kids adored it. In New York Fred Allen listened to the show with his children, and the hilarious Mrs. Nussbaum on *Allen's Alley* started using the "howdy doody" line. Soon the whole country was saying "Howdy Doody."

Then the kids in the studio audience at *Triple B Ranch* started to ask where Howdy Doody was. Big Brother Bob would explain that there was no Howdy Doody, that it was just a voice he did for a character called Elmer. But that seemed like a ripoff to the kids, especially the less gullible older ones. Smith noted disappointment on some faces. "Where's Howdy Doody?" they would chirp every week. Soon Bob Smith realized that there had to *be* a Howdy Doody.

So Bob changed Elmer's name to Howdy Doody and went upstairs in the RCA building to talk to the television people.

At that time NBC television consisted of just a few hands. Niles Trammel was president. Warren Wade was the executive in charge of television. Owen Davis ran casting. Fred Coe was a producer. Ben Grauer was the news editor and reader as well as quiz-show host and all-around on-camera personality. (Old television hands often say that American television was literally invented around Ben Grauer.) Also on the scene was producer Martin Stone, who packaged *Author Meets the Critics* and a quizzer called *Americana,* also hosted by the ubiquitous Ben Grauer.

Marty Stone was a thirty-two-year-old lawyer from New York who had gone to Yale Law and then clerked for Judge Irving Lehman. In the Navy, during the war, Stone had worked for Edward Stettinius in the Lend-Lease program. Afterward he had returned to New York to practice law. Almost by accident he fell into radio broadcasting, producing a book-chat show on an NBC Blue Network affiliate in Albany, New York. A rave review of this show, *Speaking of Books,* in *Variety* caused NBC's Warren Wade to approach Martin Stone with an offer. "Ever heard of television?" Wade asked. Stone said that he had seen some closed-circuit boxing matches on television while in the Navy. Wade, with a vacant half hour to fill on Sunday nights, told Stone to come to the television offices on the sixth floor of the RCA Building, and *Author Meets the Critics* was born. At the time, there were only fifteen thousand sets on NBC's network, but *Author Meets the Critics* caught on. The public liked it, and the celebrities loved the novelty of being seen on TV by their children as well as by the high-income families in the northeast. At the same time Stone was also producing a radio show for WEAF, so he recognized the young WEAF morning guy, Bob Smith, when he ran into him one day in the summer of 1947 on the sixth floor.

"One day I bumped into Bob," Stone recalls, "and he said to me, 'I understand you're in television. I'm *dying* to get into television. Boy, I can play piano, I can sing, I'm a member of the Magicians' Club.'" Martin Stone already knew about Bob, because Stone's six-year-old daughter, Judy, was a regular listener of *Triple B Ranch,* and he thought Bob might be good on television. Stone asked if he could bring his daughter down to the *Ranch* studio that weekend for her birthday, so she could meet Bob. That way, Stone felt, he would get a feeling for Bob's rapport with children beyond the constraints of a radio studio.

That Saturday, Martin Stone and his daughter went down to the *Ranch,* and Bob Smith poured it on. Bob knew full well that this performance was also his audition for television. In the middle of the show Bob brought out the Elmer voice. "Well Hooowwwdy Dooooooody, boys and girls!"

Pandemonium. The children laughed themselves sick in the studio before Stone's eyes. "Hyuh Hyuh Hyuh. Gosh, Big Brother Bob! Hyuh Hyuh Hyuh!" The kids dissolved with joy at how stupid this sounded.

After the show, Martin Stone collared Smith. Together they went into a studio, and Stone got Smith to cut an acetate disk to replay at Judy's classroom birthday party the following week. This acetate still exists. Over the scratchy surface noise Big Brother Bob can be heard auditioning his brains out, playing his piano and singing "Happy Birthday." He interviews Judy Stone with the unctuous fervor of a born-again pitchman. Then he brings out the Elmer voice for the coup de grâce: "Well, *Howdy Doody, Judy!!*" On the acetate Smith says hi to Judy's mom, gets her teacher's name right, and generally shines with corny raw talent. When Martin Stone played the acetate at his daughter's birthday party and the kids heard Elmer say, "Howdy Doody, Judy," they fell apart.

Martin Stone knew he had something. And Martin Stone, as Bob Smith later put it, had a way of opening doors at NBC. Stone was a charismatic and good-looking lawyer/producer who had the ear of some key people at NBC, including General Sarnoff's son Robert, then beginning his career at NBC as an ad salesman.

There were actually many factors working synchronously to produce the first kids' show at NBC. First, Warren Wade wanted to put puppets on television, maybe even in the daytime. Then there was the young NBC staff producer Roger Muir, who had been on Wade's staff at Astoria. Muir had wanted to get a children's show on the air for months. Then there was Bob Smith, who had an act that seemed ready for television with only slight modification. Bobby Sarnoff, the son of the head of the company, was also interested. All these men had children who had nothing to watch on their daddies' TVs. One day in the autumn of 1947 Warren Wade asked Martin Stone if there was any place in the home for television in the daytime. "Warren," Stone replied, "I don't know for sure, but I do know that my kids will watch a *test pattern*. And my wife is always telling me to do a show that begins at five P.M. to keep the kids occupied while Mom makes dinner." Stone was speaking the gospel truth.

Sometime that fall, Marty Stone went back to see *Triple B Ranch*. This time he took Warren Wade with him. Wade was of course familiar with Bob Smith from WEAF; anyone who listened to that station in the morning knew that Bob Smith was the perfect disc jockey — warm, personable, honey-voiced, talented and eager to entertain, funny and intimate.

Best of all, Bob was also an ardent and relaxed salesman, as happy to read a commercial with passion as he was to spin a record or tell a story about Mrs. Huffnagel back in Buffalo. But it was Bob Smith's total control and mastery of the *Triple B* audience — both in the studio and over the air — that convinced Warren Wade that Smith could handle the same job on television. Warren Wade saw that when Bob Smith spoke to them, children actually listened, and did so with rapt attention.

Finally, early in December 1947, Martin Stone called Bob Smith and said he wanted to put him on television somehow, in some format. At the same time, Warren Wade and Roger Muir decided to put a kids' show on as an experiment, the Saturday evening after Christmas, one show only. These two factions — the NBC brass and the "team" of Smith and Stone — came together in the office of NBC's casting vice president, Owen Davis, Jr. Davis had also wanted to get children's programming onto NBC and had even begun negotiations to lure Bob Emory and his *Small Fry Club* to NBC. He also had on hand one of the premier professional puppeteers in America, Frank Paris. Paris was one of the great puppetmasters of his generation, and Owen Davis knew that his huge company of lifelike marionettes would be a sensation on television's limited screen.

A week before Christmas, NBC gave Roger Muir the go-ahead for the post-Christmas show, and Muir knew he would have to scramble to put together an hour of children's programming from scratch in two weeks. Fortunately Frank Paris and his crew had a thirteen-part puppet serial called "Toby Tyler at the Circus," about the adventures of a little boy who ran away and joined a carnival. Bob Smith was to act as the show's host, singing at the piano and talking with the children who would sit on folding chairs and be Bob's on-camera audience. Between Toby Tyler's adventures and Bob Smith's contests and games, they could show old silent films from a library that NBC had bought from Warner Brothers for fifty thousand dollars. These old films, misread by the electronic eye of the Iconoscope and thus speeded up when projected through TV's kinescope process, were seen for years on *Howdy Doody,* thus introducing the Baby Boomers visually to the world of their grandparents. The films included early pictures by Ben Turpin, Charlie Chase, Stan Laurel (without Oliver Hardy), Buster Keaton, and Bobby Dunn, a sort of fake Chaplin tramp character.

Bob Smith did his Elmer voice for the NBC group, and Martin Stone explained the appeal of the character and the subsequent audience demand to *see* a character they thought was called Howdy Doody. Someone asked Frank Paris if he could make a puppet that looked like Elmer sounded. In his pronounced and exaggerated lisp, Paris said that yes, of course, he could make a puppet that looked like anything, but the puppet couldn't possibly be ready by the December 27 air date. Deciding to go with the Elmer voice and fake it with the puppet, NBC told Paris to build Howdy Doody. The puppet, the network insisted, had to look dumb. It was an oaf, a lout, an imbecile like Mortimer Snerd. NBC and Frank Paris settled on a fee of five hundred dollars for the marionette, with NBC retaining the ownership rights to Howdy Doody. At the end of the meeting Bob Smith asked: "When do we go on?"

"Next week," Muir replied.

As in an old movie, Smith said: "Saturday! Well, gang, we can do it, can't we?"

Of course, it wasn't that easy. First, somebody had to come up with some material, and fast. Frank Paris's act was only good for fifteen minutes. Roger Muir filled some time by hiring vaudeville acts from Radio City Music Hall: a magician, a circus-type dog act, and a quick-sketch artist. But Bob Smith would have to speak and sing for the rest of the show. This is where *The Howdy Doody Show*'s creator and first writer, Eddie Kean, comes into the story.

Eddie Kean was *Howdy*'s chief writer, philosopher, and theoretician for the show's first eight years (until my father assumed those duties). Between 1947 and 1954 Eddie Kean wrote almost every line spoken and every note sung on *The Howdy Doody Show*. And remember that, for almost all that time, *Howdy Doody* was a "strip show," broadcast live five nights every week. For those eight years Eddie Kean came up with every major creative decision, story line, and character on *Howdy Doody,* material today imprinted in the brains of my generation. Bob Smith may have invented Howdy's character, but Eddie Kean created the world Howdy lived in.

In late 1947 Eddie Kean was twenty-three years old and a writer on Bob Smith's morning show as well as *Triple B Ranch*. Related to the actors Paul Muni and Boris Thomashefsky, Eddie had spent his childhood summers at an upstate music camp called Camp Paradox, eventually becoming a counselor. Part of his job there had been to produce a musical extravaganza at the end of every summer for the neighboring girls' camp. Paradox was a famous music camp, and Kean had been preceded in these duties by the likes of Richard Rodgers and Arthur Schwartz. Like many camps of the day, Paradox indoctrinated campers with local Indian lore and legends. These would also later rub off on Howdy's show.

In 1941, at the age of seventeen, Eddie Kean had enlisted in the Navy, which sent him to officers candidate school and then put him on the bridge of a landing craft. Eddie and his shipmates steamed from Boston to Okinawa in 1944, the 125-foot ship making a maximum speed of eight knots. During this excruciating voyage Eddie often sat the midwatch, from midnight to 4:00 A.M., humming along to the sixteen-inch Armed Forces Radio Service records supplied by the Navy. Every night he listened over and over to a record called "Laura" while he sat in the conning tower and jotted down song ideas. Eddie saw action in the ferocious battle for Okinawa when his flotilla of 120 ships was attacked by kamikaze planes, with devastating results. Eighty ships were lost, and Eddie Kean considered himself lucky to have survived the war.

After his discharge, Eddie finished his studies at Columbia University and then paired with his friend Bob Unger to form a song-writing team. They wrote a novelty song called "Where Is Sam?" but the music business was even harder to break into then than it is now, and the song went nowhere until Eddie wrote a letter to the syndicated columnist Walter Winchell, who answered Eddie in print and told him to keep plugging away. The column was read by a Tin Pan Alley song-plugger named Enoch Light, who called Eddie and published "Where's Sam."

Wednesday was song-pluggers' day at Bob Smith's office at WEAF, the day Bob would buy new tunes and jingles for his daily show. One day Enoch Light showed up and played "Where's Sam" for Smith, who loved it, sang it on his show, and then recorded it for RCA (with the Herman Chitteson Trio). Eddie came to the recording session and met Bob, charmed him with his youth and vigor, and was soon hired to help provide Bob's morning show with chatter and jingles for thirty-five dollars a week. Later on, when Vic Campbell became ill, Eddie began to write *Triple B Ranch* as well. When Bob Smith first went to be interviewed by Warren Wade at WNBT, Eddie went with him just to see what the inside of a television studio looked like.

Eddie remembers the meeting. "Wade said he wanted to do a kids' Christmas show for one hour. There was no thought of a series, and Wade had no awareness of any character like Howdy Doody. He just told Smith that he wanted a kids' show on the tiny budget that he had." At that meeting Eddie Kean was offered and accepted the job of chief writer for the show. Asked for a title off the top of his head, Eddie thought of Frank Paris and the Howdy Doody puppet he was making. "How about *Puppet Playhouse?*" Eddie offered.

Wade met with Bobby Sarnoff and Martin Stone to talk about what time the show would go on. Wade was pushing for a late-afternoon slot, but Stone remembers Bobby Sarnoff saying to him, "*You* pick the time." So Martin Stone suggested 5:00 P.M., and the era of daytime television began.

Feverish preparations for *Puppet Playhouse* began less than a week before the broadcast date. This doubled the workload of Bob Smith's young assistant and gofer, Bobby Keeshan, an ex-marine who had enlisted in NBC's page corps after the war. These uniformed guides, doorkeepers, and messengers operated on the theory that if NBC's broadcasters were knights of the airwaves, then they deserved to be served by young pages with quiet restraint and politesse. A page had about six months in uniform to ingratiate himself with some office somewhere at NBC and be hired at the end of his term. It was up or out at NBC! Keeshan first met Smith while he was manning the fourth-floor page station outside Smith's office at WEAF. Every morning Smith played different songs on the piano over the air, and gradually Keeshan was assigned the task of going to the library and finding out what year the songs had come out so Smith would have some chatter. Then Bobby Keeshan started handing out prizes on *Triple B Ranch.* When Keeshan's page job expired, Bob Smith hired him as a forty-dollar-a-week office manager. "I had him interview the song-pluggers," Smith said, "and answer the mail. He was just a gofer, a stooge." For *Puppet Playhouse,* Keeshan wrote and rewrote the cue-cards as Eddie Kean's bits of dialogue started to trickle in.

Meanwhile, in NBC Studio 8A, puppeteer Frank Paris set up the low-slung puppet bridge from his touring "Toby Tyler at the Circus" revue, which he had adapted for television. One of Paris's crew was a skilled twenty-year-old puppet handler named Rhoda Mann. Rhoda would later play a key role as the puppeteer who manipulated Howdy himself, but back in 1947 she was both scared and thrilled at the prospect of working on television. In Rhoda's Bronx neighborhood, where she was the only daughter of strict Polish immigrants, she didn't even know anyone who owned a television.

Rhoda was working for Frank Paris, the best in the business, because she could really *walk* a marionette. Rhoda had a kind of family fondness for puppets. Her father painted the faces on dolls for the famous Effanbee Doll Company, for which he also designed the legendary Dydee doll, the first doll that wept. When Rhoda was eight, her father brought home one of the company's nine-string marionettes. When she proved naturally adept at walking the difficult puppet, her father brought home two more. Rhoda Mann was performing on a near-professional level for her schoolmates by the time she was nine years old. She had learned a trick whereby she could make all three of her puppets dance, using a special control bar that let her hold the puppets' bodies with one hand and move the legs with the other. Soon word of Rhoda's talent spread to the small world of puppeteering, an ancient art and a tight-knit fraternity. String marionettes have been found in dynastic Egyptian tombs and were popular with the ancient Greeks. European writers from

Goethe to Pepys described touring puppet companies, while in France the great playwrights wrote sketches to be performed by marionettes. In the eighteenth century, popular puppet plays included *Dick Whittington* and *Merry Andrew*. Spectacular puppet theatricals were performed in the London of Charles Dickens. One production of *Noah's Flood* included a flooded stage and puppets representing hundreds of animals. These arts began to die with the advent of film in the twentieth century, but were kept alive in America by puppeteers like Tony Sarg and Frank Paris, until the advent of television almost killed puppeteering completely.

It so happened that Frank Paris had the same agent as Rhoda's exotic neighbor Ali Ben Ali, the Moroccan Wonder Man, a magician for whom Rhoda worked as an assistant after she graduated from high school in 1944. Frank Paris met Rhoda somewhere on the vaudeville circuit and tried her out on his masterpiece, the Carmen Miranda puppet. When Paris saw Rhoda wiggle Carmen's hips, he said, "OK, lady, you got a job."

The job involved touring with "Toby of the Circus," Paris's two-hour spectacular featuring fifty-three different marionettes. But before Rhoda's father would give his daughter permission to go on the road with two grown men, Paris and his assistant, he demanded to meet them. Later he came home and told his wife there was nothing to worry about. "Frank was *very* gay," Rhoda remembers. "For the next three years I lived through all his boyfriends and crises."

Over the next years Rhoda Mann learned her trade from the best there was. "Not only was Frank the best puppet-builder of all time," Rhoda says, "he could make them come to life! Frank had puppets that stripped off their clothes, puppets that smoked cigarettes and ground them out with their heels, puppets that could blow bubbles. He even had a puppet that could juggle. Even today I still don't quite believe he could make marionettes do what they did. It was unbelievable."

After appearing in vaudeville all over the country and in a triumphant series of shows at Madison Square Garden and Radio City Music Hall, Paris got the first call for *Puppet Playhouse*. Rhoda recalls many tense hours at NBC while producer Roger Muir, who was also directing the program, invented the camera angles needed to televise a puppet show. There was also consternation because NBC wanted a character named Howdy Doody on the show, and

Paris was fretting because he couldn't build it in time for the premiere.

Adding to the confusion were the other acts — Prince Mendez the magician, Nino the sketch artist, and the Gaudschmidt Brothers' Dogs. As Eddie Kean watched the Gaudschmidts run their big black Alsatians through their paces in Studio 8A, he had a sensation of *déjà vu;* then he remembered that he had seen this act twenty years earlier when his father had taken him to see some vaudeville at the age of four.

Finally, on the day after Christmas, *Puppet Playhouse* was run through by its cast. Anxiety was very high. Both cast and crew sensed they were on the edge of some kind of breakthrough; none of them had ever appeared on television before, so no one was prepared for what was going to happen.

Puppet Playhouse was scheduled to be broadcast over the NBC Network at 5:00 P.M. on Saturday. It started to snow Friday afternoon and didn't stop for twenty-four hours. The *New York Times* for December 27 reported that a record twenty-five-inch snowfall was crippling New York City and the entire northeast. The *Times* movie page advertised John Wayne in *Tycoon,* Henry Fonda in *The Fugitive,* Gregory Peck in *Gentleman's Agreement.* Jean Cocteau's *Beauty and the Beast* was playing in Greenwich Village, and *Bambi* was at Radio City Music Hall. Duke Ellington's orchestra was playing Carnegie Hall. At a movie theater on West Fifty-seventh Street, Ronald Reagan was starring in *Voice of the Turtle.* Over on Broadway one could see Ethel Merman in *Annie Get Your Gun* or John Gielgud in *Crime and Punishment.* The original *Streetcar Named Desire* was at the Barrymore. Judith Anderson was featured in *Medea,* and Leonard Bernstein was advertised as the conductor of *The Cradle Will Rock,* Marc Blitzstein's "vivid proletarian drama."

If you turned to the *Times* radio page, you saw what was going to be on TV that night. CBS had basketball, the Knicks against Chicago. DuMont had college basketball — Rutgers versus Seton Hall. And then there was NBC's kiddie program, misidentified in that day's paper as *Puppet Theater.*

Because of the enormous blizzard that had just dumped tons of wet snow on New York, Broadway was dark that night. The movie and vaudeville palaces didn't open for business, and Duke Ellington and his band stayed home. Bobby Keeshan couldn't reach the studio because of the snow and so missed the debut of *Puppet Playhouse.*

But the show went on. Bob Smith played the show's theme song

36

on a ukelele (off camera, to get around a union ban on playing live instruments on television). The song Smith played was called "It's Howdy Doody Time," with words written by Eddie Kean to the tune of the old French cancan "Ta-Ra-Ra-Boom-Der-É." Bob sang: *It's Howdy Doody time, it's Howdy Doody time, Bob Smith and Howdy too, say howdy do to you. Let's give a rousing cheer, 'cause Howdy Doody's here, it's time to start the show, so kids let's go!*" Then Smith billboarded the show — Frank Paris and Toby Tyler! Prince Mendez! Nino the sketch artist! The Gaudschmidt Brothers and their Dogs!

There was no videotape in those days, and if anyone made a kinescope recording of the first *Puppet Playhouse* it has unfortunately been lost. No one remembers much of that first show, except for the moment when, near the end of the hour, it was time for Bob Smith to introduce his friend Howdy.

Since there was as yet no Howdy Doody, Eddie Kean came up with another angle. Bob Smith said something like, "Well, kids, have we got a surprise for you! As an extra-special treat tonight I brought my friend Howdy Doody along. You know, Howdy does the *Triple B Ranch* show with me here in New York, and a lot of you kids have asked to see what he looks like. Well, I wanted Howdy to come on the show today, but he says he's too shy to come out of this drawer in my desk here and say hello." Then Smith leaned over and said to the desk, "Hey, Howdy boy, are you still in there?"

Cut to a shot of the drawer. Then, over the television speaker, came the Elmer voice in all its stupid glory: "Gorsh, Mr. Smith, Ah'm in here but Ah'm too darned bashful to come out! *Hyuh Hyuh Hyuh Hyuh Hyuh Hyuh!*"

Then Smith said, "C'mon, Howdy boy! The kids wanna see you!" But the drawer wouldn't budge. When the camera was off him and on the drawer, Smith had Howdy say, "Aww gee, Mr. Smith. I'm just too bashful. *Hyuh Hyuh Hyuh Hyuh.*" This provoked much mirth from the proto-Peanuts sitting on folding chairs in the audience.

And that was it. At six o'clock the whole cast gathered and waved goodbye as the primitive credits rolled over *Puppet Playhouse.* About a dozen kids in the studio had seen Bob Smith play the piano and do some gags with an invisible puppet in a drawer. They also saw Frank Paris's puppets, some vaudeville acts, and a bit of what Eddie Kean had billed as an "old-time" movie. There had been no commercials. *Puppet Playhouse* was "sustained" by the network, meaning NBC had paid for the show. When they turned out the blazing studio lights in 8A, everyone congratulated each other and commiserated about how hard it was going to be to get home through the driving snowstorm. Of course there was too little applause for anyone — Bob Smith, Roger Muir, Martin Stone, or Warren Wade — to gauge how the show had done. No one had any idea of how many people had watched. In fact, nobody even really knew exactly how many television sets there *were* in the country at the time.

NBC paid Bob Smith seventy-five dollars for that first show, and Smith gave Eddie Kean twenty-five to write it. When they went home on Saturday night — Smith to New Rochelle and Eddie back to his writer's pad on Central Park West — neither of them had any idea of what was in store.

Bob Smith, Howdy Doody, and Bobby Keeshan as Clarabell on the steps of the U.S. Capitol after participating in "I Am an American" Day, May 1948. (EDDIE KEAN COLLECTION)

Three

A Star Is Carved

THINGS WERE QUIET around NBC for a few days after the first show. It was the holiday season, and many people were away. But the following Tuesday a review in *Variety* catapulted *Puppet Playhouse* to fame; for thirteen years after that nobody looked back. American television exploded in 1948 largely because of Howdy Doody and his relentless power to capture the minds of children from ages two to nine.

Most *Howdy* veterans think the big snowstorm had everything to do with it. "We were blessed by that incredible snowfall," Eddie Kean remembers, "because the weather was so bad that the audience was literally captive. You couldn't even walk on the street that day. In that era there might have been one television set in every apartment house, but you could bet that every kid in the building was there watching it. And, thanks to the snowfall, the response was *incredible*." And not only from *Puppet Playhouse's* intended audience — the children of New York, Philadelphia, Schenectady, and Washington, D.C. — but from their parents as well. Because almost every set capable of receiving a station in NBC's television network had been tuned to *Puppet Playhouse,* the parents of these children had gotten an hour's worth of total and complete peace and silence from their offspring. The children of the affluent northeast were *catatonic*. Thousands of mothers made dinner in tranquillity. Thousands of postwar Baby Boom fathers put their feet up and read the paper. For that one crucial and tormented hour between five and six on a winter's eve — we call it "the suicide shift" in our family — the parents of young Baby Boomers knew the sweet solace of quiet. And there were some parents who watched along with their kids. They saw Bob Smith at the piano singing in his rich, perfect-pitch baritone, and they liked it. They thought it was OK, even nice that the kids were getting to spend time with this friendly and nonthreatening guy who obviously loved children and wasn't even trying to sell them anything.

But it wasn't Bob Smith's vocal skills or Frank Paris's marionette artistry that *Variety* noted in its rave review of the first show. It was the baby-sitting that *Variety* noticed. "In the middle-class home, there is perhaps nothing as welcome to the mother as something that will keep the small fry intently absorbed and out of possible mischief. This program can almost be guaranteed to pin down the squirmiest of the brood." Other writers took note of the show that week, especially the New York *Herald Tribune*'s influential columnist John Crosby and the widely syndicated Billy Rose. By the middle of the week, NBC executives, with the pleas for more *Puppet Playhouse* from their wives and neighbors having been validated by the New York media, began to tell Warren Wade that he possibly had television's first hit.

Puppet Playhouse had originally been planned as a trilogy. Warren Wade's idea had been to have Roger Muir produce one kids' show with Bob Smith; NBC producer Fred Coe was to have produced another with Ed Herlihy as host; and another producer, Eddie Sobel, was to have put together a third show with Paul Winchell and his dummy Jerry Mahoney. The three, collectively entitled *Puppet Playhouse,* were to have been presented on consecutive weekends, with the show that received the best response getting the network's OK to stay on the air.

But after the initial success of Bob Smith and his Howdy Doody act, the other producers dropped out. Warren Wade called Muir into his office and told him to go ahead and do another show.

So on January 3, 1948, *Puppet Theater,* as it was listed in the *New York Times,* went on the air again. There was still no Howdy puppet, still no commercials, but no snowstorm either. This time Bobby Keeshan made it to the RCA Building in plenty of time to make his television debut in a sports jacket, handing out prizes to Bob Smith's juvenile guests as they fidgeted on their folding chairs. During the break in the show when they showed the Old-Time Movie and the studio lights were shut off to cool down the studio for a few minutes, Bobby Keeshan assumed a new duty, getting Bob's little guests to stop talking and shut up. Frank Paris and his crew ran through another episode of "Toby Tyler at the Circus." (Paris's main puppet, the little boy Toby, was dressed in a checked shirt, jeans, and cowboy boots and would prove to be very popular.) There were different vaudeville acts on the second show, but the response was the same — an overwhelming demand for more. The Monday after that second show, Roger Muir went back to Warren Wade's office on the sixth floor. Wade looked at Muir and said, in his best colonel's growl, "Let's do it again!"

The *New York Times* listed the third Howdy Doody show as *Puppet Television Theater,* but it was more of the same, with the addition of the elderly Doc Whipple. The resident organist at Radio City Music Hall, Doc played a great carny-style organ and would play *Howdy*'s theme song and commercials off-camera for years. Whipple had started out in the old nickelodeons and was very skilled at accompanying the Old-Time Movies.

By the end of January 1948, after several more shows, it was obvious that *Puppet Playhouse* was a smash. The president of NBC, Niles Trammel, told Warren Wade to tell Roger Muir to get ready to broadcast two nights a week, on Thursdays and Saturdays.

By then television was already catching fire. Most TV receivers were still set up in bars and saloons, but one could now buy a seven-inch RCA set for $180, which put television within reach of at least the upper regions of the American middle class. New York had eight daily newspapers and six television channels. Although broadcasts averaged only two hours per night, the programming was execrable — "ill-conceived, awkward and dull," in the words of one contemporary critic. Television owners had to choose between boxing, pro wrestling, the roller derby, lectures, and some live drama. The kids' shows were witless and boring. In this morass of video pulp, *Puppet Playhouse*'s gentle marionettes and whimsical songs, as well as Bob Smith's undeniable presence, stood out like a beacon of hope. Many television pioneers saw the show as television's best chance of being accepted in the American home.

Meanwhile, Frank Paris had finished and dressed his new Howdy Doody puppet, which he unveiled at a staff meeting in January 1948. The marionette was ugly to the point of being grotesque — Frank Paris's faithful depiction of Bob Smith's stupid Elmer voice. Howdy had a hideous grin and big jug ears and wore a blond fright wig. He was dressed in the vest, bandanna, and chaps of a cowboy and sported elbow-length work gloves. This monstrous puppet was proclaimed marvelous and the very personification of Howdy Doody by all concerned, and Eddie Kean was told to write Howdy out of the drawer. On the next show Smith was depicted talking to his shy pal, still in the drawer. The camera cut to Smith, then back to the drawer, which now had strings protruding from it. Bob Smith opened the drawer and — socko! — Howdy Doody stepped out in all his loathsome glory.

The kids were riveted. Soon Howdy and Bob were joined by two of Frank Paris's stock company of marionettes. The new characters, adapted from "Toby Tyler at the Circus," were Mr. Huff, the manager of the circus they all worked for, and Huff's prissy and indecisive stooge, Eustace. The earliest scripts Eddie Kean wrote all involved Bob Smith and these three characters in situations where Bob and Howdy were allied against the machinations of the other two. By February 1948, however, Eddie Kean had a new character to write for — the legendary Clarabell Hornblow.

Clarabell, as played by the ex-page Bobby Keeshan, was an infantile and occasionally dangerous clown who served as Bob Smith's foil and scapegoat, much as Bobby Keeshan himself served Bob Smith. The character evolved by accident.

Bobby Keeshan's first job on *Puppet Playhouse* had been to seat the studio kids, supervise them, and keep them quiet. Then one day when the show was running late Smith was doing a stunt with a couple of children and asked Bobby to bring the kids their beanies. Keeshan appeared briefly on camera in his sports coat, prompting Warren Wade, watching on a monitor, to ask Martin Stone, "Who the hell is that?"

After this happened a few more times, Colonel Wade got tired of seeing a civilian on the show. "Get that guy into some kind of circus outfit," he ordered Roger Muir.

So they took Bobby Keeshan downstairs to the costume department. It turned out that NBC had two clown suits, one with polka dots and one with zebra stripes. Clarabell became a striped clown. Several different versions are given to account for the fact that Clarabell was mute. Some *Howdy* veterans say that Clarabell didn't talk because Keeshan couldn't speak lines. Bob Smith maintains that Warren Wade heard Clarabell say "thank you" on one of the earliest shows and got nervous. In those days the radio talent union was trying to organize television people as well. Wade was worried that if AFTRA took over video actors (as they of course would later do), then NBC would have to pay AFTRA scale to Keeshan. So the story goes that Clarabell stayed silent on Warren Wade's orders.

Bobby Keeshan remembers the period very well. "I worked in the clown suit for several shows, and then someone said, 'That looks fine, but wouldn't it be better if he wore makeup to go with the clown suit, and then we could make a character out of him.' So I got together with Dick Smith, who *was* the makeup department at NBC in those days, and we created this character with a bald pate that had to be applied very skillfully and took a long time every day.

"There was no real reason Clarabell couldn't say lines," Keeshan continues. "It was often said that the reason I didn't say lines is because they didn't want to pay me. But that wasn't the reason at all. I think that actually they had no faith in my acting ability, which was probably well-founded. I was twenty years old and had none.

"But then I went and did a lot of research into clowns, and it became evident that all the classic clowns were pantomime clowns. They were mute. There was never a classic talking clown. From medieval days, clowns did pantomime."

So they gave Clarabell a box with two horns on it. The right horn was for yes, the left horn meant no. When Clarabell had to communicate with Bob Smith or the puppets, he would honk and gesture frantically, with great exaggeration. And the others still didn't understand him at all. Martin Stone sums up the situation: "Keeshan blew a horn so they wouldn't have to pay him."

"Clarabell *caught on*," Eddie Kean recalls. "Bobby Keeshan was unskilled enough to make a perfect clown for that time. He had no theatrical training, he wasn't about to put on a show of his own, he was an oaf — a perfect foil. In fact, I've often thought that if we had hired one of the great clowns of the day, like Emmett Kelly or Felix Adler, to play Clarabell, the character would not have succeeded. Because Clarabell would have been too sharp. It would have seemed too staged for television. I'm not knocking Keeshan at all, because I was as inexperienced a writer as he was an actor. None of us really knew what we were doing, and it gave us the excuse and the ability to be completely original."

For his early services on *Puppet Playhouse,* Bobby Keeshan made five dollars a week from Smith. Later, when the show started being broadcast twice a week, Smith tipped Keeshan an extra fifteen dollars every week. As the show continued to grow in the spring of 1948 and NBC added Tuesdays to the schedule, Smith persuaded NBC to pay Keeshan thirty-five dollars a week.

Under those burning video lights, clad in a full bodysuit and an hour's worth of heavy greasepaint and wig, Bobby Keeshan sweated buckets. And with his prop, the seltzer bottle (which had been brought in to the studio by Roger Muir from his bar at home), Clarabell drove the children nuts. When Clarabell let loose with that dreaded seltzer bottle and drenched the benign and paternal Bob Smith with a blast of fizzy soda right in the face, it fulfilled the wish-fantasies of every five-year-old who had ever wanted to let Mom or especially Dad really have it, just once, right in the kisser!

And Clarabell's behavior! His manners! Wait — he *had* no manners. Clarabell was a terrible clown, stamping his foot with petulance, pouting like the most truculent three-year-old imaginable. The kids in the studio saw this and laughed themselves silly. The children at home laughed so much that their mothers came in from the kitchen and watched, too. The interaction between Smith and the clown was so dumb and predictable that even the moms had to laugh. And when Clarabell actually chased Smith around the studio, brandishing the seltzer bottle, the studio kids screamed. Sometimes, the NBC custodial staff quickly learned, the younger kids wet themselves with delight.

Later that year, when NBC decided to telecast *Howdy* as a strip show, five nights a week, Bobby Keeshan asked Warren Wade for eighty dollars a week to play Clarabell, the top television attraction in America. Wade said OK to the eighty dollars, but told Keeshan that he would also have to edit film for NBC. Keeshan refused to do this, so he and Wade settled on seventy-five dollars per week. "Finally, they very reluctantly made a deal with me," Keeshan remembers, "and I became one of the first salaried TV performers."

As much as the earliest *Puppet Playhouse* shows were praised by journalists and parents, the show was also criticized from the first for getting children too riled up and excited just before the dinner hour. But nobody had the slightest idea of how to put on a kids' show without getting the kids to froth a little. From the beginning, Eddie Kean insisted that the show never display a gun or any other weapon or any form of violence. What Eddie wanted was rivalries between characters, just like in everybody's family — sibling rivalry and conflict between the generations. "Buffalo Bob" had not yet surfaced; on *Puppet Playhouse* he was called Mr. Smith — the father-figure.

At this point, Eddie Kean developed the "shell game" and "chase" gags that would see *Howdy* through more than a decade. In the shell game, the seltzer bottle would get switched and Mr. Smith would get wet. Furious, Mr. Smith would chase Clarabell through some kind of impromptu set. Kean recalls that "the studio was so small that you couldn't really have a chase unless you put some obstacles in their way. We used everything — phone booths, trap doors, countertops, anything. But it worked every time, because the children got hysterical when Mr. Smith chased Clarabell." Most of the show's slapstick, in fact, evolved from Eddie Kean's memories of successful vaudeville acts he had seen with his father, acts that Kean reduced and translated for juvenile use.

No commercials aired on *Puppet Playhouse* in its first three months, except house ads for the NBC network. But in March 1948 there was a flurry of press comment about the show. Arturo Toscanini told the papers that he watched Howdy Doody with his grandchildren. The fact was, *everybody* watched with their children; children were even taken to bars to watch *Puppet Playhouse*.

So, slowly, ads began to air on the show. The first was a commercial for the Polaroid Television Filter, a plastic screen to place on the television set to cut down the glare. (The jittery black-and-white picture on an American television screen was no brighter then than it is today, but its glare terrified some customers. Articles appeared in popular magazines stating that the glow of the television set was possibly very harmful. In this atomic age, people were afraid that too much television radiation might even be fatal.)

Even when he only had to write two shows a week, Eddie Kean had to flail around for material. Since 1948 was a hotly contested presidential election year, Eddie decided that Howdy Doody should run for President of the kids. On March 4, Howdy was seen reading the Constitution and deciding that he was qualified to run for President along with Harry Truman, Thomas Dewey, and Henry Wallace. Howdy announced that he would run and displayed two (human) assistants who could only say "yes sir" and "Howdy Doody for President." Howdy asked the kids at home to write him "thingamajigs" — new ideas for his campaign platform, which at that point consisted of such reforms as bigger ice cream sodas, more playgrounds, higher allowances, and the like.

The campaign took off immediately. On March 6, Howdy got congratulatory telegrams from Tex and Jinx, Perry Como, Sammy Kaye, and Fred Allen. A "Howdy Doody for President" poster dominated the set. When mean old Mr. Huff spotted this, he subjected poor Howdy to withering ridicule for running for President. Huff's yesman, Eustace, couldn't have agreed more. Howdy, desperate for a campaign staff, tried in vain to get Eustace to come over to his side.

On March 9, Howdy left for a secret mission on Staten Island. Later, he was seen scribbling on a Magic Manuscript paper, trying to write his campaign theme, "Howdy Doody for President." (Actually, this stunt backfired. The prop man, Bernie Morshen, had prepared a large piece of cardboard with lines for music notation. Then notes were written on the cardboard with an invisible chemical solution. During the show, off-camera, Mr. Smith dipped a brush in a jar of liquid marked INK and went over the notes already on the cardboard. This second liquid caused the notes to appear when it reacted with the first chemical. But the fumes from the reaction proved to be toxic, and Smith and the crew started to gag on camera as the cardboard began to smoke! Although it did look like Howdy was writing real music, Smith, Keeshan, and the crew were almost gassed to death by ammonium sulfate.) At the end of the show, Howdy asked the kids at home to keep those platform suggestions coming.

On March 11, Howdy and Nino the sketch artist — still on the show! — illustrated some of the home viewers' thingamajigs. Thousands of letters came in suggesting such further platform planks as a ten-month school vacation and one-cent ice cream cones. At one point on the same show, Howdy sang "Road to Mandalay." At the line "where the flying fishes play," a large herring — supposedly thrown by Mr. Huff — landed on Mr. Smith's desk with a splat and broke up the whole crew. Smith was laughing so hard he could hardly finish the show.

Howdy's request for thingamajigs generated so much mail that Roger Muir wanted to further test his audience. He asked Warren Wade if they could give away a few campaign buttons as a premium. How many, Wade wanted to know. Muir ventured that ten thousand buttons with the picture of the puppet and the slogan I'M FOR HOWDY DOODY might be enough. The idea was simple: Howdy would announce that anyone who wrote in to the show could get a free button. Although some of the salespeople weren't sure they could give away that many buttons, Wade told Muir to go ahead, and Muir placed the order.

By the end of March, *Puppet Playhouse* was on three times a week — Tuesday, Thursday, and Saturday. On March 23, Bob Smith made the initial offer of a Howdy Doody campaign button to anyone writing in to one of the five stations that carried the program. (By then Baltimore's WBAL had signed on as an NBC video affiliate.)

The result of Smith's first announcement, and the four that followed it, literally *made* television in the eyes of the business community, which had hitherto only had ears for radio.

What happened? Nothing less than a marketing landslide of historic proportions. The following day the mailroom called up and complained to Roger Muir that they had been inundated with six thousand pieces of mail for Howdy Doody. NBC affiliates were reporting eight thousand letters in Philadelphia, six thousand in Baltimore, three thousand in Washington. On March 26, NBC issued a press release saying that twenty thousand letters had been received, all asking for buttons.

Five more times in the next ten days, Bob Smith offered free Howdy Doody buttons. Another thirty-five thousand requests came in. A week later the total had reached sixty thousand, and the mailroom refused to accept any more. Muir was afraid for his job, and Smith thought he'd have to come up with the cash for sixty thousand I'M FOR HOWDY DOODY buttons. But everyone at NBC was flabbergasted. Sixty thousand requests represented one third of the estimated number of working television sets in the United States. At a meeting, the NBC vice president for sales, George Fry, told the Doody people to calm down — they had nothing to worry about. "Are you crazy?" Fry exclaimed. "We'll have this show sold out in two weeks." Actually, it was *less* than two weeks. After NBC published a survey indicating that one in three television sets in America was tuned to *Puppet Playhouse* three days a week between 5:00 and 6:00 P.M., NBC president Niles Trammel rang up Ed Little, the president of the Colgate Corporation, and sold him two segments of the show. Then Continental Baking, bakers of Wonder Bread, bought two segments. Then Ovaltine. Then Mars candy. By April 1948 the program was sold out for years ahead, with two sponsors every day.

By then, the Howdy for President storyline was going great guns for Eddie Kean. Kean fed off the campaign stories of the day, such as Harold Stassen's run against the photogenic New York governor, Tom Dewey, in the various Republican primaries. Howdy was running against the mysterious Mr. X, a concoction of Eddie Kean's designed to disguise the fact that he couldn't quite think of a suitable opponent for Howdy.

Things were going fine until Frank Paris walked out and took Howdy Doody with him.

It was the specter of merchandising — and the age-old question of who owns what — that cost *Puppet Playhouse* its first Howdy Doody. It started when Martin Stone got a call from a toy buyer at Gimbel's. "You guys know you got a doll?" Stone asked what he meant, and the buyer explained that children were coming into the department stores with their parents and asking for a Howdy Doody doll. Stone knew an opportunity when he saw one, but who owned Howdy? Who had the right to sell his image and those of other puppets and cast members? It turned out that NBC owned Frank Paris's Howdy Doody puppet, and that Bob Smith owned the rights to the Howdy Doody character. Martin Stone by this time had an ironclad management contract with Bob Smith, so Stone decided to see if this television show could carve out a niche for itself in the children's toy market. But in 1948 Martin Stone had little inkling that the merchandising of Howdy Doody would evolve into a two-hundred-million-dollar empire by the end of the next decade.

Stone's first call was to Kay Kamen, the merchandiser who handled the Disney products. "Television?" Kamen said over the phone. "Who cares? Go see my brother — he handles Raggedy Ann." So Stone made the call and told Kay Kamen's brother about the sixty thousand button requests. He was impressed but wanted sixty percent to merchandise Howdy. Stone said he would call him back. "Now we had to resolve who owned what," Stone says. "And this was the genesis of the Frank Paris finale."

At the same time, someone from Macy's approached Frank Paris after a rehearsal and told him that the store had received hundreds of requests for a Howdy doll. The next day the guy from Macy's was back talking to Paris, who as usual had Howdy in a cloth bag. Smith joined them, and Paris told Bob that Howdy was his puppet and that he was going to have a share of any profits from merchandising.

But Smith, Stone, and NBC said no. NBC asserted that it owned the puppet and that Bob Smith owned the show. Paris maintained that he owned Howdy. It was a standoff. So Frank Paris stood up, holding Howdy Doody in his cloth bag, and announced, *"Well.* If you think that you own him, you just see how you're going to do your show tonight!" And Paris stormed out with his puppet.

"He was ill-advised," Kean says simply of Frank Paris, "and we never saw him again. But it was one P.M., and we had a show to do at five that night."

With no Howdy Doody to work with, Eddie Kean had to think fast. At five o'clock that afternoon a map of the United States was flashed on the NBC network. Bob Smith announced at the top of the show that Howdy Doody was flying to Portland, Oregon, to take part in the presidential primaries there. For the rest of that show the Peanut Gallery kids chuckled while they watched Howdy's progress on the map as he reported in over his radio.

By Saturday, Frank Paris had decided to move his puppets to another channel. That afternoon, Howdy called in from Oregon to say he was worried about the campaign. Howdy had finally laid eyes on his opponent, Mr. X, and discovered that Mr. X was the handsomest man in the world! Howdy was frantic, fearing that he was so ugly by comparison that surely no woman would vote for him. (This was of course Kean's spoof of the ultrahandsome Republican candidate, Tom Dewey, who looked like the man on the wedding cake when contrasted with the rumpled Missourian President Harry Truman.) Howdy told Bob that he was going to have his face remodeled by a plastic surgeon so that he would be the best-looking candidate in America.

It went on like this for another couple of weeks before the sponsors started to get upset that there was no Howdy to do the commercials with Bob Smith. Told that a new Howdy was being worked on, the ad people begged for anything on strings in the interim. So one Tuesday Howdy Doody radioed in that he was on his way back. The operation had been a big success, but Howdy's face would have to remain bandaged for a few more weeks — doctor's orders! Just before the show's fadeout, Howdy Doody himself came crashing through the roof of the RCA building, and the telecast ended with the new puppet dangling from the ceiling by the lines of his parachute.

Indeed, it was a new puppet, its face completely wrapped in bandages. Worked by a puppeteer named Sky Highchief, this fake Howdy had been made by a local puppet-maker named Dorothy Zuconic.

On the next show, Mr. Smith asked the Peanut Gallery, "Do you know what plastic surgery is, kids?"

"NOOOOO!"

"Well, if people think their nose is too big, they get the doctor to take a little off. It really doesn't hurt a bit! Remember, it won't hurt Howdy, but it'll help him beat Mr. X, the handsomest man in the world!"

Meanwhile, Frank Paris had gone over to a new show on WPIX, New York's Channel 11. News of his departure from *Puppet Playhouse* appeared in both *Time* and *Life* magazines as well as in Billy Rose's syndicated column, "Pitching Horseshoes," and in the earliest editions of a new magazine called *TV Guide*. NBC told the media that Frank Paris had walked out over a salary dispute, a story Paris claimed had made it hard for him to get another show on network television. So he sued NBC for damages, a suit that was later settled out of court. Years later, Paris would remember that NBC couldn't show him any kind of contract or even a canceled check to prove that NBC owned complete rights to Howdy Doody. "So I literally took my puppet and went home," Paris said.

He took Rhoda Mann with him, and that bothered Bob Smith. Nobody else could work Howdy Doody like Rhoda Mann. She was such a natural that she had quickly become used to Bob's pacing, timing, and gestures. Rhoda had perfectly coordinated Howdy to Bob's movements. Whenever another puppeteer tried it, Howdy was awkward, spastic, completely off. So one day Bob called Rhoda. "RHODA, BABEEE! It's Bob . . . Bob Smith. Rhoda, honey, no one can work Howdy like you can. Come back and work Howdy and we'll give you a hundred dollars a show!" Three shows a week, Rhoda calculated, and said yes. With regret, Frank Paris let Rhoda Mann go back to *Puppet Playhouse*.

As soon as Frank Paris left, plans for a replacement Howdy Doody got underway (the second Howdy — the bandaged puppet — was only a temporary measure). The problem was how and where to get a quality puppet fast. Fortunately, one of NBC's programming managers, Norm Blackburn, had worked for Walt Disney Studios in California. Blackburn put Bob Smith on the phone to two Disney artists, who did some drawings and sent them back east. In New York, Howdy's management chose a sort of composite that represented a friendly freckle-faced boy on a ranch. Significantly, Bob Smith had changed Howdy's voice. The old Snerdish yokel tones were replaced by a more intelligent and boyish drawl. The drawings reflected this, and these went to a young puppet artist in Los Angeles, Velma Dawson, who had also done work for Disney. Again Bob Smith got on the phone to Velma and did the new voice. Then Smith went down to Victor Recording and put the voice and some songs on acetate and shipped them to Velma. A few days later, she sent back some sketches. Smith says, "Boy, we saw one face and we said, 'That's Howdy!'" NBC told Velma Dawson to go ahead and make the puppet. For a month, NBC and the *Howdy* cast and crew waited anxiously for the third and, they hoped, final version of Howdy Doody.

Eddie Kean was now writing three shows a week. The Tuesday show had been added by Niles Trammel in response to mail from parents to the effect that their children were confused about why they could only see Howdy twice a week. Even without the show's main character, Kean played up Howdy's election into a national joke. Since you had to be *under* twenty-one to vote for Howdy, Wonder Bread was persuaded to place ballots in their bread packages. Howdy continued to tout his platform, opposed by Mr. X. If Howdy thought that the kids should have two ice cream sundaes per week, Mr. X advocated no sundaes ever. Whatever Howdy came out for, Mr. X was against. A month into this story line, Kean still didn't know who Mr. X was, except that he was running for President of the kids by proposing to abolish comic books and have school seven days a week. To supplement the old hyped-up Mack Sennett comedy two-reelers they showed as Old-Time Movies with a corny narration by Mr. Smith, Eddie Kean wrote a lot of songs for Smith and the puppets. In the afternoons Smith would record Howdy's voice on acetate, as well as all of the other puppets' dialogue. Then, on the show, Smith could talk and harmonize with the puppets, using a precise and intricate system of cuing between himself and the audio engineer. Often Smith added an on-camera ukelele or bass line as well.

It took Velma Dawson a month to make the new Howdy. For television purposes, he was almost twice the size of the average marionette, and thus quite heavy. Velma modeled him as a freckled ten-year-old and dressed him in a flannel shirt, blue jeans, a kerchief, and a cowboy hat. Howdy's mouth moved, and his eyes rolled. Howdy was as cute as a button. He was adorable! Before Velma shipped him back east, she walked him in her back yard while someone took pictures. NBC had paid Velma two thousand dollars for the puppet and all rights to same, but it was a wistful Miss Dawson who shipped the little boy-puppet back east in two crates, the head in one, the body in the other.

The crates were opened in Roger Muir's office with all hands present. There was a hush as the tops of the crates were pried loose and then a cheer of delight when Rhoda Mann joined Howdy's head to his torso and pulled him upright by his strings. Gasp! It was Howdy Doody time! On June 7, 1948, NBC issued a press release: "HOWDY DOODY WEARING NEW LOOK AFTER FACE-LIFTING ON COAST, REJOINS BOB SMITH ON NBC TELEVISION SHOW TOMORROW." On June 8, they retired the bandaged dummy and wrapped the new Howdy in bandages. NBC had been building up to this for weeks, advertising "the old voice, the new look" in the trade publications. By then

The Puppet Playhouse *puppet bridge, early 1948. Frank Paris is at left, Rhoda Mann at right. In the left foreground is an Iconoscope TV camera mounted on a wooden tripod.* (COURTESY ALAN COOK, INTERNATIONAL PUPPETRY MUSEUM PHOTO ARCHIVES)

Velma Dawson and her new Howdy marionette, May 1948. (BURT DUBROW COLLECTION)

Boston's WBZ had joined the NBC network, and children in six cities were glued to their tubes to see what the new Howdy looked like. At the end of a suspenseful show, Mr. Smith and Clarabell gently unwrapped Howdy's bandages, and suddenly there he was, smiling, blinking, a nice child rather than a horrible doll. The television-watching children of America relaxed. Howdy looked great. The nation breathed a sigh of relief.

We can see this new Howdy if we turn out the lights and put an old kinescope on a sixteen-millimeter projector and throw it on the wall. The date on the rusty old can is June 1948; it's probably from mid-June because the new Howdy is there but it's an hour-long Saturday show, before it went to five shows per week, Monday through Friday.

The kine flickers into focus with Bob telling a dopey joke that's a pun on the word *Rappahannock*. Then he sits at his piano and plays the theme. We get a glimpse of Bob Keeshan in a polka-dot Clarabell suit as Smith talks to the kids in the Peanut Gallery, consisting of a low cardboard wall in front of some folding chairs. After speaking directly to the kids watching in Baltimore and Washington, Smith narrates an Old-Time Movie while Doc Whipple plays accompaniment on the organ. Then there are commercials for Kellogg's Corn Flakes and Wonder Bread. Smith sells the cereal and the bread with the spiritual fervor of an itinerant tent preacher.

After the film, it's time for one of Eddie's quizzes, a "Peanut Puzzler." In keeping with the Howdy for President theme, which has been trumpeted throughout the show, the kids in the studio are asked to draw the White House. But of course Clarabell gets it wrong and draws a "Wide House" by mistake. When Mr. Smith upbraids him for not paying attention, Clarabell becomes irritable, disgruntled, sulky — a sort of ultimate oversized two-year-old jerk.

Then Mr. Smith sits at his upright piano, with Howdy perched on top of it. They sing a song about only crossing at the green light, the kind of thing Eddie Kean wrote to counter mail from people complaining that the show wasn't teaching the kids anything. To end the show, Mr. Smith asks the kids if they have any wishes. The first child says he wishes Howdy had an animal friend to play with. (NBC received hundreds of letters on this subject.) The second child says she thinks Howdy Doody should be on every day. The third, a tiny little girl no more than four years old, bravely tells a sympathetic and concerned Mr. Smith that she doesn't want the baseball game to be on at the same time as Howdy because they take Howdy off the air when that happens. At this point the forty-year-old kine trails off, but you get the idea.

By the end of June, Howdy was on every weekday.

Parents had continued writing NBC to say that their children were confused by the show's Tuesday/Thursday/Saturday schedule. Instead of alternating days, the parents would cry, can't you put it on every day? For six weeks Roger Muir agitated with his bosses Wade and Trammel. Smith, Muir, and Martin Stone — *Puppet Playhouse*'s ruling triumvirate — all wanted a strip show, and Eddie Kean was convinced he could write it. Of course, there had never *been* a strip show — five consecutive weekday installments, like a radio soap opera — on television before. There were people at NBC who wondered whether a strip show could really work on television.

The decision was eventually made by Bobby Sarnoff, who was selling the show to advertisers. Put it on at five-thirty, Sarnoff concluded, while Mom is making dinner. So one day in June they plastered the number 5 all over the set. It took Howdy and the gang a whole show to solve the mystery: starting the next week, Howdy was going to be on every day, Monday through Friday, from five-thirty to six! That's right, kids, you'll be able to watch Howdy and the gang — every day!

Writing five shows a week, Eddie Kean worked like a slave. He loaded scripts with as many Old-Time Movies, seltzer blasts, riotous chases, and vaudeville acts as he could; it helped that the commercials could run long and often took up as much as a third of the show. No one ever held a stopwatch to an advertiser on *Puppet Playhouse* or *Howdy*. But Kean still had to come up with a lot of fresh material, and gradually he began to add new characters to the show.

The first was an accident. As soon as NBC received Velma Dawson's Howdy and saw that it was a masterpiece, Roger Muir called Velma again and asked her for another Howdy puppet. The show obviously needed two Howdys, in case of an accident, and Muir also wanted this new Howdy's eyes to roll more and his face to be generally more animated. Velma told Muir that she thought these changes would alter Howdy's *look* too much, but Muir said he didn't care. When Velma Dawson sent Howdy II back to New York, there was grumbling at NBC. "Don't much look like Howdy," they said. So they called up Scotty Brinker.

Scotty was a furniture maker from Staten Island who owned one of the first seven-inch Motorola televisions in his neighborhood. All the kids came over to watch Howdy Doody. The only other places they could go were their fathers' taverns, which didn't sit too well with their moms. Scott Brinker watched the show one day and went down to his basement and built a sample Howdy Doody premium, a tin Howdy with a mouth that pulled open with a string. The next day he called up Bob Smith at NBC. Despite the fact that Smith performed on five early-morning radio broadcasts and five early-evening telecasts each week, and continued to do *Triple B Ranch* on radio every Saturday morning, he answered his own phone. Brinker thought he sounded friendly. Premium, eh? Well, come on down, said Smith.

So Scotty got on the ferry and went to 30 Rockefeller Plaza. It was about a month after Frank Paris had left the show, taking Howdy, Mr. Huff, and Eustace with him. Bob Smith thought Brinker's premium was cute, but what he really needed was puppets.

Bob asked Brinker, "Do you make marionettes?"

Scott Brinker had never even seen a marionette up close, but he said, "Sure!" Shortly thereafter Brinker had the contract to build that notorious dirty old man and villain, Phineas T. Bluster. But before he had even started on the Bluster puppet, Brinker was asked to come back to NBC and look at Howdy II. The executives in charge of the show told him they didn't think the puppet looked like Howdy and, since they needed more characters, they were going to turn him into a detective. So Scott took Howdy II back to his workshop on Staten Island and began to operate, shaving the puppet's nose and reshaping his chin. A tailor in Brinker's neighborhood made a suit with a cape and a deerstalker's hat. When fully dressed and strung, the Dawson/Brinker creation looked like Howdy Doody as Sherlock Holmes. It was perfect, and Eddie Kean christened the puppet Inspector John J. Fadoozle, America's Number One (here a sound effect went *BOING!*) Private Eye.

When they beheld his skillful work, they hired Brinker to build another Howdy so they could do costume changes. Brinker copied Velma's puppet, altering it slightly since Rhoda had complained that Howdy was top-heavy and hard to handle. Eddie Kean dubbed Brinker's new Howdy "Double Doody" and tried to figure out how he could get both puppets on the air at the same time.

Nobody took a vacation during the summer of 1948. Kean kept up his election-year primer on democracy. Between commercials and musical numbers, Mr. Smith would show the kids how to mark their ballots in *TV Guide* and send them in. This ballot-marking lesson was usually followed by a short lecture on the rules of a democratic election. This stuff was well-liked in Washington. In September, the conservative *American Magazine* endorsed Howdy's campaign.

In this period Kean also trotted out inventions like the Honk-a-doodle, which translated goose honks into Mother Goose stories in English. There was also the Flapdoodle, which served any purpose Howdy required, and the Air-o-doodle. Through all of this pranced and sprayed the anarchic Clarabell.

Just as Clarabell was a problem, so was Bobby Keeshan. All Bob Smith really wanted was a little band on *Puppet Playhouse,* but Keeshan had a tin ear and could barely play three consecutive notes on a simple marimba. Very early on, Eddie wrote a skit in which Mr. Smith tries and fails to teach Clarabell to play three notes in a row. Smith would get exasperated and call Clarabell a dummy. The clown would retaliate with a vicious spritz of seltzer, and there would be a chase. The kids would scream. But Smith really *was* annoyed that Keeshan couldn't play music.

In September Bob Smith added to his already taxing work schedule a weekly prime-time music series, *The Gulf Show Starring Bob Smith,* which ran until the summer of 1949. As was common in that era, the show went through several format changes — variety hour, musical quiz, talent show, and new talent (which included the debut of singer Patti Page). For a time, some of the musical pressure was off Clarabell, as Smith's ever-sharpened musical chops were in demand elsewhere.

Finally, in the first week of November, America voted for President. "Howdy had been running against Mr. X for nine months at this point," Eddie Kean remembers. "It was a gold mine for us because we got to cover every state in the union. We talked about making cheese in Wisconsin and coal mines in Pennsylvania. We tried to educate the kids and show them what this country was all about. We were all proud we got all the four- and five-year-olds acquainted with the names of the states. But during all this time, I still didn't know who Mr. X was going to be. Then, when I saw the new Howdy puppet, it dawned on me. Mr. X was Howdy's twin brother — Double Doody!"

They explained this on the air as a way of making sure that Howdy Doody got all the votes for President of the kids.

Two days after the election the headline HAIL HOWDY DOODY! appeared over the byline of radio columnist Jack Gould in the *New*

York Times. The subhead read: "He Triumphs over Mr. X, Survives Mr. Y, and Always Delights the Youngsters." The story noted that incredulous ballot-counters in all forty-eight states had declared that Howdy Doody had finished third in the presidential election, behind President Harry Truman and Thomas Dewey but way ahead of the third-party candidate, Henry Wallace. (Some Doodyville historians actually claim that Howdy Doody received about a million write-in ballots in the election, but this is impossible to confirm.)

Gould said in his column that he was particularly impressed with Smith's skill in communicating with children. "[Smith] has proved to be that rarest of souls, a man who avoids any hint of condescension toward the younger generation and makes the boys and girls feel partners in the spirited high-jinks of his wooden alter ego. [Smith's is] one of the most imaginative minds in broadcasting." After stating that the Honk-a-doodle was a much-needed machine, Gould summed up: "In the extraordinary versatility of his performance, Mr. Smith may have hit upon the answer to the academic do-gooders who bemoan the influence of the comics and the thriller radio shows and as a substitute would jam old-fashioned tales down unwilling ears. The more constructive suggestion as suggested by the success of *Howdy Doody* is to offer something wholesomely different, something [that is] equally stimulating to the youthful imagination yet is not furnished in what children might regard as a demeaning manner. For many, many reasons in fact, hail Howdy Doody."

By Christmastime, everyone on *Puppet Playhouse* was exhausted. One crisis after another had been faced and resolved. "The lifeblood of that early show was that, despite many crises, things seemed to stay natural," says Eddie Kean. "Somehow it just flowed. So many things that caught on in *Howdy,* like the election, happened because of a bad problem, like Frank Paris leaving. Eventually we got used to taking some disaster and adopting it, making good use of it. Marty Stone kept saying it was the philosophy of his whole life. When you face adversity, don't just lick it, but turn it into a plus if you can. It's a good trick."

Nineteen forty-eight had been the year television really made it to the American marketplace, the year television "broke." By December of that year, there were 127 television stations around the country. In 1949, Americans would buy eight million television sets. Vladymir Zworykin's pioneer tube, the Iconoscope, was superseded by Dr. Albert Rose's Image Orthikon tube, which required much less light and projected a better image. The Image Orthikon was also easier to operate, since the Iconoscope cameraman had to work with an image that was upside down and reversed, not the case with the Orthikon. Some media critics cried that television would cripple the Baby Boomers with fatal radiation and long-term mental problems, but others saw the flickering little tube as comfort and solace for millions of lonely people, an invention that could prevent mankind from withering in depression and ignorance.

What did the so-called lonely and depressed like to watch? Well, in 1948 cleavage was very big on television. Cleavage — or, more accurately, modestly low-cut evening dresses — made big stars out of actresses like Faye Emerson and Dagmar, who appeared on Jerry Lester's *Broadway Open House,* the first prime-time chat show on network television. Columnist Ed Sullivan, borscht belt comedian Milton Berle, and radio star Arthur Godfrey all made their television debuts that year, as did another puppet show out of Chicago, *Kukla, Fran & Ollie,* with puppeteer Burr Tillstrom, actress Fran Allison, and the soon-to-be-beloved Kuklapolitan Players. It was also the year that television ratings began. The networks and the ad agencies wanted to know how many people were watching the four hundred thousand sets in homes and bars around the country. The dreaded Hooperatings, which measured television audiences, were instituted by statistician Claude E. Hooper, much to the detriment of good television ever since.

The cast and crew of *Puppet Playhouse* knew they were in the vanguard of this revolution. Theirs was the hottest show on television, the only thing everybody watched every day. Once Martin Stone asked the president of Colgate why he was advertising an adult product, Halo shampoo, on the show. The distinguished Mr. Little replied that he was selling more Halo on *Puppet Playhouse* than he was on the *Colgate Comedy Hour.* For this, Martin Stone still credits that ultimate salesman, Bob Smith. "Bob could leap across the camera, through the lens," Stone says. "He could project complete sincerity. He could talk to the kids on their own level. Plus, he was genuinely in love with what he was doing. He didn't even have to work that hard at being a star. He was himself — *sui generis!*"

Reflecting on those vanished days, Martin Stone describes Bob Smith almost as if he had had some kind of weird power over children. "He would do the commercials," Stone recalls in amazement, *"and kids would go buy the stuff."*

At the time, Martin Stone had a management contract with Bob Smith. Stone arranged for NBC to compensate Bob by paying him thirty-five hundred dollars a week for *Puppet Playhouse*. More importantly, Stone reserved the crucial licensing rights to Howdy for Smith and himself. According to Smith, when Martin Stone finally cut the licensing deal for Howdy Doody, Stone kept fifty percent while Bob Smith and NBC split the remaining half. Smith felt a little funny about this, but toy-makers were flooding Stone's office with requests to manufacture everything from Howdy Doody watches to Howdy Doody toilet seats. Martin Stone assured Bob Smith that they would make a fortune from it, and they did.

Watching this from the sidelines was Clarabell — Bobby Keeshan, who was then making about a hundred dollars a week. Clarabell, who was ridiculed and belittled daily by Mr. Smith on network television. Resentment began to simmer in Keeshan's gentle heart. Forty years later, with a lot of water having flowed under the proverbial bridge, some of the resentment still lingers between the two men. Speaking of Bob Smith's early success, Robert Keeshan, TV's Elder Statesman, grudgingly allows: "It *had* to be Bob, because in those days you couldn't get anyone else to work in television. If an actor was making a living in radio or the theater, he was being paid, at least, which certainly wasn't the case in television. It was Bob because there wasn't anybody else."

Bobby Keeshan as Chief Featherman. (EDDIE KEAN COLLECTION)

Four
Meatballs and Spaghetti

Pushing goods to children is an abomination, and allowing the most popular shows to float along on the surface, buoyed by the ratings, clearly abdicates adult obligations to children.
— Martin Mayer, *About Television*

IN 1949 comedian Milton Berle conquered television for adults with the same force with which Howdy had mastered the children of America.

My father had been working for RCA for two years by then, and he was itching to find a job on the NBC television network. Like many veterans, Howard Davis hadn't had much idea of what career he would pursue when he returned from the war. He had been raised in the large family of a circuit-riding Methodist country parson in southern Missouri during the Depression. After the war, fond memories of a boyhood along the Mississippi weren't enough to keep him from New York, where the real action was, then as now. Before leaving England, after his discharge, Howard had studied economics at the University of London. This and his love for the English language, he felt, would see him through to his first job in the big city.

Back in '39, Howard had been one of those countless country boys who hitchhiked north to work at the World's Fair in New York. Like all those others, he had been impressed by the early TV broadcasts at the Fair. So on his return to New York Howard gravitated toward the personnel office of RCA. His first job was as a public-relations man at the RCA Exhibition Hall on West Forty-ninth Street, across from the RCA Building.

The Exhibition Hall is the site of my earliest memories. It had a huge art deco glass window facing the street; inside were demonstrated such technoglories as the new ten-inch RCA TV (black-and-white, of course), the new electron microscope, and the ultranew microwave oven (which wouldn't be bought by the public for another twenty years). Down a long sloping ramp parallel to the Forty-ninth

Street window was the Johnny Victor Theater, a large screening room with plush red seats. I was first taken to the Exhibition Hall when I was less than three years old, and I remember sitting through (and being frightened by) Laurence Olivier's vivid color film of *Richard III* in the theater downstairs.

As for my father, a PR position at RCA was the perfect entrée for an aspiring writer who wanted to break into television. In 1949 anybody could write for television. NBC needed material not only for network programming but for its local flagship station, WNBT. So with his friend Steve deBaun, Howard wrote some scripts for a kids' show called *Tales of the Red Caboose* — sponsored, of course, by Lionel Trains. Since NBC didn't have anyone else to do it, Davis and deBaun had to direct the shows as well, using sixteen-millimeter film. In the same era Howard wrote some scripts for an early series called *Eye Witness,* which took a supposedly panting public behind the scenes of television. Ben Grauer was the host and narrator. Howard remembers writing a scene with a scantily clad girl for an *Eye Witness* show about NBC's costume department. There was a very pretty girl in her underwear around that day, he recalls, a twenty-one-year-old NBC contract actress named Eva Marie Saint.

During that time Howard got to know some of the people running NBC. There was the autocratic General Sarnoff at the head of the organization, the one-time wireless hero transformed into a wartime brigadier who had served in Washington. Sarnoff's chauffeur, Harry O'Brien, was a legend around the company and — like most RCA/NBC people — hung out at Hurley's, an old Irish bar on Forty-eighth Street and Sixth Avenue that had defied the Rockefellers and held on to its corner location surrounded by the granite blocks of Rockefeller Center. Howard remembers the rumors buzzing around NBC in 1949 about NBC's dynamic new programming chief, Sylvester "Pat" Weaver. Everyone at the network knew that Pat Weaver represented a new era at NBC.

The old NBC had been all radio. It had gotten so big that it had to split into two radio networks — the Red and the Blue. Eventually the government stepped in to break this monopoly, and the Blue Network was sold and later evolved into the American Broadcasting Company (ABC). When my father joined NBC in 1949, radio far surpassed TV in audience, sales, and importance. Howard's pay for a prime-time TV script was fifty dollars, compared to the radio writers' guild minimum of $250. The big NBC stars who passed through Kaufman & Bedrick, the NBC drugstore/soda fountain/lunch counter, were the radio household words — Fred Allen, Eddie Cantor, Jimmy Durante. None of them was really interested in television.

Milton Berle changed their minds. Most of the great radio comics — Bob Hope, Red Skelton, Fred Allen, Burns and Allen — held off their TV debuts until the early 1950s, when TV was better established. Milton Berle, who owned Tuesday nights in America as early as 1949, was the exception. A young comic from the borscht circuit and Broadway, Berle hadn't been a radio star. His humor looked original on television since it relied on highly visual sight gags, not on joke telling. Berle appeared on TV in heavy showgirl makeup and Carmen Miranda pineapple headdress drag, and his popularity was unbelievable. Restaurants, movies, and theaters would actually close on Tuesday nights rather than compete with Berle's *Texaco Star Theater*. Broadway was devastated when Uncle Miltie literally kidded the piss out of America (in 1949 municipal water authorities began noting alarming and unprecedented drops in American reservoirs during the commercial minutes on *Texaco Star Theater*).

Pat Weaver, NBC's new dynamo, was emblematic of these changing times. By then the three networks — NBC, CBS, and DuMont — covered a television service quadrant roughly cornered by Boston, Chicago, Saint Louis, and Washington (DuMont would eventually be replaced by ABC). Milton Berle had a Hooperating of 75, which meant that for every million televisions in existence then, 750,000 were tuned to Berle. Pat Weaver was the first television executive in a position to react to an audience of this size; once he had the American people, he invented modern television for them.

Weaver had been ad agency Young & Rubicam's "man from the sponsor" on the Fred Allen show, and had then come to NBC as first head of programming, eventually becoming network president. While at NBC he would literally stage a revolution in TV management, wresting control of his shows away from their sponsors. He invented the "Spectacular," or one-hour special. Later, he would move television away from variety and vaudeville and toward magazine-style telejournalism. But first Weaver rode a crest of success created by Howdy Doody and then the national landslide of Milton Berle. Weaver had another big success when he aired another puppet show from affiliate WNBQ in Chicago. Weaver put *Kukla, Fran & Ollie* on the NBC network at 7:00 P.M. weekdays, an hour after *Howdy*. Not only did Kukla get Howdy's audience, but it also appealed to adults, just arriving home from work at that hour. Kukla was more sophisticated than Howdy, with tongue-in-cheek dialogue between hand-puppets Oliver J. Dragon and Kukla the Clown, moderated by actress Fran Allison. *Kukla* was the first hip show on television, and the darling of a lot of people in show biz and politics. The actress Tallulah Bankhead was a big fan of the Kuklapolitan Players in those early days and would always show up at the RCA Exhibition Hall when Tillstrom and company came in from Chicago to broadcast from the Johnny Victor Theater. Pundits, columnists, and other media critics read all sorts of subversive material into *Kukla* that Tillstrom would deny was ever there.

My father paid his first visit to the *Howdy Doody* set around this time, in 1949. Of course, I was watching regularly at home by the age of two (this slot is today filled for that crowd by *Sesame Street*), but my father often worked late in those days and only saw *Howdy* on monitors at the Exhibition Hall. Sometimes, after leaving his office around 9:00 P.M., Howard would walk across the street to RCA and take the elevator to the eighth floor. There, in Studio 8H, which had been specially built for the purpose, Arturo Toscanini conducted the NBC Symphony's national radio broadcasts. This was an era in which both NBC and CBS maintained broadcast orchestras that were the equal of the great metropolitan symphonies of the day. One day Howard was up on the eighth floor trying to arrange to get into that night's Toscanini broadcast when he stopped in at Studio 8A to watch Howdy rehearse. Howard knew most of the show's technical crew as "the Astoria crowd" — Warren Wade's fellow Signal Corps veterans, including Roger Muir and Robert Rippen, who had replaced Muir as Howdy's director when Muir's increasing duties as producer made him unable to juggle both jobs. Howard also knew the stage manager at the time, Dominick Dunne, a young guy in his first job whom they all called Nicky. Then there was the boom man, Bud Yorkin, and a cameraman named B. J. Bjornson. My father had walked into a rehearsal, and the whole crew was howling over some ribald malaprop that Bob Smith had just caused Howdy to come up with. The atmosphere was unusually warm and familiar in the studio, and Howard Davis decided that the set of *Howdy Doody* would be a nice place to work.

Howdy Doody was inaugurated President of the Kids of the United States in January 1949, to much hype and hoopla on the part of NBC.

This was a big problem for Eddie Kean, whose nine-month election scam was now over. *Puppet Playhouse* had to change, and drastically. These changes began early in 1949. The name of the show was changed from the outmoded *Puppet Playhouse* to *The Howdy Doody Show* for easier recognition. Then Eddie Kean changed Mr. Smith's name as well.

The existential questions arose: Who was Mr. Smith, anyway? And what was his relationship with Howdy Doody? "It was never stipulated," Eddie Kean says. "All I knew was they had met one day and became friends. We never tried to explain anything beyond that." Kean suggests that Martin Stone came up with the name Buffalo Bob, and Smith told an interviewer that "Eddie Kean came up with the idea that my great-grandfather was Buffalo Tom, the Great White Hunter of the Sigafoose Indians; when Buffalo Tom passed on to his Happy Hunting Ground he left his title and pioneer suit to his next of kin. I was that person. So sometime in 1949 I was given the suit, officially named Buffalo Bob, and as far as I know I'm still the Great White Leader of the Sigafoose Indians."

At the same time, a new set was built with a better puppet bridge, a bigger Peanut Gallery, and more doors for slapstick entries and exits. For the first two years Eddie Kean had set the show at the Howdy Doody Circus, which had evolved from Frank Paris's Toby Tyler show. Now Kean pitched Howdy's circus permanently in the town of Doodyville. It was around this time that one show featured an Indian celebration to recognize the Indian roots of Mr. Smith; he was renamed Buffalo Bob. Using the primitive fade-and-dissolve technology of the Image Orthikon cameras, Buffalo Bob materialized on the Doodyville set in his new pioneer costume with the rampant buffalo on the back.

Attending and presiding over Mr. Smith's transformation into Buffalo Bob was Doodyville's resident Indian, Chief Featherman, headman of the Tinka Tonka tribe, played by Bobby Keeshan. Featherman and all the other Indian material derived from Eddie Kean's indoctrination into Indian lore at his old summer camp. "You have to remember that *Howdy* was never a big-budgeted show, even in its prime," Kean says. "We always had to be resourceful, making the most of what we had.

"For reasons I can't remember, it seemed appropriate to have an Indian character, even before Buffalo Bob came along. An Indian also seemed a good thing to play Clarabell against, because neither of them would know what the hell the other one was. Plus, we had Keeshan pestering us all the time for a speaking part. But we only had a budget for one guy, so we had Keeshan play Chief Featherman because I wanted an Indian so badly. So what do you do next? You have Clarabell afraid of the Featherman since they can never meet anyway; you have Chief Featherman on an eternal search for Clarabell. If you mentioned Featherman's name, Clarabell put on his roller skates and fled. This began in 1948, and for a year we made a national epic of the hatred of the Featherman for the clown. Fortunately they never met, because that was as much of a story line as we ever had. It also took Keeshan at least fifteen minutes to do each makeup. It looked to the kids as if *something* was going on, but of course nothing was ever happening."

Kean's next inventions were more puppets to populate Doodyville. Since the election only three puppets had been used — Howdy, Double Doody, and the Inspector. Now Eddie would invent new puppet foils for Howdy. These first two were Mr. Bluster and Dilly Dally.

Bluster and Dilly were direct descendants of Mr. Huff and Eustace, who had disappeared along with Frank Paris. "I hate to say this," Kean says ruefully, "because it sounds like plagiarism, but Bluster was modeled on Huff, the manager of Toby's circus. Mr. Bluster was a know-it-all type, and Dilly Dally was his lackey and slave.

"The role of Mr. Bluster was always to want what Howdy had, or want to do what Howdy was doing. It was rivalry like in the home. If Howdy had a circus, then Bluster wanted all the kids to come to the Bluster Circus instead." Kean initially intended the Phineas T. Bluster character to be an old-fashioned circus promoter like P. T. Barnum, but eventually Bluster evolved into a cantankerous old man named, reportedly by Roger Muir, in honor of the blustery old NBC war-horse Warren Wade.

"With Mr. Bluster we tried to create a new kind of kids' villain," Kean remembers. "We wanted a lovable villain like a child's crusty and half deaf grandfather. With Bluster you were always on Howdy's side, but the element of fear was never there. The element of *concern* was there, but never fear."

Mr. Bluster was drawn and designed by Milt Neal, a former Disney artist and cartoonist who had joined *Puppet Playhouse* in 1948 as a sketch artist, replacing the original Nino. Neal was used frequently on the show because he could produce large drawings for television quickly and accurately. His sketches for Bluster went to Scott Brinker on Staten Island after Brinker had finished Double Doody and the Inspector. Brinker built Bluster as a sclerotic old coot in a three-piece suit, bowler, and spats. When Scott brought the Bluster marionette into the kitchen to show his wife, Edith, she made him drill air holes in Bluster's carrying box because he looked so real.

There was a collective gasp in Martin Stone's office when Brinker took Bluster out of the box, then out of his cloth bag. The whole show — cast and crew — was awed by Phineas. He was like a character in every family in America. Now they needed a new puppeteer to work him and a voice to bring Mr. Bluster to life as vividly as Howdy Doody was animated by Bob Smith.

They had the same problem with regard to Dilly Dally. As built by Brinker, he was a dim little boy in a baseball cap and letter sweater, always willing to follow any person (or puppet) he met. Dilly was Bluster's foil, according to Eddie Kean: "What did we do with Dilly Dally? Well, if Howdy had a circus, then Bluster wanted to be the boss of the circus. He used Dilly because Bluster was a big user of other people. He was always able to manipulate and bamboozle Dilly Dally into aiding his schemes to take over the circus. Bluster was always able to hoodwink Clarabell as well, since Clarabell always helped anyone who befriended him." Eventually, Kean points out, Dilly Dally declared his independence from Bluster and became a character in his own right.

Two puppeteers were hired in 1949 to work Mr. Bluster and Dilly Dally. First hired was Bill Lecornec, who quickly became the infamous Chief Thunderthud as well, making the expletive "Kowabonga!" a household word. In a cast that included an out-of-town disc jockey like Smith and two naive youngsters like Keeshan and Rhoda Mann, Lecornec really stood out. He was a confirmed bachelor in his thirties, lived in Greenwich Village, and enjoyed a drink.

Lecornec was born in 1915 to a poor family in Marin County, California. In 1931 he won a scholarship to the Fairmont School of the Theater in San Francisco, later touring California during the Depression in a traveling company that did Broadway plays and *Alice in Wonderland* (Lecornec was the White Rabbit). He grew into a dark and handsome young man and was advised by all to go to Hollywood and try for the movies. "But I didn't want to go to Hollywood," Lecornec recalls. "I wanted to go to New York and be on the stage." Along the way, Lecornec learned to work marionettes. After the war, Lecornec came to New York and landed a role in the Broadway musical *The Firefly*.

Rhoda Mann had been working Dilly and was relieved when Lecornec was hired. She says, "Bill was a very talented man with a wonderful speaking voice. He also did interesting voices, could move well, was nice-looking, and had a wonderful sense of humor. I had started Dilly Dally and then they brought Bill in because he could sing. He had done some summer stock and knew how to work puppets, so he was just what we were looking for."

Lecornec today doesn't remember how he got the job. But it was obvious to everyone that Bill marched to a different drummer. "Bill was separate from the rest of us," Keeshan says. "But there was no easier guy to get along with. He never said a bad thing about anyone, and we laughed with him a lot. He was accident-prone, was chronically late to rehearsals, and always had wild excuses. There would be fires in his apartment and five major tragedies a week. Plus he was a little flaky and had difficulty remembering his lines. We had to dance around him all the time, trying to bring him back."

"It seemed like I went up there forever," Lecornec says, recalling his audition for *Howdy*. Boy, were they fussy! They — Roger Muir — kept auditioning me doing different voices. [He demonstrates:] 'Deelee Deealley!' 'DIILLYY DAALLLLEE!!' Finally they said they'd give me a chance. So they put me on, and I was scared to death because I had hardly ever seen television at the time, let alone been in a studio. Jeezus! But I told myself it was a steady job, and I did do Dilly Dally very well; and since Dilly was an important part of the show, at least I felt that my voice was now rather important. I felt like . . . Miss America!"

Shortly after they hired Lecornec to work Dilly, they hired Dayton Allen, another young actor/puppeteer, to work Bluster. Dayton, still described forty years later as a comic madman by those who knew him, changed and dominated *The Howdy Doody Show* over the next four years. His comedic energy, practical jokes, outrageous behavior, and amorous adventures are still remembered and recounted by *Howdy* veterans and older hands at NBC. *Dayton*, they still exclaim, shaking their heads when they hear his name. *What a madman!*

Even today it's hard to get a straight answer from Dayton: picture a millionaire semiretired actor who thinks he's a scream toying with an interviewer who has intruded on a lush August afternoon in the country.

QUESTION: Dayton, where were you born?
DAYTON: Near Mom.

Dayton Allen. (COURTESY DAYTON ALLEN)

Q: No, really.

DAYTON: I tell everyone I was born in Dayton, Ohio.

Q: That's not true, is it?

DAYTON: Yeah. No, it's not true, that's right. Then we moved to New York.

Q: Were you born in Dayton?

DAYTON: No. Nobody that I knew ever was born there. I was born in New York at Lloyd's Sanitarium because they couldn't afford Madison Square Garden. This was in 1831.

Q: Were you born in Manhattan?

DAYTON: We think so, yeah. But my mother lied a lot. We lived in Jackson Heights but then we moved to Africa 'cause I wanted to be near my grandparents. You know — *Roots!* And we've been eating them ever since.

Q: Please, Dayton. When did you get into radio?

DAYTON: When I found a big enough set, because otherwise you can break your hip.

Actually Dayton Allen Bolke was born in New York in 1918 and started on WINS radio in 1939. "I spun records, did characters and voices. I did a million things. I was so great that I was even better than I thought I was." During the war the Army put Dayton in Special Services, and he entertained the troops with an impersonations act, working with bandleaders like Ray Block. After the war he did radio stand-ins and soap operas for ten dollars a shot until he made his television debut in a rowdy early puppet show called *The Oky Doky Ranch*. It was broadcast on the DuMont network on Thursdays at 7:00 P.M. from its downtown studios in Wanamaker's department store and featured Dayton working and doing voices for a grotesque thirty-inch marionette, Oky Doky, which, Dayton says, "was a four-hundred-pound lummox I used to work from a platform." Ostensibly featuring a gang of kids in games and contests with a dude-ranch theme (sound familiar?), *Oky Doky* went on the air in November 1948 and lasted until Dayton left a few months later. In Dayton's loving hands *Oky Doky* quickly got a reputation as a violent and crazy show, with puppets bashing each other over the head and plates and furniture flying all over the set.

"So in 1949," continues Dayton, "I was doing *Oky Doky*. One day I walked into the men's room on the third floor of NBC and I met Bobby Keeshan — who I imagine is still there. He said, 'Hey, you do a lot of voices. We're doing a thing here called *Howdy Doody*.' As

idn't know! They were doing it down the hall in 3A. So I went
there with Keeshan and met Bob Smith and he said, 'We're
doing a thing with puppets. You ever work puppets?' I said, 'Are
you kidding? *They* never worked *me*. I *gotta* do it that way.' "

Bob Smith only had to take one look at Dayton Allen's goofy
rubberized mug; he only had to hear the aggressive, spontaneous,
and unquenchable spritz emerge from Dayton's huge mouth to know
that Dayton was just what they were looking for. "We needed a
puppeteer who could do voices," Smith later remembered. "Dayton
could do a million voices but didn't know a puppet from a horse-
ball. Of course he said he was a great puppeteer."

"So I went on *Howdy Doody,*" Dayton relates, "and the first thing
I did was Mr. Bluster. I didn't really know shit about marionettes,
so I used to come in early and rehearse in front of a mirror. Eventually I had Bluster working like a live person." Bob Smith agreed.
"He wound up making Bluster breathe. It was uncanny!"

In the beginning, Dayton worked three shows a week at twenty-
five dollars a show. In addition to Bluster, he did voices for the
Inspector, Mr. Bluster's Spanish brother, Don José Bluster, and many
others, including the Flubadub. Designed by Milt Neal as an amal-
gamation of different animals, the Flubadub was to be Howdy's new
pet; it was also written in as the cover story for Bob Smith's desperately needed two-week vacation in February 1949. Before he left,
Smith told the kids he was departing on a hunting expedition to
find the Flubadub, a gawky and woolly-headed creature with a flow-
erpot hat. The Flub had a duck's head, the ears of a cocker spaniel,
a giraffe's neck, a dachshund's body, a seal's flippers, a pig's tail, a
cat's whiskers, and the memory of an elephant. "She shouldn't be
too hard to spot," Buffalo Bob told the Peanuts.

One week later, a notice signed by Bob Smith appeared in the
Kids' Korner section of *TV Guide,* apologizing because the kids at
home hadn't been shown a picture of the Flubadub as the old Buffalo
had promised before he left. Actually the Flubadub puppet, an extremely complicated marionette being built by Scott Brinker, as
usual on the shortest of notice, simply wasn't ready yet. The following week, the Buffalo returned from his first vacation in two years,
looking tanned and eager to get back to work. NBC was as anxious
for Bob's return as the kids, since he was irreplaceable; no one else
could talk to the children right through the camera and sell them
toys and candy they didn't need. When Smith wasn't around, the
sponsors complained.

Anyway, Eddie Kean started writing material for the Flubadub, a harebrained mutant Dayton Allen voiced in a high-pitched scream. The Flub started out as a problem eater; since he was from a Caribbean island, all he wanted to eat was flowers. Then parents began to write and call NBC to protest that their children — the Baby Boomers — were eating flowers in the back yard because they had seen the Flubadub do it on television. Eddie Kean was stunned. The children were eating flowers? What kind of power did he have? Under pressure, Eddie quickly changed the Flub's favorite food to spaghetti and meatballs. *"Meatballs and spaghetti,"* Dayton would scream. *"Meatballs and spaghetti!"* Soon the children changed their tune as well. And Eddie Kean had learned one of the earliest lessons in television — that young children will imitate almost anything they find interesting on the tube.

By this time Howdy Doody was being seen by about five million children every day on twenty-five live and kinescope stations across the country. In February 1949, *Howdy Doody* inaugurated the new New York–Chicago coaxial cable, which opened Chicago to network televison. This boosted the total television audience to between fifteen and eighteen million.

Rhoda Mann was working Howdy that February day, which she remembers with bemused horror. "That was the year they brought Dayton in," she says, "and he scared the hell out of me at first. I was just a little girl from the Bronx, and here was Dayton, who was always ready to expose himself. *Aaargh!* And of course he had his hands on me all the time. On the first day of the coaxial cable we were on live from New York to Chicago, the entire network. Usually, when Dayton and I were up on the puppet bridge, we would hang up our mikes during the Old-Time Movie and relax. But on the day of this special broadcast I stayed up on the bridge, which was very narrow. I still had my chest mike on, and somebody in the control room hadn't turned it off. I was bending over watching the movie on the puppeteers' monitor, and Dayton came up quietly behind me and put his hand between my legs. I was startled and furious and I blurted 'Jesus Christ, Dayton! Keep your goddamned hands off of me!' This went out over the whole network." Rhoda laughs ruefully and says, "I think they docked Dayton a week for that one."

In April 1949 Howdy Doody won a Peabody Award. The George Foster Peabody Award for broadcasting was a big deal in the radio world and was considered an honor for anyone in television as well. In citing it as Outstanding Children's Program of 1948, the award committee described *Howdy* in glowing terms as a "beguiling puppet show, which, in a brief span of time, has devised a formula that is frequently educational, never frightening or offensive, and is invariably hailed with rapture by children themselves." The Peabody brought with it a certain sheen of academic prestige, and was pointed to for years by *Howdy*'s producers when (as often happened) they were accused of vulgar commercialism and irresponsibility by outraged parent groups.

Until May 1949 Howdy Doody stayed in New York, content to do his show from 30 Rock. But Howdy was such a star that children and even adults began demanding to see him in the — pardon the expression — flesh. So that May Buffalo Bob, Clarabell, and Howdy Doody flew to Washington to participate in a bond-selling government promotion called "I Am an American" Day. The three characters were posed on the steps of the Capitol with the vice president of the United States, Alben W. Barkley, and most of the members of Harry Truman's cabinet. At the close of the ceremony, while the Buffalo, Clarabell, and Howdy were posing for pictures with the various dignitaries, one of the latter group shocked Bobby Keeshan by whispering into his ear: "Clarabell, you've got more brains in your ass than the vice president has in his head."

The problem with taking Howdy on the road was that he was really one of a kind. "We've rebuilt Howdy several times," Smith told a reporter at the time, "but we've never been able to duplicate the original." On their return trip from Washington, Smith recalled, "Howdy was stored in an unpressurized part of the plane. When we landed we discovered his head had split open. We had to rush to patch him up in time for the show." After that there were several attempts to build another Howdy from Velma Dawson's original mold, but the results never seemed to perfectly match the real thing. "I guess it's the same as no two people ever looking exactly alike," Smith mused at the time. When he wasn't working, the original Howdy was kept in a locked puppet closet. No insurance company would write NBC a policy on its most unique asset.

In June Howdy flew to Chicago with Rhoda Mann to inaugurate the first split screen between New York and Chicago; in New York, Buffalo Bob would be holding a balloon on the right side of the screen. "Now, when the balloon pops, you kids here in the Peanut Gallery and at home will see Howdy on the other side of the screen!" Bob Rippen, Howdy's director, was frantic with nerves. The split screen was being done via telephone lines, but at that time there was no direct feed to New York. The signal had to jump from Ohio to Pittsburgh to New York; the effect couldn't even be rehearsed because the telephone lines were in constant use and couldn't be tied up. Rippen remembers pacing the floor of the control room and shaking with fear. The first split screen in live broadcast history! The whole country would be watching, and NBC couldn't rehearse it! Then Bob Smith came in and grabbed Rippen by the shoulders in that take-charge manner he had. "Ripp, calm down. It's gonna be all right, buddy." When the Buff popped the balloon, Howdy Doody popped onto the screen next to him, from a thousand miles away.

This was also the era of the "Howdy Daddy Show," the first time adults ever sat in the Peanut Gallery. The Howdy Daddies included NBC celebrities like Milton Berle, Sid Caesar, Paul Winchell, Bennett Cerf, disc jockey and bandleader Skitch Henderson, Tex McCrary, Morey Amsterdam, and others.

Beneath the placid and extremely lucrative surface of *The Howdy Doody Show,* the program's social fabric was beginning to slowly tear. Although he was careful not to upset his mentor/protégé relationship with Bob Smith, Bobby Keeshan complained about poor working conditions at NBC: cramped studios, crammed schedules, no dressing rooms, and no privacy. Keeshan had to put on his clown makeup in a studio closet. "The production facilities at NBC were so tight that we'd go off the air at 5:58:30 and at six P.M. sharp the camera would swing around to the other side of the studio and the same crew would start telecasting a musical show with Johnny Andrews and his Singers. It was so hectic we didn't have any time to think." Keeshan also complained that he couldn't do commercials because Clarabell wasn't supposed to speak. At that time the ad agencies' writers had refined Howdy Doody's commercial pitch to the point where it had the impact of a fastball in the face. The way it worked was that Bob Smith would hold up the product — Kellogg's Corn Flakes, Ovaltine milk powder, a Three Musketeers bar — in his right hand, look into the camera, and tell his audience about the product with the same wholesome sincerity with which he delivered Eddie Kean's concerned messages about being nice to animals and looking both ways before crossing the street. Then, when he had finished, the Buffalo would say, "Isn't that right, Howdy boy?" And the camera would cut to a tight shot of Howdy with the product. Howdy would respond, "That's right, Buffalo Bob! And kids, when you're shopping at the store with your mom, be sure to tell her to get Wonder Bread [or whatever] today!"

It was double reinforcement, and for thirteen years it worked like a charm on affluent postwar American children. Whichever actor did the commercial was paid extra for it, and Bobby Keeshan wasn't getting any part of it. Eventually, with much pleading, Keeshan convinced Smith and Muir to throw Clarabell a crumb and let him stand next to the product now and then.

Up on the puppet bridge, a precarious ten feet over the stage, Rhoda wasn't thrilled either. There were rumors that Smith and Muir were looking for a young actress to play in the show, and Rhoda felt insecure. The previous year, when Howdy went to a daily show, Smith and Muir had tried to cut Rhoda back. But Rhoda's talent, her special way with the difficult Howdy puppet, had saved her, and they called her quickly back. "Rhoda, baybee!" Smith had again cried over the phone. "We need you back full-time!"

But if Keeshan and Rhoda were grumbling, Dayton Allen and Bill Lecornec were thrilled to be working on one of the most popular shows in America. As he got used to his new surroundings, Dayton Allen relaxed and was himself. According to Eddie Kean, "One day somebody made the mistake of introducing Dayton to Howdy's new female floor manager. And Dayton said, 'Floor manager, huh? I guess you've seen just about everything.' The girl said, 'Uh-huh,' and Dayton said, 'How about this?' and takes out his big pecker and walks around holding it in his hand. Everybody died from either embarrassment or laughter. But I could only look toward the rear of the studio and pray that the writer from *Time* who'd been hanging around all week wasn't standing there with his notebook open."

Gradually, Eddie began to create characters for Dayton and Bill. "Dayton is one of the funniest and one of the most versatile men I've ever met," Kean says. "I always admired him enormously and was also scared to death of him because of his mouth. Oh God! He was funny and filthy. He'd do these vulgar double entendres in rehearsal or have Bluster's hand in Howdy's crotch. The crew would be shrieking and hysterical. Dayton was the kind of naturally gifted comedian who could say anything and you'd be foaming with laughter. We hired him for his mouth, and soon after I started to write live characters for him." The first was Ugly Sam, who was actually the first live character on *Howdy Doody* besides Buffalo Bob and Clarabell. Sam was a wrestler in a striped union suit who never won a match and was an utter moron. Then there was an old cowhand named Lanky Lou. (At one point it was in vogue for the mothers of cast members to make appearances on the show. Bob Smith's mother, Emma Schmidt, appeared on network television as Buffalo Emma, while Dayton's mom came on as Lanky Lou's mother, Lanky Lulu.) Another Dayton character was Pierre the Chef, who cooked for Howdy's circus. But Dayton's most popular character was Sir Archibald, an English explorer in a pith helmet and flowing beard who was forever searching for the lucky left leg of the Lima llama.

Kean also created several live characters for Bill Lecornec, who was more of a singer and an actor than a comedian. There was Oil Well Willy, a prospector who did cornball Western humor with Buff and Howdy. There was Dr. Singasong, an "ole professor" type in a top hat who could harmonize with the Buffalo. And there was the role that was to last for Bill Lecornec's entire career in television — the legendary and immortal Chief Thunderthud.

Thunderthud was the dynastic chief of the Ooragnak Indian tribe; as written by Eddie Kean, the chief was really the last of the cigar store Indians, a dumb red man with a lounge lizard's waxed mustaches and firewater on his breath. *Ooragnak* was of course *kangaroo* spelled backward, a typical Keanism, and the whole concept of Thunderthud was equally ridiculous. "When Chief Featherman caught on," Kean recalls, "we decided to have a rival Indian chief, and we used Bill. But Bill was a flamboyant actor who outshined poor Keeshan, who had trouble delivering any line that was tougher than 'Featherman no like Clarabell.' " Thunderthud very quickly became popular and stayed a favorite character for years. He became famous for his all-purpose expletive and greeting, "Kowabonga!" — which was coined by Kean at a script meeting and immediately became a national catchword. "*Kowabonga* was a nonsense word that originally meant an expression of anger, like 'dammit!' But the way Bill first said the line, it sounded more like an exclamation of surprise, and that's mostly the way we used it." Years later, Baby Boom surfers weaned on *Howdy Doody* would scream "Kowabonga" on an ecstatic wave. Young officers in Vietnam, incredibly, used it as a battle cry.

The merchandising of Howdy Doody began in earnest in November 1949, a month after the show's cast and crew had celebrated Howdy's four hundredth show. As Martin Stone remembers: "One day the head of Western Printing said to me, 'You have a comic book, Howdy should be a comic.' I asked him what the deal was, and

Dayton as Pierre the Chef.
(EDDIE KEAN COLLECTION)

Dayton as Ugly Sam, the wrestler.
(EDDIE KEAN COLLECTION)

Dayton as the explorer, Sir Archibald.
(EDDIE KEAN COLLECTION)

Bill Lecornec as Chief Thunderthud, with Phineas T. Bluster and the Flub-adub. (FROM A POSTCARD IN BURT DUBROWS COLLECTION)

he said, 'We pay you a royalty.' I was surprised to hear they paid a royalty, because I thought that the publicity would be so good that we ought to pay them!

"It was this kind of incident," Stone muses, "that showed me that what was important to control was the property rights. The script was very important, because it determined the course of the show and therefore its value. We had the biggest children's audience in the country, and we didn't even mind that NBC was using us to sell advertising. From almost the beginning we were more interested in merchandising." To this end, for the rest of his career, Howdy Doody would be used as a billboard for every conceivable kind of merchandise tie-in.

The new Howdy Doody comics were announced on the air in November. The comics began as Sunday-newspaper funnies and expanded into regular comic books the following year, 1950. A kinescope of the show that announced the new comics has survived. Turn the lights down and check out a good example of a typical *Doody* show of the late 1940s.

"SAY, KIDS, WHAT TIME IS IT?" the Buffalo asks. "IT'S HOWDY DOODY TIME!" the kids yell back. Then, with Double Doody (for some reason) sitting on top of his upright piano, the Buffalo plays the *Howdy Doody* theme and sings along with the Peanuts.

Clarabell walks on, holding a bottle of Halo shampoo. The Buff has the kids sing the Halo song, which every kid in the country knew by heart — "*Halo everybody, Halo* . . ." Then they show a sixty-second Halo cartoon featuring Goldilocks and the three bears.

After five minutes, we finally get some exposition. Oil Well Willie is talking to Don José Bluster on the puppet stage. (Don José was the second of the Bluster triplets. The third, Hector Hamhock, had a thick English accent, in contrast to the cheesy Puerto Rican accent Dayton used for Don José. Eddie, when asked why the three Bluster brothers had different accents, explained that their mother birthed them on a cruise.) Willie and Don José are glad that things are back to normal after Phineas tried to steal a thousand dollars to take over Howdy's circus on behalf of the Bluster brothers.

Next we see Howdy and the Buff, whispering together and excluding Clarabell, who has a tantrum. Then Howdy announces the beginning of the Sunday comic strip. "And don't worry, kids, because Clarabell won't be in it!" At this insult, Clarabell goes berserk. He stamps his foot and pouts like a two-year-old. The performance has little grace or charm. Keeshan's Clarabell is like a lumbering child who has lost control; at any second he may pull out his seltzer bottle and give the Buffalo or Thunderthud a blast. (Although he wasn't supposed to, Keeshan occasionally soaked the front rows of the Peanut Gallery as well.)

Smith goes on to say that Clarabell won't be in the comic because the clown drew a mustache on artist Milt Neal's only copy of the Mona Lisa. Then Milt Neal, in an artist's smock, brings out his easel and announces that he refuses to draw Clarabell. In a rage, Clarabell whips out the seltzer and spritzes the Buffalo. The Peanuts are worked into a frenzy as the characters chase each other around.

They break for a commercial, another long Halo ad. Soap dulls your hair, the Buffalo is saying, but Halo *glorifies* it. But Smith's words are drowned out by the Peanuts; some of the younger kids are still zizzed up from the last sketch and are shouting and pointing at Clarabell, interrupting the spot for a moment. (The sponsors hated it when the Peanuts couldn't be controlled. Soon after, more stringent measures would be taken to assure Peanut passivity.)

When he finally finishes selling the soap, the Buffalo takes a minute to welcome twelve new cities to the NBC network. Now all the kids in Atlanta, Kansas City, Minneapolis, Jacksonville, and North and South Carolina can join the Doodyville gang. Then another segment reflects the show's office politics and petty hatreds: Buffalo Bob tries to teach Clarabell to play three consecutive notes on a xylophone, but the poor clown gets flustered trying to please the Buffalo and can't quite get it right. So Buffalo Bob humiliates Clarabell with much the same vehemence that Bob Smith, the man with a perfect sense of pitch, constantly needled Keeshan about his inability to play music.

Next they bring out Milt Neal again, this time with his sketch pad, and Neal quick-draws that Sunday's first Howdy comic. When Neal is finally persuaded to let Clarabell be in the comic, all is calm again in Doodyville. But then the Buffalo provokes Clarabell by pasting a mustache and beard on his sketched likeness. The clown, humiliated twice in the same show, sees red. Out comes the seltzer, and the Buffalo is again soaked. "YOU STUPID CLOWN!" shouts the Buffalo, but soon the camera zooms in for a close-up two-shot of reconciliation.

"OK, Clarabell," Smith tries, "go start a movie for us on the Scopedoodle." But Clarabell is being a jerk. (Look carefully at Keeshan in freeze-frame. With fury in his eyes, Clarabell stands there dumbly. He looks goofy but sinister, shambling, dissolute. Something about Clarabell makes your hair stand on end.)

After the old Ben Turpin silent, narrated by Buffalo Bob with character names drawn from his old neighborhood in Buffalo (Bertha Schlegel, Charlie Schwichtenburg, and Holda Hannawinkle), the show does a quick wind-down. There's a Three Musketeers ad, a bit between Howdy and the Inspector, and a last fast sketch where Clarabell becomes terrified and phobic when Chief Featherman's headdress falls on the hapless clown from above.

What have we just watched? A typical early show from about a year before Howdy's prime, in which the cast sells a merchandising spin-off, in this case the new comics. Today the old kine seems crude, exploitative, and unfunny. But in November 1949 it was state-of-the-art video, and hilarious. And while the room is dark I look over and catch my seven-year-old daughter staring with total fascination as the grainy Buffalo Bob belittles and berates his hapless clown.

Almost forty years after it was first shown, the old Howdy kine can hold a child's attention as well as a show featuring Howdy Doody's great-grandchildren, the Muppets and the Fraggle Rock creatures.

In December 1949 *Howdy Doody and the Air-O-Doodle,* a 78 rpm phonograph record released by RCA Victor, hit the *Billboard* charts and for a while sold thirty thousand copies a week. Bob Smith proved to be as natural a recording artist as he was a disc jockey and video host; over the years the various Howdy Doody records sold in the hundreds of thousands and were eventually even merchandised with Little Golden Books, the Baby Boomer's first library.

On the last day of 1949, professional wrestlers Primo Carnera and Antonino Rocca (the Mr. T and Hulk Hogan of the day) appeared on *Howdy Doody* to promote some matches NBC was televising (how little things have changed). In the course of a show in which he and Carnera were to teach Clarabell how to wrestle, Rocca inadvertently felled the poor clown with a flying drop kick. Nothing ever went right for Clarabell. Nothing.

NBC's publicity department marked Howdy Doody's triumphant entry into his decade, the 1950s, with a press release dated January 10, 1950. The release announced that Howdy Doody had been granted a fourteen-year U.S. patent (number 156,687) on himself. And so began the era from which Howdy would emerge as much a national icon as President Eisenhower, Marilyn Monroe, or Elvis Presley.

My own vague memories of television begin around this time. Aside from *Howdy Doody,* my earliest exposure to TV seems to have been war footage, assembled from Signal Corps archives and captured enemy film. In 1949, NBC began broadcasting *Sands Point Navy Training Program,* which consisted of Naval Air Reserve training films shown at the now-unthinkable hour of nine-thirty on Saturday mornings. But this was soon supplanted in my own mind by the expertly edited, brilliantly scored, and martially stirring series *Victory at Sea,* which mesmerized me with its shifting images (ships, tanks, bombers) and Richard Rodgers's evocative sound track, which made World War II sound as romantic as a fabulous Broadway musical. That's what I remember about early television — Howdy Doody and war documentaries. Much later, when I saw battle footage and other filmed atrocities from Vietnam on the evening news, they didn't seem so shocking to me. I was used to that. Watching war films on television reminded me of — childhood!

The thing about Howdy Doody that puzzled me as a three-year-old was — who was he? If Buffalo Bob wasn't Howdy's father, then who was? And if Howdy Doody was really a boy, where was Howdy's mother? Nobody I asked had the answers to these questions. My father, who I knew worked at the television studio, didn't know. Many years later, when I interviewed him for this book, I asked Eddie Kean who Howdy was, and Eddie said that even *he* didn't know. But Eddie did say that "Howdy Doody wasn't a cowboy, he just hadda be something. He was the right thing for merchandising. The cowboy thing happened because it sounded like a cowboy name."

Still, the question persists, Who *was* this Doody?

Fortunately, there is an answer. It was pieced together by *Howdy Doody* researchers, cultists, and fanatics, who spend their lives hunting down esoteric Howdy collectibles and memorabilia at tag sales and flea markets. They even publish nostalgic and sentimental newsletters about life in Doodyville, nearly thirty years after that company town shut down for good, its heavy industry replaced by cheap, shoddy goods. These unrepentant Doodyites assembled a cryptobiography of Howdy back in the mid-seventies, using the three basic Howdy texts that had descended to them from the misty and remote Howdy Era. The first of these texts were the twenty-seven Simon & Schuster Little Golden Books that Eddie Kean wrote, beginning with *Howdy Doody's Circus,* published in September 1950. The Howdy Doody Golden Books were huge sellers, especially when Buff and Howdy plugged them on the air, which they did frequently. Further analysis was also applied to the second series of Howdy texts, the long-running Dell comic books packed with obscure Doodyville inhabitants, place names, and events, which were supervised by Eddie Kean in order to keep the comics in reasonable sync with the show. The third major set of Doody texts comprises the hard-to-find two-year story line (again written by the tireless Eddie Kean) for the syndicated Howdy newspaper comic strip and rotogravure Sunday funny (drawn by the tyro cartoon artist Stan Lee, who would later create Spiderman and other paper heroes).

According to the Doodyologists' deconstruction of the textual data, twin sons were born to the wife of a ranch hand named Doody in the small town of Doodyville, Texas, on December 27, 1941. (Doody, incidentally, is in fact a respected family name in the Midwest, chiefly around Saint Louis, Missouri.) The boys' father named his sons Howdy and Double. Their earliest years growing up on a cattle ranch are shrouded in the red dust of the arid Southwest. The researchers discovered that Doodyville had been named after the boys' rich uncle, Uncle Doody, after he struck oil nearby. When the twins were six, Uncle Doody died and left them a plot of land in New York City. Now, Howdy Doody had a cherished dream of having his own circus, while Double Doody wanted to stay in Texas. When NBC offered to purchase the land to build a television studio, Howdy's father, Mr. Doody, arranged a deal so Howdy could have his circus. NBC built the circus, surrounded it with TV cameras, and appointed Buffalo Bob Smith as Howdy's guardian. (Bob Smith retained ownership of his own name and image with respect to licensing. So Buffalo Bob never appeared in any Howdy book or comic.) After a tearful farewell to his Texas family, Howdy arrived in New York in December 1947, and the rest is history.

There were tremors in Doodyville in 1950. In June Bobby Keeshan was fired from the role of Clarabell. Apparently Keeshan's inability to play an instrument or read a line finally became too much for Smith, Muir, and Eddie Kean, who was always having to invent sketches that could be performed on a hundred-station national television network by an actor with very little natural talent. Keeshan also made management nervous because he was heavily involved in the new AFTRA union for TV actors, which had evolved from the old radio union. And there was another aspect to this. Howdy Doody was drawing increasing complaints from parents and the Parent-Teacher Association. Letters continued to come in to NBC every day to say that all the chases and seltzer spraying were getting the children too excited just before dinner. The scapegoat for this was, naturally, Clarabell. Moreover, whenever someone from the show came in contact with one of the great clowns of the day — Emmett Kelly, say, or Felix Adler — or indeed talked to anyone with any knowledge of clowns, all they heard was what an unfunny clown Clarabell was. A *real* clown was a mime, a juggler, a con artist, and occasionally a musician. But Bobby Keeshan's clown couldn't do much except hold up a product and squirt seltzer. Yet — and this is what really got to the real clowns — in just one night Bobby Keeshan's loathsome Clarabell was seen by more children than would ever see the greatest clowns in those clowns' lifetimes.

So in June 1950 they fired Bobby Keeshan, the first television actor. Roger Muir called him up and told him that Howdy was letting him go. Keeshan was devastated. That very night he was replaced on the air by the new Clarabell, a sensational, theatrically trained dancer and mime named Gil Lamb. At last, everyone on the show thought, a Clarabell with some talent. But it didn't occur to them that Clarabell fans might not like the new clown. The first problem was that whereas Keeshan's Clarabell had been short, pudgy, and graceless, the new Clarabell was about six-three and gangling and moved with the obvious panache of a dancer. Second, Keeshan's infantile and regressive misbehaver was replaced overnight by a gentle, almost shy Clarabell, a sensitive clown who wouldn't even squirt a fly.

The next day all hell broke loose. Outraged viewers called NBC's affiliates to complain.

That wasn't Clarabell, you idiots!

Who are you trying to kid?

Do you people think our children are morons?

That's not Clarabell!

When Gil Lamb appeared a second time, a tall and Apollonian clown, even the children of NBC executives started to complain at dinner: "Daddy, why are they trying to fool us? They're not showing the real Clarabell." Eventually, so much pressure was put on the network and the show that Martin Stone told Roger Muir to call Keeshan and get him back. Reluctantly, Muir showed the famous Gil Lamb the door, and Bobby Keeshan, whose lumbering Clarabell would never be duplicated even by the two talented men who would later replace him, was given back his clown suit, his bicycle horn, and his trusty bottle of warm seltzer. NBC issued the following extraordinary press release on June 23, 1950:

CLARABELL IS BACK — ALL IS FORGIVEN

Clarabell the clown is in good graces with Howdy Doody again.

After two weeks' suspension from the NBC network television program (Mondays through Fridays, 5:30 P.M., EDT) the mute clown with the talking horn is back with the puppets, trying to keep out of trouble.

He was let go two weeks ago because he wouldn't stop squirting seltzer water on emcee Bob Smith and persisted in being a general nuisance. He also raised the ire of the cast by hiding Howdy's "lucky left leg," the rabbit foot which the pint-sized cowboy keeps as a souvenir of Phineas T. Bluster's recent trip to South America [from which he returned with his long-lost twin brother, Don José Bluster].

Clarabell spent his enforced vacation hunting for clown jobs on other NBC shows. No one wanted him.

Clarabell the Clown is played by [a] 23-year-old New Yorker, Robert Keeshan, who used to be an NBC page boy. By taking lessons from [the Ringling Brothers' Circus star] Emmett Kelly and other professional clowns, Keeshan has developed his pantomime on television to a point where he is now one of the best-known clowns in the U.S.

Life in Doodyville was a pressure cooker. Part of this was due to Eddie Kean's story-line technique. When he got an idea he would run with it, only rarely outlining a long-term plot. For years this kept the prop people awake all night, as scripts that came in at five o'clock in the afternoon often called for elaborate painted props and backdrops to be ready by first rehearsal at one o'clock the following day. Often Kean would have no idea where a storyline was heading. One of Kean's plots could meander along for months before some twist or turn would suggest a good wrap-up. Many of his colleagues didn't understand how he had the nerve to go on the network this way, yet Kean insists he was never more than a week ahead on scripts. If he wasn't sure which direction a story line should take, he would study the kids in the Peanut Gallery to see what material was engaging their imagination and catching on. Often Eddie would mingle with the Peanuts' young parents, who watched the show on monitors in the ninth-floor viewing room while NBC intimidated their children downstairs. Eddie kept tabs on the reactions of the parents. If a bit or character drew negative comments from parents, Eddie would never use it again.

But by 1950 there were plenty of complaints about the entertainment that Howdy was dishing out at five-thirty every weekday afternoon. The show, many parents carped, was obnoxious and strident. One contemporary account describes *Howdy Doody* as "a veritable breeding ground for just about every juvenile habit extant. On the theory that kids are great imitators, the parents are becoming a little weary when Junior flits (like Clarabell) into the dining room, blinks when he talks (like Howdy Doody) and shouts (like the entire cast) when he wants something." These complaints escalated throughout 1950 until, that fall, a private group of self-appointed censors that called itself the National Television Review Board, supported by *Reader's Digest* and the PTA, placed *Howdy Doody* on its "Objectionable" list, indicating that they found the show "loud, noisy, and confused." The Board was right; it was.

NBC swore that it would get the show back on track. The network held meetings for parent groups so Eddie Kean could identify the problems and, it was hoped, write a show that would not be objectionable to anybody. So what did the parents say? "Half of them complained the show was too silly and didn't teach the children enough," Kean says. "The other half demanded that we not try to indoctrinate children or attempt to teach them anything. In the end we were as confused as the parents."

One result of all of this was that Eddie phased out the confusing long story lines that meandered for months. Now every week comprised a five-day story line that would be closed out on Friday by a new song written by Eddie, "The Goodbye Song."

"That was the sentimental, lengthy song we used to shut down the show on Friday," Eddie recalls. "It went, *'It's time to say goodbye, goodbye until next Monday, when we'll all be with you again.'* Every major character participated, singing an eight-bar phrase, and the hostilities of the week's scripted conflicts faded into the good feeling that nothing can impart as music can."

I still know the words and melody to "The Goodbye Song" by heart, and often catch myself humming Eddie's Brahmslike tune when I'm in a certain mood.

Howdy Doody *merchandising goes on the road: Buffalo Vic Smith (Bob's older brother) with one of the fake Clarabells, circa 1953.* (BURT DUBROW COLLECTION)

Five

Hucksters and Whores

We were real hucksters. You might say we were real whores.
— Bob Smith

THE SCREAMING DOUBLE LINE that slowly edged its way up to the Jordan Marsh department store on Washington Street in downtown Boston on a brisk day in September 1950 was eight blocks long. Store officials had expected a modest turnout of young televiewers, perhaps a couple of thousand at best, when they hired the Howdy gang — Buffalo Bob, Clarabell, and Howdy himself — for a personal appearance in the toy department of their store. Yet before the day was out more than thirty thousand children from all over New England had filed past Jordan's Howdy merchandise displays. Instead of tinkling out a few tunes on his trusty upright, the Buffalo had performed a half-dozen sets of songs from the show, throughout the day. And the wonderful thing, Jordan Marsh officials thought, was that the Buffalo didn't even seem to mind.

By then, of course, *The Howdy Doody Show* was exploding like a reactor whose cooling systems had failed, becoming much bigger than anyone had foreseen. NBC estimated Howdy's daily audience at upward of eight million children. (About half of these kids saw Howdy "live" on the network that ran as far as Kansas City. The other half saw the same show two weeks later via kinescope recordings on their local stations.) This audience was roughly triple that of any one of *Howdy*'s competitors, including *Hopalong Cassidy* and *Captain Video*.

The show itself, however, was just one part of it, because 1950 was the year that the merchandising of Howdy took off with a crazy momentum of its own. Not since the prewar days of Mickey Mouse had there been such a strong influence on children's things — toys, clothes, accessories, anything anyone could think of. By the end of the year American children had bought fifteen million Howdy comic books and five hundred thousand record albums, some of which, notably *Howdy Doody's Christmas*, stayed on the *Billboard* charts for months. Howdy's image decorated lamps, sweatshirts, wallpaper, lunch boxes, everything. Merchandising experts estimated that the gross income from all Howdy paraphernalia added up to fifteen million dollars in 1950 alone. Out of this figure, it was reported, Buffalo Bob Smith earned royalties ranging from two and a half to ten percent.

For the privilege of having the team of Buff and Howdy hawk their products, five carefully chosen sponsors each paid NBC about sixty-five hundred dollars a week and considered themselves blessed to be able to do so. Reasons for this were easy to find. When Mars Candy paid Howdy to tout a new coconut bar, Mounds, the company sold a quarter of a million bars by the end of the first week. When Howdy offered a premium to any kid who visited a Poll Parrot shoe store one week, the sponsor reported that two and a half million kids had dropped by the chain's stores, all over the country. One executive told the *Wall Street Journal* that advertising on *Howdy* had pulled him out of the red, increasing his business forty-two percent. And when Ovaltine offered a Howdy Doody mug in return for an Ovaltine jar lid, a hundred thousand jars moved over countertops the day after the broadcast. I can remember making my Dad buy Ovaltine when we went to the store. I hated the stuff but desperately wanted the mug.

Every day hundreds of letters poured into Martin Stone's office requesting tickets for the Peanut Gallery, which held forty children at a time. At one point, to handle the overflow, Stone booked Madison Square Garden and sold out the big hall in a matter of hours. In 1950 alone, Buffalo Bob turned down more than forty lucrative personal appearances at three thousand dollars saying he didn't have time between his morning radio show and *Howdy* every day. Indeed, *Howdy* was so big that in the early summer of 1950 the Buffalo finally had to turn the drive-time radio program over to bandleader Skitch Henderson. And there were still so many requests for personal appearances that Smith and Stone decided to send Bob Smith's older brother, Vic Smith (an upstate TV retailer who only vaguely looked like Bob), out on the road with actors in Clarabell suits to open supermarkets and cut ribbons at shopping centers. Buffalo Vic, as he was billed, had briefly substituted for his younger brother on the air, in May 1950, when Bob had taken sick with flu; but Vic would stay on the road with his fake Clarabells for years.

* * *

Eventually these merchandising campaigns began to influence the course of the show. The tail began to wag the dog. Up until 1950, all of *Howdy Doody*'s characters, both human and on strings, had emerged solely from the imagination of Eddie Kean. But Princess Summerfall Winterspring emerged from a merchandising meeting.

She was Martin Stone's idea. Stone knew that *Howdy* was geared to little boys more than girls, and he wanted to change that. Since an all-male *Howdy Doody Show* had been able to routinely grab eight million children, perhaps a strong female character could draw a few million more little girls. "I remember a long session on this," Stone says. "We needed to add material for girls, and I said we could sell a hell of a lot of dresses if we had a little girl on the show. So I came up with the Princess; her name was the only name on *Howdy* that I take credit for. I thought Summerfall Winterspring would allow us to sell seasonal clothing. It allowed symbols — sun, snowflake, leaves, whatever. Ask Eddie — he came up with the puppet."

Eddie agrees. "The thought of having a female character was generated by the merchandising office. We all knew that Marty Stone had said we could sell a lot of dresses if we had a female character. This was the only character on *Howdy* up to that point that wasn't my idea. I *abhorred* girl puppets from my days at camp. I thought they were boring, and I was very leery of having a girl puppet on the show. The nature of *Howdy Doody* was very zestful, exciting, noisy, adventuresome slapstick comedy. I wondered how a squeaky little girl puppet's voice could even compete.

"I was wrong," Eddie Kean now allows.

But it took them about ten months to get a Princess puppet they could fall in love with. Milt Neal's original drawings of a darling black-braided Indian maiden in feather bonnet and buckskins turned out to be extremely hard for Scott Brinker to duplicate. In the end it took months of conferences, sketching, modeling, and carving to produce the diminutive Indian charmer that finally made her debut on *Howdy Doody* in October 1950. Eddie Kean didn't like it. "In abhorring the thought of a girl character," he says, "I tried to think up anything to glamorize her. So I made her the magic princess of the Tinka Tonka tribe, with an enchanted necklace that would tell the future when the Princess rubbed it. And she was the princess of the seasons, which accounted for her costume and her name — it was very mellifluous, and it just happened to be the order of the seasons as well. What the hell seasons had to do with anything I don't know. It just seemed Indian-appropriate."

True to Martin Stone's instinct, the Princess puppet was a hit, and Summerfall Winterspring frocks started to move across America's counters. When sponsors saw this, they wanted their own puppets too. Around that time, a Poll Parrot puppet appeared in Doodyville. The parrot was worked and voiced by Dayton Allen, and it sold a lot of shoes.

But behind the Doodyville cameras at 30 Rockefeller Center things were not so placid. By Thanksgiving 1950 word was circulating around the cast and crew that Bob Smith and Martin Stone, who hitherto had owned all rights to the Howdy Doody character and story line, were trying to sell the show. By Christmas the rumor was out in the open. Smith and Stone were negotiating to sell NBC the biggest show in the country, a combined television and merchandising empire potentially worth hundreds of millions of pre-inflation dollars. On Madison Avenue, on Wall Street, and in Hollywood, the word was out. Howdy Doody was for sale.

It had started back in September, when an old law-school class-mate had called Martin Stone and said, "For God's sake, do something fast!" By this time, the word on the Street was that Stone and Smith were making a fortune out of Howdy Doody. Continental Baking was paying a hundred thousand a year merely for the right to print Howdy's picture on the end-seals of their loaves of Wonder Bread. The Welch's Grape Juice empire was paying a fortune in licensing fees to put Howdy on their jelly jars and juice cartons. This was real money in those days, and Wall Street was taking notice of a new growth industry — Howdy Doody.

Martin Stone's classmate was calling because earlier in 1950 Congress had passed a new tax law that said one could no longer receive capital gains from ideas per se — including books, movies, or television shows. (This law supposedly had been passed after General Dwight Eisenhower had been allowed a controversial capital gain on his best-selling memoir *Crusade in Europe*.) As soon as this law was passed, all the big TV stars stampeded the networks in an orgy of renegotiating and deal-making. Everyone who could, sold out — lock, stock, and Berle. Uncle Miltie, still extremely hot in prime time, received a lucrative thirty-year contract with NBC. Bob Hope traded himself for a television station in Denver. NBC lost two big shows, Jack Benny's and *Amos & Andy*, when CBS bought them away for capital gains. The long knives were out in the skyscrapers of midtown Manhattan.

So Martin Stone and the Buffalo decided to go all out when their contract with NBC expired toward the end of 1950; this would allow them to cash in before the new law went into effect on January 1, 1951. Stone spent the fall negotiating for all he was worth. First he went to NBC and told them that there would have to be a new deal. Then he went down Fifty-second Street to CBS, where he pitched Howdy Doody to that network's czar, William Paley.

"How'd you like to have Howdy?" Stone asked Mr. CBS.

"I'd love it," Mr. CBS replied.

Stone then told Paley that NBC had the right of first refusal on Howdy, and the shrewd Paley told Martin Stone that he didn't want to set up NBC. The meeting was really a waste of time. Paley and Stone both knew NBC would match any offer CBS made for their kiddie gold mine.

Martin Stone went back to NBC after seeing Bill Paley and offered Howdy to Niles Trammel, who asked Stone the price of the show. Stone said he felt Howdy was worth a million dollars. Fine, said Trammel; but then what would be your incentive to stay on the show and make it a success?

NBC soon put together an offer. It seemed that one of the board members of NBC's parent company, RCA, was also a senior partner at Lehman Brothers, the old New York investment firm that also served as RCA's financial adviser. This executive's name was Paul Mazur. Mazur happened to know exactly how much Howdy Doody was really worth; his sister was married to Jack Kaplan, who owned Welch's Grape Juice. A year earlier Kaplan had come to Stone and said he was going to use Howdy to break the hold orange growers had on the American juice market. Stone suggested plastering Howdy all over the grape juice, which had the inevitable results of unbelievable sales in a manner of weeks and quick penetration of Concord grape drink into the marketplace and down the gullets of the Baby Boomers.

Mazur's plan called for NBC and Lehman Brothers to form a new company called KAGRAN (the word was an amalgam of the first letters of the names of Lehman Brothers executive Frank Mannheim's children, Katherine and Grant). This company bought Howdy Doody from Smith and Stone for a million dollars over a ten-year period. The Buffalo got $175,000 in cash, plus $250,000 in firm debenture bonds in KAGRAN with interest-bearing coupons, which would yield income for ten years. Martin Stone also received some cash, plus forty percent of KAGRAN. NBC and Lehman Brothers each owned thirty percent.

The KAGRAN deal was signed just in the nick of time, on December 26, 1950. The Buffalo, under the terms of his new contract, actually had to take a cut in salary, from thirty-five to about fifteen hundred dollars a week, "play or pay," for the next six years.

Almost at once, the rumor percolated among Howdy's cast and crew that relations were strained between Bob and Marty. Although word filtered out that Bob and Marty's deal was the industry's second biggest capital-gain buyout after Jack Benny's, it became clear that Bob wasn't happy. Before 1951, Bob Smith had held the copyright to the *Howdy Doody Show* and all the Howdy merchandise. After 1951, the show and the merchandise were copyrighted in the name of KAGRAN, the biggest chunk of which was owned by Martin Stone. "That son-of-a-gun Marty got everything but the skating rink," a sour Buffalo murmured to Howdy director Bob Rippen.

The KAGRAN deal was the end of the original *Howdy Doody* — three years of relative innocence, innovation, and experiment, with spectacular, even historic success. Everything had been improvised so quickly that no one on the show had ever had a really clear idea of where the show was going. All this changed with the KAGRAN deal. Everything got bigger now that Wall Street was in the game. The money involved became astronomical, and the sponsors took over the show.

"Things changed as different advertisers came in," Stone remembers. "They all wanted to tie in some way, using our characters in promotions for their products. It was the Poll Parrot shoe people who instigated the personal-appearance approach in their shoe stores" — by insisting that Buffalo Bob, Clarabell, and Thunderthud show up in shopping centers on weekends to help sell shoes. (This was fairly lucrative for KAGRAN if not for the actors. Records show that Bobby Keeshan got only twenty dollars per appearance.) Poll Parrot also produced a Howdy record — to be given away as a premium with each shoe purchase — that was heavily promoted on a single *Howdy* show early in 1951. The following day the J. L. Hudson department store in Detroit ordered a thousand extra records. Macy's in New York and Gimbel's in Philadelphia each sold out its whole stock of Poll Parrot products. So successful were the *Howdy* promotions in that era that at one point Martin Stone proposed that KAGRAN take a percentage of Welch's gross sales instead of a licensing royalty in a forthcoming grape-juice campaign involving Howdy and the gang.

Whoever controlled *Howdy*'s script owned a guaranteed gold mine of insider merchandising info, since the script ballyhooed the clients' products with as much fervor as it spun out the Howdy story lines. The show chimed out memorable little jingles —

> *Brush your teeth with Colgate (Colgate Dental Cream!)*
> *It cleans your breath (what a toothpaste!)*
> *While it cleans your teeth.*

— whose words and melodies are etched into the memory of a generation, and Buffalo Bob accorded commercial characters like Happy Tooth and Mean Old Mr. Tooth Decay the same respect and reverence as any of the Doodyville civilians.

The truth of the matter was that the networks had discovered that children's love for repetition, predictability, and regularity perfectly matched the needs of television advertising. The collective mind of my generation was a blank page upon which was crudely scrawled, *"Brush your teeth with Colgate . . . ,"* and other commercial propaganda.

So utterly Pavlovian was the reaction of America's young children to anything hawked on the *Howdy Doody Show* that there developed around 1951 an inevitable but energetic backlash against children's television. The eminent European psychoanalyst Bruno Bettelheim railed against TV's negative influence on innocent minds. The poet John Ciardi, in the pages of the augustly middle-brow *Saturday Review of Literature*, thundered: "Children's programs are an offense to civilization. . . . The cartoon shows are a disgrace. The emcees of kids' shows are sickening oafs. The tone of the shows is barbaric. I hold TV to border on moral corruption and civic disloyalty." Professor Louis Kronenburger, a respected academic, wrote that television was "the greatest cultural calamity in this country's history."

Priests and bishops begged their young flocks in Sunday school to give up *Howdy Doody* and its inferiors — *Rootie Kazootie, Smilin' Ed's Gang* — for Lent. Doctors all over America started diagnosing maladies like "TV tummy," which supposedly afflicted children who became overstimulated by programs such as *Howdy Doody* and the violent Farmer Gray cartoons.

They all protested and complained, but it didn't matter. Nothing really changed. Eddie Kean still went to the ninth-floor viewing room and eavesdropped on the parents of the sequestered Peanuts. "By overhearing what the parents had to say, I could tell what the kids were talking about at home," Kean says. "This was my real report card for the scripts, not what the critics had to say. Remember, there were never any script meetings on *Howdy Doody*. The only person who consistently suggested good story lines was Roger Muir. I could only tell if something was working by going into the studio and watching the Peanut Gallery during the first half of the broadcast. If it held their attention and made them laugh, that was all I cared about. I regarded that show, my work and everyone else's, as an endurance contest rather than a skill or a job."

But if there were complaints about *Howdy Doody* and TV in general, our parents didn't care that much. Ticket requests to the Peanut Gallery poured in by the thousands every week of the year. Women would write NBC as soon as they got pregnant to say they wanted seats in four years. Whole classes and grades of elementary school children wrote to ask for tickets. But the Peanuts out there in TV Land didn't know the hideous truth, *Howdy*'s ugly secret, which was: the only way to get a seat in the Peanut Gallery, the hottest child's ticket in the United States, was to *know* somebody. It might be someone connected to the show, like a cast or crew member. It might be somebody at NBC, KAGRAN, one of the big New York advertising agencies, or, best of all, one of the sponsors. The only other way to get into the Peanut Gallery was to be the child of some celebrity with clout. General Eisenhower's four-year-old grandson, David, got into the Peanut Gallery that way, as did the son of Jackie Robinson, the baseball star.

Early on, Bob Smith learned not to underestimate how important seeing their children and grandchildren on the show was to some people. One day Smith was called out of rehearsal by Roger Muir to face Niles Trammel, normally an old-fashioned and courtly broadcasting executive, now fuming with rage and anxiety. Trammel was angry because he had promised a child a seat in that night's Peanut Gallery but had been turned back by his own pages because the child did not have a ticket. (There were, again, only forty seats in the Peanut Gallery, and the number of children admitted was scrupulously enforced both by the NBC pages who controlled access to the studios and by the New York Fire Department, which stationed a fire marshal in Studio 3A daily to make sure the limit was adhered to for the sake of public safety.) This was Trammel's network, and he couldn't get a kid into *Howdy Doody*! The situation seemed comical until Trammel informed Smith that the child was Andrew Hoover, the grandson of former President Herbert Hoover. Thirty years earlier Hoover had thundered that America's airwaves would never be sullied by advertising chatter. Now he was at home at his house in Washington, getting ready to watch his grandson on *Howdy Doody*.

The Buffalo thought for a minute before coming up with the perfect solution. "Tonight we're doing an ad for Welch's Grape Juice," Smith told his boss. "If you can guarantee that the kid will say, 'Oh, yeah!' when I ask him if he likes the drink, then he can sit next to me." That night the Buffalo told the fire marshal a white lie, explaining that the former President's grandson was the child the sponsor had sent over to do the commercial, not an unticketed Peanut. On cue, the kid gulped down his grape juice and expressed his satisfaction.

Any kid who wanted to be a Peanut, especially if she or he were five years old or under, had to pass a kind of audition after their parents brought them up the imposing elevators at 30 Rock. The first moment of truth came when the pages separated the Peanuts from their mothers, who were then taken to the viewing area on the ninth floor. If any child cried during the separation process, she or he was deemed too young or insecure for Peanutdom. This was a business, after all, and network television as well. Also weeded out at this point were children judged too old, too boisterous, or potentially disruptive. Once the Peanuts were seated in the Peanut Gallery, just prior to broadcast time, the Buffalo and Clarabell warmed them up by staging a chase-and-squirt sequence. This usually got the entire Gallery screaming and fidgeting. The kids who couldn't calm down after the chase scene were also taken upstairs to their mothers. Still, since young children were involved, spontaneous goofs were unavoidable and part of the fun. Most involved the toilet — or the lack of one. Once, in the middle of a Rice Krispies spot, a boy stood up and yelled directly into the overhead mikes, "Hey Uncle Bob! Where's the johnny around here?" Often a child in the top row of the little bleacher would lose control of his bladder; the result would trickle down the steps onto the other children, who would then begin to squirm. (This often happened after a seltzer fight.) More than once the Buffalo took his own seat in the Peanut Gallery to find it . . . wet!

Then there were the kids who couldn't keep quiet after the Buffalo had stopped interviewing them or doing an ad or whatever. The most notorious of these was the little girl who was asked by the Buffalo, "What does the superintendent in your apartment house do?"

"He collects the rent," the little girl replied brightly.

"That's fine," said Buff, and he started to move on to the next kid, but the little girl added, "And he has coffee with my mommy every morning!"

Sometime in the summer of 1951 I made my first visit to Doody-ville. My father was directing local television on WNBC in New York and could sometimes arrange Peanut Gallery tickets. I remember being dressed in a suit and getting on a train with my mother; the Long Island Railroad, the tremendous Beaux Arts glass cavern of the old Pennsylvania Station, the huge yellow Checker cab to Rockefeller Center, with its magical skating rink and its giant reclining golden sculpture of Prometheus, who, I was told, brought fire and knowledge to mankind. Then up the elevator of the mighty granite RCA skyscraper, so monumental and frightening to a sheltered child like myself. The last time I had visited my father had been at the RCA Exhibition Hall across the street. Now he was directing television shows and commercials and had an office on the sixth floor. I vaguely remember that we all had lunch at Schrafft's and that I spilled milk on the already itchy woolen shorts of my suit.

About the subsequent afternoon and broadcast of my first *Howdy* visit, I can remember almost nothing except being alarmed to discover that the seemingly jolly and stupid Clarabell was an agent of social control. He shouted at the Peanuts to be quiet before the show and told one child to shut up during the Old-Time Movie. I was shocked. I think the other Peanuts were as impressed as I was.

For years I thought I had probably dreamed or imagined this episode. Then I started to talk to other Peanut alumni, and they told me the same thing. "The excitement of being there was overwhelming," one wrote, "and I can still remember that to my great disappointment Clarabell, who was supposed to not be able to talk, actually yelled at me to be quiet when in my excitement I called to Buffalo Bob during the broadcast. My mother, who was watching the whole thing on TV in another room, saw him come over to me to scold me, and she felt it was not right. What I wanted to say to Buffalo Bob was that my mother had bought me some slippers with Clarabell's picture on them. And Clarabell ran over and said, 'Be quiet, kid!' I was more shocked that Clarabell talked than that he scolded me. He was also wearing a large silver-faced watch. Do clowns know how to tell time?"

It was no picnic, a visit to Doodyville. Many young Peanuts suffered their first bitter taste of disappointment and disillusion when they discovered that Doodyville was really just a bleacher, a puppet bridge, hot lights and big cameras, men wearing headphones, and an extremely uptight clown. Another ex-Peanut's testimony bears this out. Jeff MacNelly, comic-strip artist and Pulitzer Prize–winning editorial cartoonist, gave the following account to the *Chicago Tribune*:

"When I was five, Clarabell the clown was my great hero. One day my father got a ticket for me to be in the Peanut Gallery. Lo and behold, Buffalo Bob selected *me* to help him look for Dilly Dally's uncle. We had to walk under this machine that made snow. I stopped to look, and on coast-to-coast TV I started to ask questions about the snow machine. All of a sudden a big hand reaches out, pulls me off camera, and says, 'Shut up, kid!'

"It was Clarabell," MacNelly groaned. He went on to say that this experience planted the seed of cynicism required for his profession.

Think about it. You're separated from Mother. Herded down corridors. Unfamiliar studio. Blazing hot lights. Completely indifferent Buffalo Bob, in the flesh but ignoring you. Tension. The clown suddenly tells you or another Peanut to shut up.

Let's face it: Doodyville was a rough town.

Howdy Doody was television's point man, the one who went out first on patrol. NBC used Howdy to inaugurate all sorts of new TV technology — the split screen, matte effects, strange fades. (Later Howdy would introduce color television, videotape, and chroma-key painting as well.) In March 1951 the show pulled off another television first when NBC broadcast live, during *Howdy*'s half hour, a total eclipse of the sun as seen by a camera atop the RCA Building. I remember watching that broadcast at home and my mother telling me not to look directly into the screen. She was afraid I'd go blind! Other memories of a four-year-old vidiot include the Kefauver hearings, televised daily and watched by millions at home and in the taverns, a lurid congressional investigation of the influence of organized crime on American politics that often preempted *Howdy Doody* and drove the Baby Boomers mad with frustration. *The Gabby Hayes Show* featured the bewhiskered character actor George "Gabby" Hayes, former partner/sidekick of Roy Rogers in 1940s B-picture Westerns, notably *My Friend Trigger*. Gabby's show was produced by Martin Stone and KAGRAN, went on the network at 5:15 P.M. daily as a lead-in to *Howdy*, and was occasionally directed by my father. Gabby dispensed Western lore (born in 1885, he knew plenty) and showed clips from old Tom Mix and Hoot Gibson pictures. At 6:00 P.M., right after *Howdy*, came *Rootie Kazootie*, a local NBC show that went network in late 1950 (its original title, *Rootie Tootie*, was considered too much of a *Howdy Doody* ripoff for comfort). There was also *Smilin' Ed's Gang*, an extremely bizarre kids' vehicle that had been sponsored on radio since 1942 by Buster Brown Shoes and starred Ed McConnell, who read to his audience from a demented storybook that followed the adventures of Ghanga the East Indian Boy. The show featured strange cutaways to the same cheering audience every week and Smilin' Ed's oft-repeated command: "Pluck your magic twanger, Froggy!" (Any American between the age of thirty-five and forty-five who doesn't remember this should turn in his or her Baby Boom membership immediately.)

My father wasn't working for Howdy yet, but as an NBC employee he knew as early as the late 1940s that the show was a wild and woolly place to work. If the Peanut Gallery was the hot ticket for the kids, the notorious *Howdy Doody* afternoon rehearsals were the talk of the whole RCA Building. These run-throughs of the evening's script generally took ten minutes for the actual story line and about an hour for each of the sponsors. Rehearsals were the time when the men from the shoe company or the bakery actually got to shmooze with the cast and see what they were paying for. Often the *Howdy* rehearsals turned into impromptu "blue" parodies of that night's show for the benefit of the assembled clients and NBC executives. Word got out that down in 3A the puppets were humping each other in rehearsal and old standard Howdy jingles like "Cross the Street with Your Eyes" got new lyrics after lunch.

Although some *Howdy Doody* veterans credit Buffalo Bob for the blue rehearsals, most lay the blame squarely on the shoulders of Doodyville's resident prankster, Dayton Allen. Thirty years later Dayton is still remembered in the halls and elevators at NBC for his jokes, stunts, and raunchy humor. He is chiefly remembered because an entire generation of television pioneers were terrified of getting into an elevator with him. He was a comedian who was perennially in character (his own), compelled to perform, relentlessly *on* at all times. Dayton's was, according to one of his former colleagues, the kind of humor that came from shock value. Elevators in particular made him do crazy things. If a woman walked into an elevator already occupied by Dayton and a friend, Dayton might unzip and display for the friend's benefit. Another Dayton trick was to ask women he encountered in elevators to have sex with him. Occasionally, this technique was said to have produced positive results; at other times it got him into trouble. The most famous and probably apocryphal Dayton-in-the-Elevator story concerns the time he propositioned a woman who wanted to go up. She supposedly turned out to be David Sarnoff's wife, who fortunately didn't recognize the young actor in flashy sports clothes who was bothering her in her own husband's building.

"The rehearsals were unbelievably dirty," one of the cast recalls. "Dayton would have Bluster exposing himself or grabbing Howdy, and everybody would have a good laugh. But we did this to relax. Doing a kids' show all those years, we would've gone crazy if we'd played it straight."

One of Dayton's favorite games was putting filthy language into Mr. Bluster's mouth in rehearsal and threatening to repeat the obscenities on the air. This drove the straitlaced producer, Roger Muir, right up the wall; he and everyone else knew that Dayton was almost nutty and brazen enough to do it. But of course Dayton never slipped. Off-camera, Bluster was lecherous as well as foul-mouthed: just as Dayton could barely keep his grabby hands off his fellow puppeteer, Rhoda Mann, his puppet Bluster was always bumping and grinding all the other Doodyville marionettes — Howdy, the Princess, even Dilly Dally.

Eventually this preshow ribaldry led to problems. One day a tour group was going through the RCA Exhibition Hall watching that day's rehearsals on a live but soundless feed on the Hall's monitors.

They beheld the Doodyville puppets going down on each other. There were complaints, and the gang cooled it for a while. On another occasion, David Sarnoff saw something he didn't like on one of the private feeds that ran from every NBC studio direct to his office upstairs, and a stern memo came down. But the dirty *Howdy* rehearsals were tolerated and even cherished at NBC (some clients and executives went so far as to bribe pages just to be allowed to stand in the back of the studio and watch) until one afternoon when some VIP group was led on a tour through Studio 3A and beheld Bluster with his head between the knees of the hallowed Princess puppet.

Bob Rippen was still directing *Howdy* in those days, and as director he was supposed to run the rehearsals. But it was impossible, he recalls, to keep the cast in line. "The rehearsals got very dirty. Bob was quick with a double entendre and liked to turn innocuous things into a sexual situation. He would regale the crew with dirty jokes and was in general the ringleader of the famous blue rehearsals." Rippen tried as hard as he could to keep a lid on, but it was so hard. "Dayton Allen was out of control, not only in front of the cameras, but also behind them and out in the halls, where he'd make outrageous remarks to the Peanuts and proposition their mothers at the same time."

Finally NBC called Rippen and Muir on the carpet. They had already turned off the mikes on the Exhibition Hall monitors so the *Howdy* goings-on wouldn't offend the tourists; now they wanted to close the rehearsals to everyone. And just what was that bunch down in 3A trying to prove, NBC wanted to know. Did they want to slip up on the air, maybe repeat the much-dreaded "Uncle Don" incident? (This refers to a legendary 1930s radio blooper in which the host of a kids' radio program finished a show, inadvertently left the microphone on, and said, "That takes care of the little bastards for another week." This went out over the airwaves, and Uncle Don was never heard from again.)

One short-term solution that NBC tried was to literally draw a curtain around *Howdy*'s corner of the studio so that only executives and clients could watch. Eventually the crew worked out a new lookout system during rehearsals. If Scotty Brinker hung a false penis out of Howdy's fly during the run-through and Dayton started ad-libbing, for instance, they might hear Bob Rippen call out over the studio intercom: "Uh, Bob? Do you have the nickelodeon script?" There was, of course, no such thing as a nickelodeon script; this was a warning that the pages were bringing in a tour or a celebrity or NBC brass.

Although there were rarely any major slip-ups on *Howdy,* the fact that they were broadcasting live, five times a week, caused a fair share of goofs and bloopers. "The best times were when Dayton broke Smith up on the air," Rhoda Mann remembers. "Dayton would ad-lib something slightly off-color but way above the heads of the kids. Buffalo Bob would fall apart and have to duck off camera while he was trying to regain his composure. Then Ugly Sam or whoever Dayton was doing that day would come back on camera, say the Buffalo's lines, and act normally. Eventually, it got to be an ego thing for Dayton, and Smith would get angry that Dayton was cracking him up and then upstaging him."

"What can be said about Dayton?" Bobby Keeshan says. "There's nothing that can be said about Dayton that can be exaggerated. He's a madman, the original madman. He came to my wedding in 1950. When the toasts were being given, he stood up and began to talk, and when we left three and a half hours later he was still doing a monologue. He never sat down. First people were embarrassed, then they just started talking, but Dayton just kept going.

"Bob [Smith] thought Dayton was the funniest person he ever met," Keeshan continues, "because Dayton never stopped doing routines. They got along great at first, until it became obvious that Dayton was the most popular man in the studio, at least with the stage crew and the cameramen. Bob resented that, so they were forever trying to top each other."

In a famous incident, one night Dayton was parked with a young lady at a rest stop along the Saw Mill Parkway. Dayton and the girl were going at it until he noticed a cop at the window with a flashlight. "All right, outta the car!" Dayton zips up, and the cop says, "Let me see your license." And Dayton says, "Oh, can you get a license for doing this, officer?" The cop had to laugh. When Dayton told him he worked on *Howdy Doody,* the cop went nuts. He made Dayton run through all his characters — Bluster, the Inspector, Flubadub, the whole cast. "If I give you a citation," the cop said, "my kids'll never speak to me again. Is this worth a bottle of scotch to you?" Dayton looked at the cop and said, "No thanks, officer, I don't drink."

Eventually Dayton talked himself out of the citation by inviting the cop's children to the next day's show. He arranged for them to sit next to Buffalo Bob. They loaded up the kids with toys and merchandise, all to keep Dayton from getting a citation.

In time, everyone who worked with him discovered that Dayton gave new meaning to the concept of chutzpah, nerve, balls. He was chronically late for rehearsals and liked to say he didn't get up before five for anyone. "The truth was," Rhoda Mann says, "Dayton was so good at reading the cue-cards, working Bluster, and ad-libbing that he didn't need rehearsals. He considered rehearsing a kids' show beneath him, and it got to be an ego thing." It became so much of an issue that at one point Roger Muir fired Dayton for being late to an important rehearsal. They waited a day, to let the message sink in, before they called Dayton back to Doodyville.

Howdy Doody was still riding high, but by the fall of 1951 someone noticed that KAGRAN wasn't selling as many Princess Summerfall Winterspring dresses and moccasins as they had projected. Various explanations for this were put forth. The Princess puppet was cute but didn't generate much audience interest, and consequently millions of little girls weren't watching *Howdy Doody*. And the puppet was voiced by Rhoda Mann, who was not a trained actress. ("Rhoda did the voice — atrociously!" the Buffalo remembers.)

"They knew the Princess puppet hadn't caught on," Eddie Kean says, "because the merchandisers weren't asking for Princess hand puppets and dresses. There was no demand. Then someone had the idea to turn the puppet into a live character. At a meeting, someone said, 'We gotta get a young girl who can sing.' "

As a result of that meeting, KAGRAN auditioned, hired, and immersed into the bawdy mayhem of *Howdy*'s locker-room vulgarity a seventeen-year-old chorine named Judy Tyler.

My Princess Summerfall Winterspring.

But let's face facts. Even though Judy was only a teenager, she was already a street-smart tough cookie who was married to her vocal coach and exuded stardom like most girls her age exuded naïveté.

What can you say about a girl who lands a job dancing in the chorus of the Copacabana at the age of fifteen? Her real name was Judith Hess, and she was born on October 9, 1934, in New York City. Her parents were show people, bit players who fought in the trenches of Broadway in the 1920s and '30s. Judy's father, Julian Hess, blew trumpet with bandleaders Paul Whiteman and Benny

Goodman, among others. Her mother, Lorelei Kendler, had been a beautiful chorus girl with the Ziegfeld Follies. The Hess family resided on the Upper West Side, and Judy's childhood was spent shuttling between acting, piano, and dance lessons. She studied for twelve years at the famous Ballet Arts School in Studio 61 at Carnegie Hall, and starred in the usual school productions, most notably as Cinderella. While at Teaneck (New Jersey) High School she was a cheerleader and started to enter beauty contests; she won her first, Miss Stardust of 1949, on her first try and was proclaimed the most photogenic girl in the country. And she was *something,* with her long black hair, her dark eyes and perfect full eyebrows, a big singer's mouth rimmed by vivid red lips, a stunning complexion, and a figure like — a dream.

And she had been . . . around.

Judy's not here anymore to speak for herself, and didn't give many interviews in her day. So let's talk to her first husband, Colin Romoff. In 1950, Colin was a twenty-five-year-old ex-Marine who had fought at Tarawa; he was making a living playing piano in the hood joints of his native Manhattan. It was the era when Fifty-second Street between Fifth Avenue and Broadway was a paradise for jazz lovers. On any given night you could hear Billie Holiday, Coleman Hawkins, or Dizzy Gillespie in the basement of some brownstone. Romoff played in pseudo-high-class dives like the Salle de Champagne and the Gold Key Club. "I taught myself to play piano well with singers — the art of the accompanist — and soon I was starting to coach as well: 'Here's how to do it, honey.' Early in 1950, I was playing after hours at the Gold Key Club, a posh little mansion with a butler on Fifty-sixth between Fifth and Sixth. The Copacabana was nearby, and the girls who worked in the chorus there liked to pop in after their shows. Judy Garland used to come in, very late. Anyway, one night I was playing the usual Gershwin and Cole Porter, and in come the Copa's showgirls, one more beautiful than the other. There was one extremely gorgeous girl, very young, who stood out from the others. She came walking toward me, and I've never forgotten how that felt! She was young, natural, good-looking, high forehead, healthy, clean-cut, exquisite! Absolutely!

"She sat on the piano. I thought I had been around some myself, but when she sat on the piano and said she liked the way I played — I almost died. She said she'd heard that I coached and asked if I could show her a few things. She said she had been dancing at the

Copa for about eight weeks but wanted to be a singer. Later that morning I walked her home. She lived at the Dover Hotel — to which I was not invited up, by the way."

So Colin Romoff wrote Judy an act, and in 1951 they got married and began working together at various shady after-hours rooms around midtown. Judy appeared under her stage name, Judy Tyler. The clientele was mostly assemblymen and hookers; their shows were often stopped by police raids or gangster rivalries. One night they were playing the Gold Key's main room. "It was owned by a guy who had a gun on him," Romoff says. "He was on the pad with one precinct, and at some point somebody at another precinct got wind of this illegal all-night place. So one night Judy and I are holding the floor at one in the morning — everything pitch-dark but a pencil spot on her, sitting on the piano — and the police barge right on the stage. The owner took out his gun, pointed it at a uniformed police lieutenant, and said, 'Hey, pal, I'm gonna make the right phone call and you're gonna be on Staten Island.'"

Such was the world from which my beloved magic princess emerged.

Judy was still in high school when she began to make television appearances. She was a featured singer on *The Music Store,* an early variety show on New York's Channel 11, and also sang on Ed Sullivan's *Toast of the Town* and another weekly variety program hosted by Walter Winchell. Eventually somebody from *Howdy* saw her on WPIX — Bob Smith says it was either Roger Muir or Marty Stone. But it was Stone who said to the Buffalo, "This is the most vivacious thing I've ever seen, on or off television."

At that point, in the fall of 1951, KAGRAN and NBC had been looking at girls for a couple of months. Hundreds of ingenues, starlets, and young singers had been auditioned and then sent packing. Princess Summerfall Winterspring not only had to look something like the Princess puppet, she also had to have the same kind of hypnotic charisma that Buffalo Bob had, that unconscious ability to step through the camera and into your living room.

Judy Tyler's audition is vividly remembered by all who participated. It took place in a conference room equipped with a piano, on the sixth floor of the RCA Building. "She auditioned for Eddie, Roger, Bob Smith, and me," Stone recalls. "She brought her husband and lied about her age. But she sang 'The Trolley Song' and got the job." Then Judy sang "Over the Rainbow" and the *Howdy* executives looked at each other in disbelief. It sounded just like Judy Garland. Then she sang "I Got Rhythm," and it sounded just like Ethel Merman. No, *better* than Merman.

Eddie Kean remembers, "We started to audition for a girl who could look like an Indian and sing like a nightingale. And Judy was perfect for the part. She was marvelous. If we'd auditioned every budding actress in the United States I don't think we'd have found any better."

"We were working the joints," Colin Romoff says, "and we heard there was a casting call for the Princess on *Howdy Doody*. We did 'The Trolley Song' for Martin Stone and Bob Smith. They couldn't possibly have *not* taken her. She was everything they were dreaming of. There were a lot of pretty girls walking through that door, but none of them had what Judy had. She was cute, and she wasn't afraid. She wasn't cloying, just really cute. They hired her immediately; it turned out they were desperate for a girl character."

There was a moment of silence after Judy and Colin had finished their numbers, as the NBC and KAGRAN people huddled. Then Martin Stone walked over to Judy and said, "We'd like you to do the show. Do you have an agent?"

No, Judy fibbed.

Then Stone asked how old she was.

Eighteen, Judy lied. Was she married? Judy lied again and said no.

See me in my office tomorrow, Stone instructed.

The following day, Judy arrived with her husband, her parents, and her agent. They told Stone that Judy was only seventeen and started talking money, but Stone quickly disillusioned them. Judy would be paid flat scale only — three hundred a week, and not another dime. "At the end of the meeting, Judy asked for an advance," Stone says. "They [Judy and Colin] were so broke I don't think they even had carfare back to their house." At this meeting, Kean and others noticed that at the previous day's audition, Judy had been wearing a tight-fitting bra to suppress her ample breasts and make her appear younger.

Judy Tyler made her debut on *Howdy Doody* late in 1951. Eddie Kean handled the transition from puppet to live character by having Chief Featherman decide that the Princess puppet was needed at home to care for her aging parents. So Featherman was seen escorting her back to the ancestral lands of the Tinka Tonka tribe, where she was installed in an elegant private tepee and given an ample pension of wampum. The Featherman returned from the land of the Tinka Tonkas with a new princess from his tribe. I remember watching this at home: after an elaborate "Indian" ceremony, a curtain parted in Studio 3A, and there she was. She was so beautiful that I held my breath while the Buffalo put his arm around her shoulder and introduced her to the Peanuts and the whole country. The Peanuts looked at the beautiful teenager with a wide-eyed and awed collective gaze. She wore a costume of simulated buckskin fringed with white and black feathers. All over her costume she wore symbols of the four seasons: a sun for summer, a leaf for fall, a snowman for winter, and a bluebird for spring. These also appeared on a light-blue crown over her braids, on the breastplate of her jacket, and on a golden necklace around her neck. The genius of casting Judy was that she looked *exactly* like the Princess puppet, so much so that at first the Peanuts were too startled to respond to her chattery laughter and perfect singing. They just stared. So did I.

The new Princess Summerfall Winterspring was an immediate sensation on American television. The elaborate transformation ceremony not only turned a puppet into a girl, it also turned an unknown but precocious talent into the most popular character on daytime TV, overnight. It wasn't only the kids who were interested. Suddenly, for some reason not entirely clear to the kids, many of their fathers wanted to watch too. Judy was smart, curvy, and obviously young and dewy. There had never been anything like her on television before. *Variety* raved: "The effect [of the new Princess's dramatic entry] was like a breath of fresh air. The harshness and crudeness which so many parents objected to in Howdy Doody now appears to have been largely a case of too much masculinity."

Everybody on the show was thrilled with Judy. All the men fell in love with her immediately. Bob Rippen remembers her as a "terribly bright and beautiful young girl who just bubbled. She was all show business and charmed the whole crew." But one cast member wasn't so thrilled. This was Rhoda Mann, who was fired again almost as soon as Judy was hired.

She remembers the experience with some bitterness. "Bob Smith had perfect pitch and never let anyone forget it," she says. "I couldn't sing on *Howdy* because Bob made me too nervous. I worked the Princess puppet, but I just couldn't sing her little song. When they auditioned Judy, she told them that she could work puppets, so they thought she could work Howdy. So they fired me. It was right after my father died, and I was very upset. Roger Muir just called me in after a show and let me go."

This, of course, had happened to Rhoda before. Sure enough, once again, after only a week, Rhoda's telephone rang. "Bob Smith got on the phone and said, 'Rhoda, baybeeeee! Sweetheart! We loved the way you work Howdy.' And I went back because I was desperate.

"Of course Judy couldn't work Howdy! And Dayton couldn't work Howdy and make him play the piano or ride a bicycle or get Howdy's mouth in sync with Bob's voice. Dayton was good, but Howdy was an impossible puppet. His head was too big and heavy for his shoulders; it wasn't weighted properly, and people had trouble balancing him. Normally the puppet's head hung forward, and I learned to compensate for this and Howdy's other flaws. I restrung him, but he was still a mess. Once his legs fell off during a show. Howdy was sitting at the piano, and when I lifted him up his legs fell off, so I had to sit him right down again. Bob couldn't understand why Howdy wasn't walking over to the Colgate sign until he saw me gesturing frantically. It was absurd."

After hiring Judy, Roger Muir, Howdy's producer and resident father-figure to cast and crew, worried about protecting this innocent girl from the show's foul-mouthed and twisted cast, especially the uncontrollable Dayton Allen. (Many *Howdy* veterans say they didn't even know Judy was married until she had been on the show six months.) "I was worried that the group would corrupt this young kid," Muir says. "I was concerned that they would spoil this young and innocent performer. But soon, at least in terms of foul language and corruption, I learned I had to be concerned the other way."

At first, when Judy arrived, the cast toned down their notorious rehearsals in deference to their new star's tender age. Then one day something riled Judy during rehearsal and she began to curse. It turned out that this seventeen-year-old singer could swear with the élan of a fishwife. So, quickly, the *Howdy* rehearsals resumed their naughty ways. NBC executives and agency men would roar with glee when Dayton made Bluster's head lean on Judy's large bosom and emit groaning noises. "Say, Howdy," Bluster would gulp, "how's

Judy Tyler as Princess Summerfall Winterspring. (COURTESY LORELEI HESS)

the Princess? *What a pair of lungs on her!* My God! But you're too young to think about that, m'boy. You'll get headaches!"

"Judy had a filthy mouth," Scott Brinker remembers, "and Smith egged her on. Ripp [Bob Rippen] would get sore and storm into the studio and yell at Judy while Bob and Dayton smirked in the corner. But Smith liked to make her show off her foul mouth when it suited him. Then Smith would egg Dayton on and the rehearsal would go out of control and get so dirty they had to lock the doors. Some of the Poll Parrot reps really went for this stuff. It got so they couldn't rehearse the commercials because they were laughing so hard."

Yet Judy displayed a strong integrity of her own from the beginning. She may have been all–show biz, but she didn't like hanging out with *Howdy*'s cast in those days. Her friends on *Howdy* were the show's working people, people like Scott Brinker and wardrobe mistress Kitty Dalton. Judy always did her own makeup, and was expert at it. She'd start an hour before she went on and never let anyone else touch her face.

"She was a tough cookie," Dayton Allen says. "She knew everyone, and she'd been around the room a few times. When she came on, I was cynical at first because they had a big hype for the papooses now there was a girl on the show. But she was honest and open, and we got along great."

Was she as beautiful as everyone says?

"She probably looked more beautiful on the air," Dayton says. "But she had a good singing voice and good timing. Bob and I used to have a lot of laughs with her."

The new Princess Summerfall Winterspring was a sensation. When she sang Howdy's reelection campaign theme, "I'm for Howdy Doody," the Peanuts swooned. I was deeply in love with this girl before I was five years old. Overnight KAGRAN's merchandisers and licensees began to scramble for Princess products. The Princess was such a star and heroine to the children of America that soon their parents began to write to NBC's corporate sponsors, demanding to see the Princess on the prime-time variety shows. Not long after joining *Howdy,* Judy had a thirteen-week stint on Milton Berle's show, then appeared on *The Colgate Comedy Hour* with Eddie Cantor and on *All-Star Review* with Jimmy Durante.

Such was the clamor surrounding the advent of the show's new Princess that NBC decided to put Howdy on its radio network as well. *Howdy Doody* made its network radio debut on December 19, 1951, with an hour-long Saturday-morning show featuring Bob Smith, Judy Tyler, Dayton Allen, Bill Lecornec, and Clarabell. (Clarabell's "voice" was portrayed by an audio man blowing a bike horn so KAGRAN wouldn't actually have to pay Bobby Keeshan.) The show consisted of little sketches between Buff, Howdy, the Princess, Flub-adub (Dayton), and Dilly Dally (Bill), centering on a bit of whimsy involving a man from Mars. (Since Eddie Kean had his hands full with the TV show, a writer named Bob Cone was hired to script the radio program.) Judy Tyler sang "White Christmas" and "Santa Claus Is Coming to Town" while the Buff comped expertly on piano. With an hour to fill — even an hour loaded with commercials — *Howdy* needed some extra guests. On that first show, Milton Berle and his daughter Vicki guested to plug (ironically) an upcoming Berle program with Mickey Mouse and other Disney characters. Then Gabby Hayes, whose show, like *Howdy,* was owned and operated by KAGRAN, told a rambling Western yarn that ended with his trademark, "Yes sirree Bob, it's a true story!"

The *Howdy Doody* radio show was an instant hit and sold out its ad time within the first few weeks. As always, not everyone was thrilled. The *Variety* reviewer complained that some of the material was over the heads of the younger children and that the commercials were overdone. "In some pitches," the reviewer carped, "Smith overdoes the entreating uncle bit." NBC, in the broadcasting industry's trade press, advertised Howdy's radio show as a fabulous medium "in which to sell your product to tiny and moderately large urchins." And it was. Two and a half million kids listened to every Saturday broadcast.

Bob Smith's first love, even then, was radio, and he loved doing the radio show, which he ran like a combination Lutheran choirmaster and drill sergeant. It was a music show as much as possible, and Smith worked his little Princess hard. Judy was very talented, but she wasn't a quick reader of music. The notes had to be pounded into her, and she had to sing a lot of songs; when she did duets with the Buffalo, he would take the harmony part because Judy didn't have a perfect ear. But she had a great voice and worked hard to learn the music.

This was the era of Eddie Kean's best jingles, Howdy Doody's greatest hits. Songs and jingles from both the TV and radio programs (like "The Popcorn Song," "The Lollypop Song," "Clarabell," "I'm the Inspector," "Meatballs and Spaghetti," "The Friendship Song," and "The Howdy Doody Navy") found their way onto hit albums like *Howdy Doody and the Air-O-Doodle* and *Howdy Doody and You,* staying on the charts for months. At one point, three *Howdy* albums were on the *Billboard* top-twenty chart simultaneously; this kind of success especially gratified Eddie and the Buffalo, both musicians at heart. As Kean said, "My greatest pleasure in my eight-year association with the show derived from the dozen or so record albums we did with RCA Victor. They gave me a chance to undo my music frustrations. Composing the songs and then hearing them back in the studio with the band and the whole cast was a huge kick."

By the end of 1951, *Howdy Doody* was beginning to enter its year-long prime. Now *Howdy* wasn't just a television show for kids; it was an institution that contemporaries already realized would have an impact on the generation for which it was intended. It was no coincidence that a young cartoonist named Charles Schulz decided to call his new comic strip *Peanuts* after watching Chief Thunder-thud walk up to the Peanut Gallery and say, "How, Peanuts!" in his usual greeting.

In those days the most influential broadcast columnist in the country was John Crosby, who wrote about television for the *New York Herald Tribune.* Here's what Crosby had to say about Howdy in his prime:

RADIO AND TELEVISION

By JOHN CROSBY

'It's Howdy Doody Time'

Howdy Doody occupies a very distinctive and not entirely enviable niche in the annals of the television industry. This children's program, its producers claim, has been seen by more people than have witnessed either Milton Berle or Sen. Kefauver, simply because it's been on oftener (five times a week, half an hour, for more than three years) and in so many more cities (forty-nine).

The fact that Howdy—you don't use his last name any more than you use Tallulah's—has been observed by so many people so often should not be confused with popularity. Much of Howdy's audience is composed of reluctant adults who would like to wring Bob Smith's neck. To an adult, Howdy 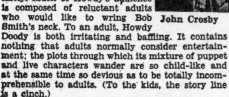 John Crosby

Doody is both irritating and baffling. It contains nothing that adults normally consider entertainment; the plots through which its mixture of puppet and live characters wander are so child-like and at the same time so devious as to be totally incomprehensible to adults. (To the kids, the story line is a cinch.)

After witnessing it once, the exasperated parent is likely to head for the cellar or the roof to escape the darned thing. Howdy Doody, however, is pretty hard to get away from unless you live in an awfully large house. From the moment it opens with a chorus of forty children piping "It's Howdy Doody time" at the top of their &%$#($% lungs to the closing, the program is conducted at a noise level roughly five times that of Berle, or about twenty times that of Frank Costello.

Bob Smith, the inventor of Howdy, is dressed in a costume which is a mixture of an African explorer and Hopalong Cassidy. Howdy is a freckle-faced Huckleberry Finn of a puppet. Clarabell is a male clown who can't talk and issues her—pardon me—his signals by means of an auto horn. Are you getting confused? You must be over nine years old, then. For the benefit of parents who wonder when they can get rid of Howdy, the age group is from two to nine. After that they graduate—or should graduate—to Hopalong. If he's still mad about Howdy after age nine, send him to a psychiatrist.

Despite the complete lack of sense to you and me, Smith, a former piano player on an early morning radio program, seems to have figured the emotional level of the age two to nine group brilliantly. This puppet now grosses $300,000 a year for Mr. Smith, which is about $100,000 more than Faye Emerson, a non-puppet, earns. It's also more than Uncle Miltie earns. (Uncle Miltie is a horse who may or may not win the Kentucky Derby, in which case I may or may not revise my figures.)

Besides his television appearances, Howdy Doody can be found in department and other stores in a variety of manifestations. Howdy Doody merchandise—including cowboy shirts, albums, school bags, balloons, balls, bedspreads, belts, buttons, chairs, puppets, crayon sets, dolls, draperies, ear muffs, piggy banks, umbrellas, pinwheels, lamps, greeting cards, jams, ice creams and—oh, brother, this is the end—eggs—is sold to the tune of $15,-000,000 every year. So far as I know, the Howdy Doody egg, just a plain hen's egg, is the first indorsed egg.

In 1948, this woodenhead—not Smith, Howdy—ran for President. He polled more votes than Henry Wallace, though not quite so many as Harry Truman. His platform: two Christmases and one school day a year, more pictures in history books, double sodas for a dime and more movies.

Some 10,000,000 children watch the show, depending on when their bath hour is, and almost anything Howdy says receives grave and rather alarming attention. One premium offer on the show drew 785,000 letters, or roughly ten times the mail Truman gets on a major speech. Howdy has enormous influence, mostly for the good. He has persuaded millions of moppets to brush their teeth and is credited with driving thousands of them to the dentist.

In 1952, he may run again on a Mars candy bar platform. Don't be at all surprised if he wins.

Part Two

1952–1960

Children who have been taught, or conditioned, to listen passively most of the day to the warm verbal communication coming from the TV screen, to the deep emotional appeal of the TV personality, are often unable to respond to real persons because they arouse so much less feeling than the skilled actor. Worse, they lose the ability to learn from reality because life experiences are more complicated than the ones they see on the screen, and there is no one who comes in at the end to explain it all. The "TV child" . . . gets discouraged when he cannot grasp the meaning of what happens to him. . . .

If, later in life, this block of solid inertia is not removed, the emotional isolation from others that starts in front of the TV may continue. . . . Thus being seduced into passivity and discouraged about facing life actively on one's own is the real danger of TV.

— Bruno Bettelheim
The Informed Heart

Howdy's cast in 1951. Left to right: Bill Lecornec, Judy Tyler, Dayton Allen, and Bob Smith. Missing is Bobby Keeshan, who didn't sing. (COURTESY LORELEI HESS)

Six

The Christmas Eve Massacre

I WAS FIVE YEARS OLD in 1952, Howdy Doody's prime year. At the apex of its audience and merchandising pull, with its original cast nearly intact, Howdy was an American institution as well as an entertaining and well-meaning money machine.

That was the year I left home and went to school for the first time, now an anomaly in the age of daycare and preschool. Today Mom wants to work, and frequently she has to. Back then, she did the ironing in the afternoon and listened to *Helen Trent* on the radio. At school I met the other Baby Boomers from the class of 1947. What we talked about — naturally — was what was on the tube: Howdy Doody; Roy Rogers, king of the cowboys; Gabby Hayes, presented by Quaker Puffed Oats (which they said was "shot from guns," in case anyone worried about Quaker pacifism); Sky King, the pilot; Mr. Wizard, the scientist; Rootie Kazootie (and his girlfriend, Polka Dottie); *Junior Frolix,* a local show on New York's old Channel 13 that featured the mindless and ever-popular Farmer Gray cartoons, where it literally rained cats and dogs. (These old silent cartoons are now considered too violent to be shown to young children, but that didn't bother anyone back in the fifties.)

Since I had been to the Peanut Gallery a couple of times, I was glad the other kids seemed to like Howdy Doody so much. I had a vague idea that my dad was involved with it in some way, because whenever I went to Doodyville all the guys wearing headphones behind the cameras were very friendly to him. I got to meet everyone; once, kissed by Princess Summerfall Winterspring, I had lost the faculty of speech for a few hours.

Howdy helped me in other ways. At first I was very frightened of going to school and mutinied every time my mother tried to shove me into the yawning maw of the immense yellow school bus that pulled up at the end of our suburban street. Then I saw something about a school bus — a *friendly* school bus — on *Howdy,* and it made

120

me feel more secure about the entire issue. Then there were my fears of the two handicapped children in my kindergarten class. One girl wore heavy steel leg braces, having been crippled by polio; the other twitched spasmodically from cerebral palsy. I didn't know what to make of this. No one had prepared me for kids who weren't perfect. But *Howdy* did a sequence on the March of Dimes that raised my consciousness — I had never even heard of polio before that. And then, when I looked carefully at Sally, the little girl with cerebral palsy, I was amazed to notice that she reminded me a little of Howdy, the way he jiggled about on his twelve strings. Maybe Sally wasn't so frightening after all.

Another memory from the era: my schoolmates and I were "polio pioneers," which meant that we were among the first children in the world to be mass-inoculated with Dr. Salk's miraculous polio vaccine. We lined up in the gymnasium of our school on Long Island, shivering with dread at the sight of the huge glass syringes then in use. The needle looked like a spear to me, and felt worse. A couple of children even fainted during the ordeal.

One more memory. There were two kinds of drills that my kindergarten class was obliged to learn. The fire drill was easy: the bell rings, you walk out to the playground quickly in single file. Much chaos and laughter. Then there was the air-raid drill: the bell rings, you file into the hall, press your back to the wall, and crouch with your hands over your head. We were told these drills were in case of enemy H-bomb attacks. One kid in my class told me that his brother had told him H-bombs were even bigger than A-bombs. The fire drills at school were fun and a welcome interruption of our routine; but I thought the air-raid drills were terrifying, and the other children in my class seemed scared and silent too.

Let's try another kinescope, one from 1952, and see if we can figure out what was going down in Doodyville that year.

Fade in on Mr. Bluster, coughing out a welcome. Cut to the Peanuts; they're singing the theme — *"It's Howdy Doody time, it's Howdy Doody time, Bob Smith and Howdy too, say howdy do to you. Let's give a rousing cheer, 'cause Howdy Doody's here, it's time to start the show, so kids let's go!"* Then we see Howdy and the Buffalo chatting about Clarabell's impending initiation into the Ooragnak tribe. Cut to Thunderthud, livid because he doesn't want the klutzy clown in his tribe. Cut to the Ooragnak village. "Kowabonga!" moans the chief, "Kowa-terrible!" Enter the Princess (my pulse rate goes up),

121

who asks Thunderthud what's bothering him. "Not want clown Indian in same tribe," the Chief complains. Then he has a brainstorm. "Kowa-idea," he announces. This evolves into a scenario where Thunderthud and Clarabell set out to trick each other. While this is going on, the rest of the cast takes sides: when Howdy says he's on Clarabell's side because the Chief should be more tolerant, the Princess tells Howdy she thinks he should support Thunderthud.

This is followed by a long ad for Welch's Grape Juice. When Buff comes back, he huddles with the Peanut Gallery and shows them an Old-Time Movie. Then we cut back to Clarabell's and the Chief's machinations. Watch Keeshan play the clown. His slapstick is artlessly bumbling and quite endearing. And look at Lecornec's Thunderthud — handsome, debonair, played with pencil mustache and warpaint. Another ad: Luden's Wild Cherry Cough Drops. Then back to the plot: it turns out that the Princess and Clarabell are in cahoots. The show fades out with the Princess becoming frightened when she gets lost in the woods outside the Ooragnak village.

This kine is dated January 27, 1952, and is typical of that period in the show's history — rivalry, manipulation, intrusiveness, and convoluted subplots abound. Less typical is our second feature, another *Howdy* kine from two weeks later. This is the famous one thousandth *Howdy Doody Show,* broadcast February 12, 1952.

Howdy was the first network television show to have a run of a thousand performances, and consequently this big anniversary was planned as a technological extravaganza, with live remotes from Chicago and Los Angeles feeding into the main show in New York. The main show was deemed too big in scope for Howdy's minuscule Studio 3A, so NBC moved it to the Center Theater, a cavernous hall (originally intended for the Metropolitan Opera) in the Rockefeller Center complex. NBC had refitted this hall for television as the home of the network's biggest evening shows, *The Colgate Comedy Hour with Dean Martin and Jerry Lewis* and *Your Show of Shows* with Sid Caesar.

This special hour-long Howdy tribute is of interest today because its walk-on guests tell us much about TV in 1952. The show begins with the Buffalo leading all two thousand carefully selected Peanuts through a stirring version of the theme song. Then the Princess is brought out, to a tumultuous welcome. She is pert, coltish, graceful, in contrast to Oil Well Willie, the codger/prospector played by Lecornec. They do an old bit called "Where's Clarabell?" until the clown appears in the Center Theater balcony, throws a rope over the rail, and attempts to let himself down. This suicidal gag is mercifully thwarted by the NBC pages, who drag off the protesting clown.

Before the first ad, Smith does a promo for *Howdy*'s "Kids Care" campaign. (We were in the height of the Korean War, and the relief agency CARE was using *Howdy*'s audience to raise funds for the Korean refugee population. So far, the campaign had been a success. After the first couple of spots, KAGRAN was deluged by several million quarters mailed in from all over the country.) Then Smith introduces Howdy's first walk-on guest. It's a Chicago television personality, Dave Garroway, who is about to change the nature of American television. NBC's president Pat Weaver is in the process of innovating a new mode of TV entertainment, moving away from variety and toward journalism. He has conceived a TV magazine format that will mix hard and soft news stories and appear three times a day. The morning news show is to be called *Today*. *Home* will be a noon show for housewives. And late in the evening NBC will broadcast a talk show, *Tonight*. Garroway, an affable interviewer thought to be the epitome of contemporary wry sophistication, is making his national network debut not on his own imminent *Today* show but on *Howdy Doody*.

Next comes the first remote. It's Howdy and the Flubadub, live from Hollywood. Smith, back in New York, syncs Howdy's voice with Rhoda Mann as she works the puppet in California. Dayton is the Flubadub. Then the next guest, the comedian Jack Carter, walks on in NBC's Vine Street studio and does a bit with the Flub. (There had been problems earlier in the day at rehearsal when Carter came in to do his lines and Dayton/Flub asked him how they were hanging. This agitated Carter, who was a big star back then and not ready to be "topped" by a punk puppeteer and his dummy. Carter walked out of the rehearsal, and someone had to get Dayton to apologize.) Then Carter does a serious appeal for CARE, talking about the ravages of war in Europe and Asia — sobering stuff.

After the next ad, guests and remotes abound. There's Kukla, Fran, and Ollie in Chicago. There's "Mr. Television," Milton Berle, on the set of his *Texaco Star Theater* with his daughter, Vicki. Berle talks about CARE before a long Colgate epic involving Happy Tooth's constant battle against his nemesis, Mr. Tooth Decay. Then we go back to California, where comedian Ed Wynn does a turn with the Flubadub. The show's big finale has Buffalo Bob Smith and the Princess singing the Colgate song.

This appalling situation — sponsor control of the show — was something Pat Weaver was trying to change. The previous year NBC had begun a new system of advertising called "Minute Man." Instead of selling an entire show to one company, Weaver decided to sell single minutes of time to different advertisers; this way, sponsorship would be more evenly distributed, and NBC could retain more editorial control over its programming.

So Howdy was in his prime, but there was a hint of real turmoil in the air. The daily grind of the show was difficult and relentless, and word had spread around NBC that important Howdy cast members had decided that they were being grossly underpaid. In the control room, Bob Rippen was burnt out, having directed hundreds of shows since 1948 without a vacation. So NBC made Rippen line producer of the daily show, kicked Roger Muir upstairs to oversee production, and hired a new director, Bob Hultgren, to run the control room. He was a former stage manager who had been first brought in to handle station breaks and coordinate the studio. Hultgren worked on the show for about six months and was an able director, but he had some problems directing the increasingly volatile cast. Since the work was demanding and the show was relying increasingly on remotes — Howdy Doody liked to drop in at the Rose Bowl, Macy's Thanksgiving Parade, and other nationally televised photo opportunities — NBC decided to hire another staff director to alternate with Bob Hultgren. The network was specifically looking for someone who could get a restless cast to work together.

So they hired my father to codirect *Howdy Doody.*

At the time, Howard Davis was directing local television in New York. He had pioneered an early daytime show with Kathy Norris, a former newspaperwoman around whom NBC built its early midmorning schedule. Howard had also directed some of the first tennis matches ever televised in America, directed commercials on Saturday nights for *Your Show of Shows,* and generally been on the lookout to move to the more prestigious NBC network.

It was the heyday of McCarthyism, and 1952 was an election year. Senator Joseph McCarthy was leading a witch hunt against suspected communist influence in Hollywood and television. Everyone was scared. During the campaign, the Republican candidate, General Eisenhower, sat on a podium and listened to Joe McCarthy call his old mentor, General George Marshall, a tool of the communists. Ike said nothing, and won the election. The worst of the McCarthyite groups that targeted television and radio was Red Channels; these hate-mongers put a lot of liberal radio and TV people, mostly an-nouncers and newsmen, to flight, and many never worked in broad-casting again.

Howard Davis remembers the fear at NBC. Once Bob Hultgren asked Howard if he was nervous about the fact that his NBC records showed he had taken courses at that notorious socialist breeding ground, the London School of Economics. Howard replied that he wasn't worried, since five-year Army veterans usually weren't har-assed by the McCarthy groups. Just prior to being hired by *Howdy,* Howard directed a local quizzer in New York called *It's a Problem,* hosted by Ben Grauer. In the nervous political atmosphere in which they worked, Grauer confided in Howard that he thought his career had been stymied because he had in the past espoused liberal causes. (Howdy Doody, incidentally, again ran for President of the kids in 1952, easily beating Mr. X, whose campaign was [mis]managed by Phineas T. Bluster.)

Howard Davis was recommended to Roger Muir and Bob Smith by Howdy's TD (technical director), Tom Smiley, who had worked with Howard on *It's a Problem.* So, sometime in mid-1952, Howard reported for his first day of work as Howdy's new alternate director. After about a week of observation, in which he had a chance to make notes about the workings of cast and crew, Howard took over as Howdy's director. His nervousness concerning his new network re-sponsibilities (which, happily, entailed a suddenly doubled salary) was hardly allayed by the fierce attitude problems displayed by the citizens of Doodyville.

That first day, Bobby Keeshan came up to Howard in his clown suit but without makeup. "You won't like it here," Keeshan said affably. When my father asked why, Keeshan said that the Buffalo was becoming an egomaniac. Howard says he didn't know whether or not to take this seriously, but Keeshan was obviously disgruntled. My father already knew Dayton Allen, who dominated the third-floor "green room" area NBC maintained for actors. Dayton com-plained to Howard that *The Howdy Doody Show* was too lowbrow and warned him that he would soon wish he were back in local TV. Howard was relieved that not all the cast members were so trucu-lent. He found that Bill Lecornec was a lovely guy, and Rhoda Mann was quiet and professional.

Judy Tyler, now eighteen years old, was something else. On How-ard's first day as director, after he had run the cast through his initial rehearsal, Judy told him in confidence that he wouldn't last long. "You're too gentlemanly," she said. "They're all bastards on this show." She complained bitterly about Howdy's management — Smith, Muir, Eddie Kean, and Marty Stone. Judy groused all the time, but never got mad at anybody except the big wheels. She identified with the show's working class. Her "act" of downtrodden talent, Howard remembers, was so convincing that it was hard to believe she was raking in five hundred dollars a week for her pleasant chores. This was great money back then, and she had paid vacations and made extra for promotional tours and certain personal appearances.

Howard also quickly noticed that Judy loved to shock, both off the set and on. Under the stern and watchful eye of Roger Muir, she behaved herself in the studio. But backstage she would exclaim, "Jesus Christ, if that kid in the second row coughs again while I'm singing I swear I'll slug the little shit!"

As for Buffalo Bob Smith, Howard was amused to find that he was almost the same off camera as he was on. The Buff was something of a grabber, one of those buddy-buddy guys who'd pat your bum or squeeze your arm or give you a brotherly shove just for the physical contact.

Despite all the cast's grumbling, my father decided that he was going to like working for Howdy Doody. Shortly thereafter, my sporadic visits to Doodyville became more regular pilgrimages, a routine that would continue for the next four years.

In 1952 a day in the life of *Howdy Doody* began at about nine o'clock in the morning, at least for the NBC employees who began to arrive at that hour in the show's office on the third floor of the studio section of NBC. This was toward the Sixth Avenue side of the RCA building, the only part of the giant complex with air-conditioning, necessary to counter the broiling klieg lights of the TV studios. Muir and Rippen, the producer and associate producer, usually arrived right after Bobbie Horn, Muir's secretary. The directors, Hultgren and Davis, would come in next. The writers' office was just down the hall; people liked to hang out there because it had a couch where one could relax when an idea was slow in coming. Mornings around the office were full of free-lancers with story ideas, jingle-writers and song-pluggers selling their wares, and myriad singers, jugglers, magicians, hypnotists, animal acts, cardsharps, and call girls, all trying to sell themselves. Only a few of these succeeded.

Activity always picked up in the late morning. Prop man Bernie

Morshen would come in to show Rippen or Davis one of the complicated props Scott Brinker had spent the previous night building. Brinker's wife, Edith, wrote and held Howdy's cue-cards; Eddie Kean would read Edith the script over the phone around 11:00 P.M., and Scott would go out to his workshop and start to build whatever new items the script called for. His mechanical props, painted and working, had to be in, along with the cue-cards, before the first rehearsal at one o'clock the next afternoon. Kitty Dalton, the wardrobe lady, might come in with a formal Indian gown for the Princess, whom Howdy had invited to be his date at the Doodyville prom. Set designer Elmer Tagg might show the plans for next week's special set, a small Scottish village. Jack Anderson, who handled Howdy's multitude of sound effects, would check the day's script to see what *boing*s and *wwhheeeeeeee*s were required.

Howdy Doody's crew, unlike its cast, was a harmonious bunch whose members socialized together and were proud of their skills and positions. Bob Rippen points to the Buffalo's easygoing temperament as part of the reason for the crew's camaraderie, and he adds, "NBC was a big happy family in those days, and there wasn't as much dog-eat-dog commercialism as there is now."

"I'll tell you, there were nineteen men on that crew at that time," Scott Brinker says. "NBC carried 'key man' insurance on each one. Everyone who was ever involved knows that there was no closer relationship on any TV crew than there was on *Howdy Doody*."

It didn't take Howard long to realize how well Howdy's technical crew worked together. The comradeship and cooperation between the directors and technical crew was very positive — not often the case in what Howard terms "the sorry state of affairs" in early television. Cue-cards were color-coded for each character. Bob Smith had to follow two colors, his own and Howdy's. The director had to follow conversations between puppets and people without catching Smith doing Howdy's voice. Around this time, Smith began prerecording Howdy's lines on acetate disks that were then played by the audio man when Howdy spoke. The directors' earphones and microphones were hooked into the floor managers', and the technical director's went to all the technicians'. The technical team worked in a darkened control room adjacent to the studio; the director was obliged to trot back and forth many times in the course of an afternoon rehearsal.

Air time was 5:30. The technicians would start lighting the set (if a new one had been installed overnight) around noon. The cameramen generally walked in about 12:30 and warmed up the big Image Orthikons. Rehearsal began at 1:00 if there were new ads to rehearse, somewhat later if not. Until then the cast would dawdle in the adjoining third-floor dressing area. Judy usually dressed in tight-fitting pants or short (for then) skirts, and the men wore loud sports clothes. Everybody would smoke lots of cigarettes while waiting to be called for the first run-through of the day.

Howard soon learned that the notorious *Howdy* rehearsals were indeed raunchy. Lecornec, to get a laugh, would have Dilly Dally beg for it in his horrible squeaky voice: "Oh, Pwinceth, I wanna *do* you something awful!" Sitting in the control room, seeing and hearing Dilly say this to the teenage Judy on his monitor, Howard found it something of a shock the first time it happened. Soon he also learned that Dayton Allen never rehearsed a line as written. Sometimes Bob Smith would get sick of constantly being topped and cut by his jabbering costar and put a halt to it; "Dayton!" he would snap. "Read your lines right!" Dayton would look apologetic and would make the Flubadub say, in his goofy strangled croak, "All right, Dayton, the Buffalo says to cut the shit!" The crew would laugh, and Bob would get madder. Then Dayton would read his lines right for a minute or so before having Mr. Bluster introduce himself as Phineas T. Bigballs. Or the Inspector would exclaim that he was "America's Number One [*BOOIINNG!*] Private Parts!"

As air time approached, Makeup would take the actors in turn. Actually, these seasoned pros needed little help, except when they were creating a new character. Often one of the puppeteers could be heard beseeching Eddie Kean for an extra thirty seconds to rig a difficult marionette transition. As five o'clock approached the crew would get nervous, and tempers might flare if the audio man missed his cue and the Flubadub's voice was heard over a shot of Howdy. Around this time the kids would be brought into the Peanut Gallery for the preshow warm-up ritual. This would always involve the chase-and-squirt scene to weed out the very young, the hysterical, the weak-bladdered, and the criers. (Up to the viewing room they went, without apology.) In the early days of the show, Dayton did the warm-up before the Buff came out. "Well, kids," Dayton would leer, "we're gonna have a lot of fun today — right after the show!" A couple of the older kids might chuckle at this. Then Dayton, dressed as Pierre the Chef, would continue: "Now last night, kids, there was a little boy in the front seat picking his nose during the show. Now this is something you don't do on television. So if any of you Peanuts has to pick your nose, do it now before we go on the air." This routine was designed for the sole purpose of making the cast and crew convulse with laughter as forty children dug their fingers into their noses. Up on the ninth floor, the mothers would die as they saw their kids picking away on the monitors.

Then the Buffalo would come out and the kids in the Peanut Gallery would shriek. He would tease them into a frenzy and introduce the characters as they strolled onto the set. This, it was hoped, would prevent the kids from calling out coast to coast later in the show when they beheld their favorites in the flesh. "Who's that, kids?" Bob would yell, and they would roar back, "Chief Thunderthud!" Then Buff would point to the puppet bridge as Rhoda brought out Howdy, and the Peanuts would go wild. Their hero!

But when Princess Summerfall Winterspring entered, there was usually a strange, very hushed silence. The children weren't laughing. They were impressed. The Princess looked so young. She was not much older than they. The kids' eyes would go wide and invariably some little girl, perhaps a bold seven-year-old, would sigh, "There she is." Judy Tyler would smile at everyone and quietly say, "How," Indian-fashion. All the little voices would answer "How," and often one of the smallest girls would leave her seat to take Judy's hand. (This was of course fatal and meant a one-way trip to the ninth-floor gulag.)

Then Buff would ask, "Where is he, kids? Have any of you seen Clarabell?" And naturally the clown would be right behind the Buffalo, ready to let go with another wet one. This always worked the Peanuts into near-pathological excitement.

A few minutes later, the stage manager would call for silence. Clarabell would intimidate the Peanuts with a few harsh words. The stage manager relays the director's message: "Thirty seconds!" Dead stillness . . . the lights blaze on like glory . . . hearts beating hard and . . . "SAY KIDS, WHAT TIME IS IT?"

As 1952 wore on, the discontent in Doodyville grew. Bobby Keeshan was the most dissatisfied, perhaps because as Clarabell he had to work harder than anyone else. In June he accompanied Bob Smith back home to Buffalo, where a "Buffalo Bob Smith Day" was being held to honor the city's namesake and favorite son. In September Keeshan had to travel to West Virginia, where a Boone County miner's daughter named Linda Dolan had won Howdy's big summertime "I'd Like Clarabell to Visit Me Because . . ." contest. (This

Bob, Dayton, and Judy during a broadcast of the Howdy Doody *radio show,*
1952. (COURTESY LORELEI HESS)

visit was covered by *Look* magazine, which photographed Clarabell
visiting a coal mine, auctioning pies for the Presbyterian Church in
the town of Joe's Creek, and bedding down — in his zebra-striped
sleeping cap — with the Dolan kids at night, after which Mrs. Dolan
pronounced hers "the happiest family in the U.S.")

If Howdy's cast was restive, it must be said that the show's management was also ready to make changes — but not the changes the
cast wanted. For years Buffalo Bob had been stymied in his main
desire, which was to have an on-camera band on the show. Smith
wanted Doodyville's other characters to play along with him. Despite
an attempt at music lessons, Keeshan remained totally hopeless.
Lecornec and the Princess were very talented vocalists but couldn't
play. Dayton could handle some piano but not at a professional level.
Finally, in October 1952, Buffalo Bob told Roger Muir to hire, sight
unseen, a young radio musician from Buffalo named Bob Nicholson.
Hiring Nick, as he was called, was supposed to solve several prob-

lems. First, a good musician was needed for the radio show, which had to rely on music rather than *Howdy*'s usual visual humor. Second, both Stone and Muir had been urging the Buffalo to use more music on the TV show, and having a trained musician in the cast would make it possible for Doodyville to actually field a little band. Third, Nick's joining them was a message to the rest of the cast: there was plenty of new blood around, and everybody on *Howdy Doody* except Buffalo Bob was expendable.

Whether or not this last message was actually intended, it was the message the rest of the cast got. When the implications finally sank in, there was dismay on the third floor. It was as if a large and quarrelsome family had been told by its father that he was bringing in a new older brother because his current group of children wasn't quite up to snuff. Suddenly the specter of sibling rivalry and jealousy — biochemical and thus impossible to control — invaded Doodyville like a rogue virus. The hiring of Bob Nicholson would prove to be one of the straws that broke the back of the old *Howdy Doody Show* forever.

Let's call Nick and talk to him about those times. Here he is, on a clear AT&T line from South Florida, where he lives in retirement.

Nicholson was born in Buffalo in 1918 and followed a course remarkably similar to Buffalo Bob's. A regular performer on Buffalo radio by the age of seven, he toured with a big band right out of high school and was drafted in 1942. In an Army entertainment unit, he wrote, arranged, and conducted ninety-minute vaudeville shows that were backed by a big jazz orchestra and played aircraft carriers and little guano atolls all over the Pacific. After the war, he renewed his acquaintance with Bob Smith, whom he had known as a fellow musician and radio personality. Through Smith, Nick was hired as music director at WBEN, which turned into a TV station in 1950 and soon made him the variety host on its local morning show. Nick was a good-natured and funny man, and an especially skilled musician; this was noticed by Bob Smith, who appeared on his show as a guest in early 1952. After Smith and Nick played a well-received piano duet, Bob took him aside and said, "You know, you oughta come down to New York. What are you still doing here in Buffalo, anyway?" Smith went on, "I could use a guy like you to write special material for *Howdy*. If I negotiated a firm contract for you with NBC, would you come to New York and give it a try?"

Was he kidding?

Nicholson picks up the story. "That son-of-a-gun went back to New York, negotiated with NBC, and a month later I got a call. 'Come on down, I think I've got a firm commitment for you.' " Nick met with Smith, Kean, and Muir. Over lunch at Toots Shor's, they told him that Eddie had been writing the show for five years and was overworked and starting to burn out. They were hiring Nick to take over some of Eddie's workload and act as resident songwriter and arranger. Since Nick was being put on the NBC payroll as a musician/performer assigned to *Howdy Doody,* Eddie Kean came up with a character named Cornelius J. Cobb (or Corny Cobb), a country storekeeper in Doodyville with a bent for music. Nick remembers that Eddie told him, "Bob and Howdy'll come to the store and visit and you'll get out the gut-bucket and the uke and play some music."

So Nick came to New York in October 1952 with an NBC contract and a job on the most popular show on daytime television. He was nervous, and it showed. "I was nervous every time I went on the air," Nick says. "These were live shows. It was the big time, Rockefeller Center in New York. They had told me we were reaching ten million kids every time we uncapped the lens. To me, this was kind of scary, and it felt very strange." So strange, in fact, that Nick was as stiff as a corpse both in rehearsals and on the air. One day, as Nick missed another cue, one of the directors decided that enough was enough. "That's it," he cried. "That guy can't act for shit!" As the director was about to storm into the studio, he was restrained by Roger Muir, who told him to forget about Nick's acting abilities and concentrate on setting up the next shot. Clearly, Bob Nicholson was the new fair-haired boy in Doodyville. He took his new duties very seriously, superseding Doc Whipple and rearranging such Kean classics as "Cross the Street with Your Eyes" and "Do Do a Howdy Doody Do (But Don't Do a Howdy Doody Don't)."

As in any family, there was deep resentment over the new member. Judy Tyler and Dayton were livid at the lavish attention accorded Nick by Buff and Muir. At first the rest of the cast was formal and standoffish with this new guy from out of town. There was some minor cruelty from Dayton as poor Nick tried to fit in with the rest of the gang. But, as Nick remembers it, "When I got to New York everything was great with the exception of Bobby Keeshan. In the dressing room he always used to say to me, 'It won't be long before you're back in Buffalo.' I remember these words exactly, and you can quote me. But he couldn't rattle me because it was obvious that he was untalented and couldn't do anything like read lines or play music. Once they had a three-hundred-dollar set of matched bicycle horns made for him, so Clarabell would have something to do, and he couldn't play them! He had no pitch, no timing, nothing. He resented my coming in because Bob was telling everyone I was *Howdy*'s big new talent. There was a lot of schoolboy jealousy. There were no bad words between us, but we didn't really speak. You could call it an immediate dislike. I think he felt that way because he was afraid that the real reason I was there was to take the Clarabell costume away from him."

Keeshan was no dummy. He *knew* Nick was there to take the clown suit away, and, as it turned out, he was right. Rhoda Mann remembers that Smith and Muir had Nicholson try on Keeshan's costume almost as soon as he joined the show.

Nicholson got to know the other cast members quite well. "Like most comics," he muses, "Dayton Allen was actually a serious guy. He had lots of hang-ups, and I saw a lot of serious moments when no one else was around. Of course, I learned what everyone else knew — never get in an elevator with Dayton. The minute he had a captive audience like that he was incorrigible.

"As for Lecornec, he was one of the original hippies. He lived in the Village in a very small apartment, no furniture, no TV. He was very intelligent and completely undependable. Of course it was very important that he show up because he was Thunderthud and Dilly Dally and was always written into the script. Thunderthud we could play around, but not Dilly. One time Bill didn't show up by the dress rehearsal at four o'clock; he called from Philadelphia and told Roger Muir that he didn't even know how he had gotten there. But we knew that he had gotten bombed and wound up on the wrong train somehow. That night we went on without him. Roger was going to fire him, but couldn't because everyone liked Bill too much. No one ever heard him say a bad word about anybody."

Buffalo Bob got sick that fall. He came down with pneumonia and just couldn't seem to get better. He had been working furiously, with two radio shows and five live half hours of TV every week. While he was recuperating he stayed home in New Rochelle with Buffalo Mil, as he called his wife, and their two sons, Robin, then ten, and Robbie, then eight years old. It was great for the kids, but Bob itched to get back to work. The Buffalo would watch, exasperated, as Gabby Hayes hosted his own show at five-fifteen (which, as directed by my father, would end with a barrelful of Quaker Puffed Oats being shot straight at the camera lens with a loud bang, fade to black, roll credits) before crossing the studio to host that day's *Howdy*. To try to get his strength back and avoid future exhaustion, the Buffalo gave up his morning radio show for good.

When the Buffalo came back to *Howdy* in November 1952 with his batteries recharged, he discovered that he had a rebellion on his hands. Rumor flew around the third floor that the human residents of Doodyville had decided they were being exploited. Soon there was actually talk of some kind of strike.

But all this remained secret through Thanksgiving 1952. It was the climax of Howdy's second election campaign, and there was a weekly scientific poll of the Peanut Gallery using a prop machine called the Wing Ding, which measured the noise as the Peanuts screamed and cheered for their favorite candidate. Naturally Howdy won every week. Back in 1948, ballots had been printed in TV magazines, and over one million had been mailed in. In 1952, Wonder Bread again printed ballots on the end-seals of their packages. Several weeks before the election, *TV Guide* also ran a ballot. Eddie Kean wrote a campaign theme that went, *"I'm for Howdy Doody, are you?"* The Peanuts were to respond by yelling, "YES I AM!!" The campaign slogan was "It's Your Doody to Vote." Eventually several million ballots came in during November, a bonanza for KAGRAN and for NBC, which promptly raised the show's ad rates. Howdy's landslide that year was almost as big as General Eisenhower's.

My father, who as director was closer to the cast than Howdy's real management, first got wind of the impending social unrest in Doodyville around the end of November. I remember him talking about it in hushed tones with my mother before he left the house on Thanksgiving Day to drive Buffalo Bob's shining red Model T Ford down Broadway in the annual parade sponsored by Macy's. A Howdy Doody float or balloon had played a major role in the parade every year since 1948. This year cast members donned their costumes and rode in Bob's old Ford. I remember being incredibly excited to see my dad at the wheel on television, cast in this role because he was the only one in Howdy's crew who knew how to drive the gearless old car.

*   *   *

The ringleader of the Doodyville Cast Revolution was Bobby Keeshan — ex-NBC page, the first television actor with a steady job, Clarabell the clown. Keeshan was fed up with the status quo in Doodyville. Things were getting tense, and he knew he had to make his move. He made it, and the result was disaster.

What Keeshan wanted was a new deal on *The Howdy Doody Show*. It was obvious to everyone that millions were being raked in by KAGRAN and NBC, all from the advertising and merchandising of characters the actors had created. Even though the actors were making good money for the time — between six hundred and eight hundred dollars a week (perhaps six thousand in today's money) when commercial fees were added to scale-based salary — men like Keeshan and Dayton Allen wanted a bigger piece of the action. By December Bobby Keeshan had begun organizing the rest of Howdy's cast. In a meeting with Dayton, Rhoda Mann, and Bill Lecornec, Keeshan convinced the others that, despite fairly constant assurance from Marty Stone that they were all expendable, all the actors who worked on *Howdy* were in fact utterly indispensable to the show's success. After all, Keeshan was so utterly right as Clarabell that one attempt to replace him had already been foiled by public disapproval. Keeshan's Clarabell was a national treasure! And Dayton — well, Dayton *was* Mr. Bluster. Dayton *was* the Inspector. Dayton *was* the Flubadub. Nobody could bring these crucial characters to life except Dayton Allen. What about Bill Lecornec? You couldn't broadcast *Howdy Doody* without Chief Thunderthud. Kowabonga! And Lecornec *was* Dilly Dally. Nobody else could do Dilly's crazy voice. And Rhoda Mann, they all said, was the only puppeteer who could handle the top-heavy and off-balance Howdy puppet. Each time they had tried to fire Rhoda in the past, the Buffalo had had to call and beg her to come back because no one else could make Howdy work like . . . Howdy.

The next step was to recruit other sympathizers among the remainder of the cast and the crew. Judy Tyler was approached, but said immediately that she wasn't interested. Bob Nicholson would obviously side with management, and anyway he was the cause of some of the bad feeling among the rest of the cast. Other key creative people, including Scott Brinker and Doc Whipple, were approached by the group but turned down the opportunity to join in any action. Keeshan also made several overtures to the directors, Hultgren and Davis, attempting to damage their morale by suggesting, "Everyone around here is getting rich except for the actors and directors." This was true, but the directors were NBC employees already covered by their Guild contracts, so a new deal in Doodyville couldn't affect them anyway.

By December 10, the four dissident cast members began making their move. First, they hired an agent to represent them in negotiations with KAGRAN and NBC. Then they commissioned a new set of marionettes so they could work without the KAGRAN-owned Howdy characters if they had to. Next they began to talk about doing commercials and a pilot for one of the other networks. Finally, their agent approached Roger Muir with a set of demands that boiled down to one basic issue. Bobby Keeshan, Dayton Allen, Bill Lecornec, and Rhoda Mann wanted more money.

When Muir took this demand to the network, NBC executives at first laughed. These kids are already making a fortune, they said. Then the executives started running around like chickens whose heads had been bitten off. *Howdy*'s cast is going on strike! They're trying to kill us! The sky is falling! And one can almost comprehend NBC's paranoia. Even as late as 1952, Howdy Doody and Milton Berle were still supporting the network. But while Uncle Miltie was beginning to tire (his Hooperating audience share had tumbled from a stupendous seventy-five percent to a merely extraordinary fifty percent), Howdy was still growing. The most recent ratings had given Howdy a fifty-five percent audience share and a rating of 30 in network "B-time." By way of comparison, no other show in either B-time or prime-time on any network or local station had a rating above 15 or 10, respectively. Howdy Doody was a license to print money, and damned if NBC was going to let a bunch of screwball kiddie actors take it away from them.

The bitter irony, as it turned out, was that, after ten days of frantic negotiations that were broken off too soon, the three actors and the puppeteer almost got what they wanted. But events that occurred more than a generation ago are fuzzy in the minds of all the participants, so it's hard to know what is the unvarnished truth. Better to let the principal players tell their own versions of the last two weeks of December 1952, the final bitter days of the original *Howdy* show, as best they can remember.

According to Roger Muir, "We were awfully close all around. We could've thrashed it all out. The demands the agent made for Keeshan were actually acceptable, but we weren't prepared to meet Rhoda's demands because she wasn't a performer. But the agent said he represented four clients, and it was all or nothing. NBC's lawyers said we already had an exclusive contract with AFTRA as sole bargaining agent. They told us, 'We cannot bargain with this agent, we must deal with these actors as individuals.' But the kids decided to stick with the agent, and NBC said they were off the show."

Keeshan's version is very different. "There was no cast walkout," he says. "We were fired.

"Dayton and Rhoda and Bill and I decided that, completely aside from *Howdy,* we'd like to do other things — commercials and maybe even another program. To do this we eventually went out and engaged an agent." Keeshan recalls that the agent was a friend of Dayton's who was explicitly instructed *not* to approach *Howdy Doody* with these plans. "Martin Stone heard about this, interpreted it as a union within a union [AFTRA], and blew up. So he gathered us together on December twenty-first and said to the four of us, 'You are *not* going to form a union. You are to discharge this agent immediately.' We were all intimidated because Marty was a very strong guy, but we said, look, this has nothing to do with Howdy, we just wanna do other things! He said, 'I don't want you with an agent. Get rid of him or we'll have to take some other action.' Well, we were mad. Every actor has the right to an agent, but we thought it was settled. Throughout all this, Bob Smith never said a single word. In fact, at Bob's request we did a benefit at the Brooklyn Navy Yard on December twenty-third. I rode down in the limo with Bob, and he didn't say a word about our situation. In fact, he couldn't have been warmer.

"We got back to the studio," Keeshan continues, "and prepared to rehearse that night's show. Roger Muir said he had an announcement to make and asked the crew and stagehands to gather round.

"Muir said, 'We've had a dispute with Bobby, Dayton, Rhoda, and Bill. We've decided that since they're not going to discharge their agent, we're going to discharge them.'

"This was the first time any of us had heard about this — in front of the whole crew! Bob Smith wasn't even there. So he [Muir] said, 'You're all excused. You can go.' We literally cleaned out our lockers and went home. That was the last we ever heard of Howdy Doody."

Buffalo Bob Smith tells yet another story.

"To my mind there was absolutely no dissension whatsoever among the cast," he says. "Their scale was three-seventy-five a week, and we paid extra for commercials. Finally we told the advertisers to use whatever characters they wanted and not to worry about paying them, because we doubled their scale to seven-fifty a week for Keeshan, Dayton, and Lecornec.

"Then they got an agent. Keeshan was the instigator. They took Rhoda with them and spent money on new puppets. In our eyes, they were set to go on their own show! They told us they wanted a thousand dollars a week apiece or they were gonna quit. They gave us an ultimatum.

"Roger came to me and said, 'They're holding us up.' We went to Marty, and he said, 'My God, let 'em go. Let's wish 'em all good luck!' You see," Smith adds, "nobody was irreplaceable. Absolutely not. Clarabell? You could get *anyone* to be Clarabell. And voices and puppeteers we could get — this was New York!

"Roger Muir tried to warn them that they couldn't bargain collectively with Howdy because they already had AFTRA contracts with us. It was against AFTRA code. It was like a union within a union. Roger told them that he was bound under the rules of their own union not to bargain with them.

"So when I heard about this agent they got, I said I want the cast and studio crew there fifteen minutes early today. Roger said, 'What for?' I told him not to ask me what for, I wanted everybody on the show, all fifty people.

"When we were all together, I said, 'Now, you're all going to hear some stories about what's going to happen. And these stories are going to be twisted and turned, and I want to be sure you all get the correct story.' Was I mad? You bet your ass I was mad.

"I said, 'I'm telling you why they are leaving. And if I'm not telling the truth I want them to contradict me right now so that you'll all believe what I'm telling you.' And I told them the story — the double scale, the agent holding out for a thousand a week apiece. I said, 'Well, they are making their decisions right now. They are quitting the show. Rhoda? Dayton? Bobby? Bill? Is this the truth?' They all said it was. So I looked at everybody and said, 'Rhoda, good luck. Bobby, all the best. Dayton, I love ya. Bill, best to you.' "

And then, after he fired his cast in front of the whole show, the Buffalo let fly the capper, saying, "All right, gang! Let's get on with tonight's show! We're all prepared!"

And they were. Eddie Kean had rewritten the script for that night and was already developing a new story line that would tide things over for a couple of weeks until Doodyville's regulars were replaced. That night *Howdy Doody* went on with the Buffalo, the Princess,

Corny Cobb, and Gabby Hayes, who was brought in at the last minute when management realized it was firing virtually the whole cast. Interim puppeteers came in and worked Howdy. The show went off that night without a hitch. Also without Clarabell, Mr. Bluster, and the rest of the puppets.

The worst part about it was that it was Christmas Eve. "We *always* had anxieties and problems before Christmas," Martin Stone says. "It was our busy season, with a heavy pre-Christmas sponsorship."

Bleak Christmas in Doodyville.

What really happened? Were they fired or did they quit? Keeshan says Muir fired them. The Buffalo remembers that he called a meeting and told the four cast members that they had quit. Keeshan says Smith didn't have the nerve to fire his friends himself.

I asked my father, who said he was at this meeting but couldn't remember who else had been there.

Rhoda Mann says Smith *was* at the meeting. "Our agent had told them that we would give them two weeks' notice if our demands weren't met. Bob said, 'I don't need *any* of you. You can leave *now*. You don't need to give us any notice.' " (Rhoda also swears that this incident took place after that day's show, not before.)

What really happened? What is the truth? Let's ask another witness for his account.

Bob Nicholson was there. "Bobby Keeshan was the ringleader. He got Bill, who seldom said no to anybody, Dayton Allen, who was anxious for more money, and Rhoda. Judy wouldn't have any part of it. She told them she wouldn't touch it. Clarabell was their big weapon because he was the most popular character other than the Buffalo.

"When their agent asked for a thousand a week, Muir said this constituted a secondary boycott within AFTRA. NBC Legal said forget it, we already negotiated with these people through AFTRA. So the Buffalo, Roger, Eddie Kean, and I got together. Kean said he could write them out. Roger and Bob called a noon meeting on the day of a show. The whole show came in, sat in the Peanut Gallery, and the studio doors were locked. Bob Smith made his speech. He read out the demands for high pay, which got very little sympathy from the one-ninety-per-week cameramen and stagehands.

"And Bob said, 'Now we would like to give the official reaction from me, Roger Muir, and NBC. We'd like those four people to get their belongings, leave the show, and leave NBC. They're fired.

They'll get two weeks' pay — but we don't want them around for another two weeks. We're gonna do the show this afternoon with the people who want to stay.'

"And Keeshan and the others went around and shook hands. It was all friendly, except that Bob was very angry. Everyone felt bad, but we were assured that they had been given several chances to recant along the way.

"So we went upstairs and redid that night's show. I did some old Mr. Cobb routines and Judy sang a couple of songs. And we called in another puppeteer, Rufus Rose, to do Howdy, the only puppet whose voice wasn't done by Dayton or Bill. And we were pretty pleased; they thought they could hold up the show, but we were able to do at least a week's worth of shows before we had to bring in other people. We got around the Clarabell problem by saying that he was in hiding."

The former cast members were stunned. They hadn't expected to be fired like hod carriers in front of the whole show. Within hours the entire network knew about the Christmas Eve massacre in Doodyville. Within a few days it was the talk of show biz and Madison Avenue. The four mutineers thought their careers were over.

Dayton was especially shocked. "I figured they needed me," he reflects sardonically. "I was indispensable. But it wasn't really the money. I was making six hundred a week and two hundred from the radio show. It was more that we were being harassed by Marty Stone and later Bob [Smith].

"Bob should've stood up for us," Dayton says. "But he didn't, and I never heard from him again, at least for years. It was a low point in my life."

The three actors and Rhoda had made a terrible miscalculation and had realized their utter vulnerability only after they had been canned. This was especially true of Keeshan, an untrained and inexperienced actor who had never played any role other than Clarabell in his life. The fact was that the character of Clarabell was *very* imitable by any trained actor. The part had no voice attached to it, and the face was painted on, not homegrown. (As word of Keeshan's fate spread through the business, many people associated with Howdy assumed that Keeshan's career was over for good.) Dayton and Bill were less easy to replace, but neither actor had counted on the black rage their protest would conjure in the heart of Buffalo Bob. Rhoda

Mann never had a chance; management considered her a complainer and a pain and was thrilled to let her go.

Rhoda was furious at being fired. "Smith believed his own publicity. His ego got in the way." She also remembers that Bobby Keeshan was in such bad shape financially that he had to ask Dayton to lend him money so he could pay his mortgage. Keeshan was appalled at what had happened. "I was never invited back," he says. "I was the replaceable one. Bob never considered that I had done anything to create Clarabell. He never valued my talent. But my animosity was directed toward Martin Stone, because Muir was weak and Bob Smith was easily led."

Most devastated of the cashiered actors was gentle Bill Lecornec, who had only gone along because his friends had assured him that, as Chief Thunderthud and Dilly Dally, he was totally unexpendable. The show couldn't go on without him, they had told him. And then management tossed him out like a piece of bad meat. Bill was the sole support of his family back in California. What, the suddenly out-of-work actor asked himself, was he going to do now?

A wet Bob and Howdy. (BURT DUBROW COLLECTION)

Seven

Saving Howdy Doody

A ND WHAT WAS Howdy Doody going to do? The three fired
actors had supplied the distinctive voices of all the puppets
except Howdy and played all of the male roles except the Buffalo
and Mr. Cobb. Buffalo Bob, Princess Summerfall Winterspring, and
that old coot Gabby Hayes could defend the town for a couple of
weeks, but the reality of the situation sank in pretty quickly: Mr.
Bluster, Dilly Dally, the Flubadub, the Inspector, Chief Thunderthud, Oil Well Willie, Sir Archibald, Ugly Sam, Don José Bluster,
and — most indispensably — Clarabell were all gone.

Doodyville was dead as a doornail. The place was a ghost town.

In order to save the show, Bob Smith and Martin Stone took stock
and started to rebuild the cast immediately. They really didn't have
any other choice, once they made the decision to fire the four rather
than renegotiate. They still had five live half hours a week to fill,
and Eddie Kean needed his little repertory company to sustain his
scripts. So the dear-departed citizens of Doodyville had to be replaced
as quickly and unobtrusively as possible.

As soon as the cast members were fired, Roger Muir sounded the
alarm for battle stations. Scott Brinker remembers that he and Edith
"were going off on a cruise. I'd been working twenty hours a day
building props for five years. At the last minute, as we were leaving
the house, Muir called and said, 'You can't go. The cast was fired
and we hadda redo the whole show.' He sent my wife a bunch of
orchids, and we went back to work. We were loyal to the show
because, like many people who worked on *Howdy,* we went from a
good living to a great living. We started to see money for the first
time, and we didn't want to lose it."

Right after Christmas, KAGRAN and NBC began to cobble together
a new show. The first major problem was Clarabell. They had to be
careful lest they again be perceived as trying to insult the native

intelligence of the American youth population. At first they tried the clown suit on Howdy's prop man, Bernie Morshen, for about a week, just to have a warm body standing there and honking. But Morshen was even more hopeless than Keeshan. Then, as Nicholson recalls, "They said, 'Nick, *you* do Clarabell.' I said that I hadn't come all the way to New York City to be a clown, and they told me they'd make it worth my while. So they put the greasepaint on me, and then the costume. I went on camera and looked at myself in the monitor and found I was almost a dead ringer for Keeshan's Clarabell. But the character was so popular that there were still fears that the changeover would somehow be bungled."

To pave the way for the change, Eddie Kean wrote a story line called "Where's Clarabell?" after the clown had been ostentatiously missing in action for a couple of weeks. After Buffalo Bob finally spotted Clarabell at the bottom of Doodyville Harbor, a new puppet character named Captain Windy Scuttlebutt arrived in his tugboat and discovered Clarabell imprisoned underwater in a diving suit. (I can clearly remember seeing the clown's mournful face through the wire grille of the huge old-fashioned diver's helmet.) It took a week's worth of shows for the new Clarabell to emerge from his watery abode; when the stuck helmet finally came off, the kids didn't notice it wasn't the real clown inside. In fact, though, Clarabell was transformed altogether. Gone was the goony and semipsychotic anarchist clown; in his place appeared Clarabell on lithium, an inspired musician who could play xylophone, piano, and trombone. This new Clarabell was nicer, more cooperative, even something of an artiste. (Some things, however, didn't change. Nicholson kept up Keeshan's tradition of yelling at the Peanuts every night to get them to sit still and shut up during the show.)

The next problem was puppeteers.

The short-term puppeteer whom Roger Muir quickly hired to work Howdy Doody after Rhoda was fired ended up staying with the show for the rest of its run. She was Lee Carney, an attractive blonde who lived in Greenwich Village with her actor husband, Mike King, who also worked puppets and occasionally filled in on *Howdy* when an extra puppet voice was needed. From the moment she was hired, it was clear that Lee could duplicate Rhoda's skill with Howdy. My father says that she was the best operator he worked with on the show. The hardest part of any marionette production was walking the puppets, actually lifting the feet and legs and getting them down again in a smooth flowing movement. When the KAGRAN people saw how easily Lee Carney walked the cumbersome Doody puppet, they breathed a lot easier.

But they still needed a master puppeteer to work, build, dress, and restring the rest of Howdy's puppet cast, as well as construct other puppets as new characters were written in. For this job they hired a Connecticut puppetmaster named Rufus Rose.

Rufus had been working puppets all his life, beginning in 1928 with the famed marionette troupe of Tony Sarg (where Rufus met his wife, Margo, who built all the puppets used in the last half of Howdy's run). For twenty years before arriving at Studio 3A, Rufus had been putting on his own show, *The Rufus Rose Marionettes,* in a puppet theater he had built adjacent to his home on the Connecticut shoreline. The Roses' productions of *Pinocchio* and *A Christmas Carol* had toured all over America and played an important role in the evolution of puppet performances from variety shows to full-fledged dramatic presentations.

Rufus Rose made his debut on *Howdy Doody* on December 29, 1952, six days after most of the cast had been given the boot. Used to working his own marionettes, he at first had some rough sailing with Scott Brinker's TV puppets, which were six inches taller than the conventional twenty-four-inch variety. (The larger size was necessary so the contrast between live actors and puppets wouldn't be too great. Also, since the camera picked up many more details than live audiences saw, the Howdy puppets all had oversize heads with much more animation in their faces than regular marionettes — Bluster had highly mobile eyebrows, the Inspector had a leering wink, and the whole puppet cast had movable mouths.) Almost at once, Rufus began a series of reforms. He restrung all the puppets, switching from old-fashioned woven fiber to a more malleable plastic string that prevented tangling, the bane of puppeteering. He also complained that both Howdy and Double Doody badly needed refurbishing, but both Roger Muir and KAGRAN refused to let him alter Howdy in any way. Rufus especially wanted to change Howdy's hands, which he regarded as clumsy and unprofessional, but Roger Muir was adamant: If it ain't broke, don't fix it.

One of the first tasks the Roses were given was to build two new puppets. The first was the old sea captain, Windy Scuttlebutt, who helped bring Nicholson's new Clarabell up from Davy Jones's locker. The second was a new Howdy puppet. This was actually a Howdy doll, not a marionette, needed because Howdy's strings had always gotten in the way during still-photography shoots for advertising and promotional pictures. Dubbed "Photo Doody," this Howdy was built with wire and ball sockets in its joints so it could hold position for the camera; since it was immobile, it was never used on an actual *Howdy* broadcast.

Rufus Rose and Lee Carney were great puppeteers, but they weren't voice people like Dayton Allen and Bill Lecornec. This was a big problem, because it was vitally important to get Bluster, Dilly, the Flub, and other key characters back on the air as soon as possible. Most *Howdy* people believed that Dayton was, indeed, irreplaceable; they didn't think anybody would get Bluster to live and breathe again or make the Flub as lovably nutty as had Dayton Allen.

Then, in a stroke of great good fortune, they hired the man who would save *The Howdy Doody Show.* He was a young comic and voice-man who was just beginning to get a reputation in Manhattan media circles as "The Man of a Thousand Voices."

This was the legendary Allen Swift.

He was a stand-up comic when *Howdy* hired him. Born Ira Stadlin in 1924, he had learned his craft in the borscht belt before being drafted in 1942; he spent the war as an instructor working with pilots in high-altitude pressure chambers. After the war he got his first job in a Fifty-seventh Street joint called Spivey's Place. When his agent told him he had to change his name, Ira combined the surnames of his two favorite satirists, Fred Allen and Jonathan Swift. In the earliest days of TV, he worked on shows with Bob Hope and Eddie Cantor. Then he was hired by Bray Studios, which owned the old Max Fleischer *Out of the Inkwell* silent cartoon, to ad-lib dialogue for two hundred cartoon features for use on TV.

"When I got the audition for *Howdy Doody,*" Swift says, "they had given up all hope of matching the voices of the people who had walked out. They showed me pictures of the puppets and told me to put voices on them. I had never even seen *Howdy Doody,* so I just made up some voices for the characters and they said they liked them. But, listening to the conversations in the studio, I learned that these characters had voices that already existed. For some reason, these voices were no longer available. Since my specialty was duplicating voices, I asked them about the voices and they said, 'Yeah, yeah, don't worry about it.' "

Swift told Muir and Rippen he thought he could match the voices if they had them on a recording. They were surprised and skeptical, but they gave Allen Swift some Howdy records to take home over the weekend. Of course Swift came back on Monday with all the voices perfectly matched. So he started out doing all the familiar puppet voices — Bluster, Flub, Dilly. Then they asked him to work the puppets and play Corny Cobb as well, since Nick was already in the clown suit.

"My first day on the show, they gave me Bluster to work and said, 'You're on the air,' " Swift recalls. "I'd never worked a puppet before, and I was supposed to play Mr. Cobb, too. I had a few lessons from Rufus Rose and Lee Carney and suddenly we were on the air! I worked Bluster and then, during an ad, I was tapped by Rufus. 'Down on the floor,' he whispered. 'You're Cobb!' I climbed off the puppet bridge, got on my mark, the red light winked on the cameras, I looked in the monitor and almost died of fear. I'd forgotten to put on my makeup!

"I went through the routine and the rest of the show and slunk back to the dressing room. I thought, That's it, you schmuck, you're gonna be fired your first day on the show. I was so disappointed because TV was such a clean job compared to the sleaze I'd seen in the nightclub world.

"Then Howard Davis came in and said, 'Nice show.' Then Bob Rippen came in and said the same thing. Then the producer, Roger Muir, came in and said, 'Allen, you were *great*, and the makeup was *perfect!*' After that, I never used makeup again in that character."

Eventually Swift learned of the cast firing and worried that he was scabbing, but Howdy's management assured him there hadn't been a strike or any problem with the union, and that NBC was free to turn to other AFTRA members because the four dissenters had been in violation of their own union's contract. The rest of the cast did their best to welcome Swift into the fold. "Bob Smith was like nobody I've ever known," he says. "Bob was always *on*. When he saw me in the morning he'd yell 'ALLY, BABEEEE!' and grab me in a hammerlock. And his sense of humor was different too. His idea of a joke was [saying] that the ideal wife was a deaf and dumb nymphomaniac whose father owned a liquor store.

"Judy Tyler always felt that the show was a little beneath her. So she was always a tough chorus-girl broad until the red light came on. She'd bad-mouth the Peanut Gallery kids and swear like a stevedore, but when the red light came on she was all big eyes and sweet as candy. Bobby Nicholson was also very talented and competent. He did good voices and was obviously a close friend of Bob Smith's."

With the hiring of Swift, Howdy's management was jubilant. Keeshan had been replaced. Rhoda had been replaced. Even the irreplaceable Dayton had been replaced!

But there was still one problem that lasted into January 1953, a month after the old cast had been heaved, and that was what to do about Dilly Dally and Chief Thunderthud. America's children were writing letters asking where in Kowabonga the Chief was and where was Dilly? Kids loved Dilly because Lecornec had created him as a sweet little innocent who was as childlike as Howdy's viewers. Not even the Man of a Thousand Voices could get Dilly's grating lisp exactly the way Lecornec had it. No one else could play Thunderthud with the same swish arrogance and élan. No other actor could reproduce another popular Lecornec character, Dr. Singasong. Gradually it dawned on everyone that they had to have Lecornec back in Doodyville. It was obvious to all that gentle Bill had been dragooned into the threatened cast walkout. Bill would agree to anything, they rationalized, because he was just the nicest guy around. But they wondered how they would get Bill to come back, since there were hard feelings all around.

My father saw a possible solution. Howard had a good relationship with Bill and as an NBC director was not associated with the negative aspects of Howdy's bosses. So he proposed to Stone and Muir that he be allowed to negotiate with Lecornec. Howard called Bill and invited him to lunch. At the old Headquarters Restaurant on Forty-ninth Street, he told Bill that everyone wanted him back. Howard offered Bill a good raise and emotional collateral in the form of loyalty and love. Bill was intimidated by the other protesters and didn't want to be thought of as a traitor, but he had spent a month looking for work without much luck and had a family to support. He wavered between camps for a while before finally being persuaded to come to the studio to talk.

Discussing this era, Bill Lecornec told me his version. "One day your father took me out to lunch and said, 'Bill, we need you.' And they did, because they were all fucked up. [When we left] they thought they were going to hire the greatest performers in the world. But *we* were. Anyway, your father said, 'We need you. You're indispensable!' And I had a mother and sister who needed my monthly support. That's why I came back; my family depended on me for food and rent, so I did it. I wasn't trying to be disloyal to the other people. It was Mother and Sis!" Still remorseful after all these years, Lecornec dejectedly adds, "But I *was* the disloyal one, because I went back."

Bill was welcomed back with open arms. He stayed until the very last day, the only Indian in the world with a mustache.

So Howdy Doody had been saved, but not without some losses.

Keeshan's Clarabell, for one, was never successfully replaced, at least in the minds of many who worked on the show. Nick's clown was indeed brighter, lighter on his feet, and able to play all the instruments at Nicholson's command. But Nick was more comfortable in his role as Mr. Cobb and as Howdy's musical director. Keeshan's original Clarabell had been awkward, stumbling, naive, and bratty. No one ever matched the lumbering gracelessness Keeshan brought to Clarabell. And neither of the two subsequent Clarabells ever enjoyed the role as much as its creator had.

Some on the staff didn't worry about this. When I asked Eddie Kean what his fondest memory of *Howdy* was, he replied: "When Bob Keeshan quit as Clarabell, which opened the clown to performers with musical and other genuine talents that helped broaden the scope and appeal of the show and made the writing easier." More bluntly, Scott Brinker calls Keeshan "hard to get along with. He was temperamental and had no right to be."

Keeshan had always complained when they had tried to make him learn music, saying that music would kill the character of Clarabell. And, again, Keeshan was right. The much nicer Bobby Nicholson killed the old Clarabell forever. The old Clarabell you wouldn't want in your house; Nick's clown could marry your sister and it would be OK. "Clarabell had an impishness and a childlike quality," Keeshan says today. "I think of Clarabell as the ungovernable child — that aspect of a child that rebels and resists authority. I played him that way, and tried to be protective of the integrity of the character."

It was perhaps true that Bobby Keeshan was not the most naturally talented of actors, but what talent he did have really came through in Clarabell. Perhaps it was the delighted sparkle in his eye, as if he really enjoyed blasting the Buffalo in the kisser with a spurt of cold seltzer.

A month after the firings, Howdy's handlers decided that although the shows were better, there were still a few small problems. Dayton made Bluster *breathe,* because he wore a microphone around his neck while he worked the puppet; he had perfect synchronization of Bluster's voice and action. Eventually, Nick took over Bluster's voice and prerecorded it, and Rufus worked the puppet; as a result, Bluster never again had that great spontaneity and synchronization. But they did get their Dilly back, and that was enough.

What happened to the three *Howdy* dissidents who weren't invited back to Doodyville? Right away they all auditioned for a kids' show that CBS wanted to pattern after Howdy. But CBS didn't like their puppets and passed on the idea.

Rhoda Mann started working almost immediately. First she did the voices for the *Terrytoon Circus* cartoon series. Then she started doing voice-overs for animated commercials. Her first was for two dancing clothespins in a Duz laundry detergent ad. Within a few years, she became extremely successful in this field, with sixteen commercials on the networks simultaneously.

Dayton looked for work for a while before being hired later in 1953 to play the role of Mr. Bungle, Jack Barry's incompetent assistant on *Winky Dink*. (The premise of *Winky Dink* was that children at home could draw on the TV screen by sending away for a Winky Dink kit consisting of a piece of reusable plastic laminate that adhered to the screen.) *Winky Dink* lasted only a few years, but Dayton Allen would go on to bigger and better things.

As would, of course, the supposedly untalented Bobby Keeshan. Unable to find work in television at first, Keeshan went to work for his father-in-law, who was an undertaker. But eventually he got back into television and made history all by himself.

By 1953 Howdy Doody was seen every evening on sixty NBC affiliate stations around America. Its audience was an estimated fifteen million children and adults daily. Revenue from the kids of the United States poured into the coffers of KAGRAN and NBC like a vast Niagara of bucks. The merchandising was mushrooming almost out of control as Marty Stone made deals to put Howdy's face and those of the rest of the Doodyville gang on almost every product known to consumer society. But far away on the horizon there were vague intimations that storm clouds were gathering, and that *Howdy* might be in for some heavy weather.

In 1953 a fourth television network, the American Broadcasting Company, began competing with NBC, CBS, and DuMont. Soon DuMont would dissolve and ABC would launch a formidable challenge to Howdy's reign over presupper kidvid. Then there was the specter of Miss Frances. In real life she was Dr. Frances Horwich, the teacher on NBC's *Ding Dong School,* which aired Monday through Friday at 9:00 A.M. for the preschoolers. In 1953, after social critics began to blame Howdy (and children's TV fare in general) for the rise in juvenile delinquency, street gangs, switchblades, crime, violence, and deteriorating language skills, NBC set up a Children's Program Review Committee to monitor what the network was showing to kids. This in-house watchdog group told Roger Muir to tone *Howdy* down and cut back on the screaming, chases, and seltzer fights. This wasn't much to ask, but after almost six years Eddie Kean didn't know any other way to write the show. So the slapstick and silliness remained, but the players in Studio 3A now had the sense that Someone was watching over their shoulders. It wasn't a great feeling.

Backstage, the usual madness prevailed, though somewhat less noisily now that Dayton Allen was no longer an inmate. My father remembers that he was directing a *Howdy* rehearsal from his seat in the control room one day when another NBC star, Bishop Fulton J. Sheen, wandered in and sat down to watch for a moment. Sheen did a religious and inspirational show down the hall in Studio 3B. The NBC pages referred to this show as "Holy Doody" or "Howdy Deity"; an oft-told NBC joke of the era had Bishop Sheen instructing his director: "Open on a shot of the sky, and then pan up to me." Just as Sheen sat down with my father he heard Judy Tyler on the monitor describe some other girl as "a titless wonder." Howard muttered, "Sorry, Monsignor," but saw that Sheen was laughing quietly out of the corner of his mouth.

Howdy also continued to have occasional problems with the firewater-quaffing Chief Thunderthud. Once Bill Lecornec was an hour late to rehearsal, and Bob Rippen lit into him in front of the whole cast and crew, threatening to have him fired. "Honest to God, Ripp," Bill whined, "I woke up in time, but I fell back asleep and dreamed I was here!" The whole show broke up with laughter; this was Bill's tricky way of defusing the situation. But other times he would call Rippen at two-thirty in the morning to say that he was Jesus Christ and wouldn't be able to do Howdy anymore. The next day, he'd show up in 3A sober as a parson and professional to the core. Dilly Dally was always sweetest when Bill had been a bad boy.

As the new cast settled into the Doodyville routine, Eddie began to create new characters to replace vanished regulars like Dayton's

Sir Archibald and Pierre the Chef. Allen Swift played new characters like Professor Abra K. Dabra (a magician) and a new Indian, Chief Thunderchicken, another rival of Thunderthud's to replace Keeshan's departed Chief Featherman. Chief Thunderchicken was an especially offensive characterization, an obviously Jewish Indian that Swift played in a tough "Noo Yawk" accent. Thunderchicken was dumber than Thunderthud, used occasional Yiddish intonation, and was faintly insulting to both Indians and Jews. (It was the kind of broad, vaudeville-based humor that would never even get close to children's television in these more sensitive times.) Other parts that Kean wrote for Swift included Monsieur Fontainebleau, a French artist (Swift himself was a genuinely skilled painter), and a pair of Hindu twins, Poohbah and Bahpooh, who were as offensive as Thunderchicken. Swift also did the voice for the Captain Windy Scuttlebutt puppet. Other new puppets created in this era included Buzz Beaver, which Margo Rose made in 1953; three kangaroos named Hop, Skip, and Jump; and Grampa Doody, Howdy's grandfather, who wore an old Union Army uniform and was built to ride a little bicycle across the puppet bridge. Lee Carney also began to play some minor live parts, such as Sarabell, a short-lived female Clarabell, and Princess Fryingpan Bottlewasher, a harridan counterpart of the *real* Princess.

Yet no matter how many new and original characters Eddie Kean concocted, there was still the feeling around Studio 3A that something was missing. This was never reflected in the show's ratings, and advertisers still trampled over each other to sponsor *The Howdy Doody Show,* but everyone in Doodyville was aware that some indefinable esprit was lost and would never be regained.

Sometime in early 1953 KAGRAN decided that Doodyville needed a resident animal to perk things up. The chemistry between animal acts and the hot studio lights was an unbeatable combination for spontaneity and laughs, often at the expense of the actors who had to work with the beasts. Back in 1948, within a year of the first *Puppet Playhouse,* a baby elephant had been brought out under the lights. All had gone well in rehearsal, but during the broadcast Rhoda Mann impulsively put Howdy astride the elephant's back, and the little pachyderm became so disconcerted that he wet the entire studio. As the Buffalo sloshed around in urine, the elephant began, right on the air, to trumpet and bellow in fear. Another time, a script called for Clarabell to work with a large German shepherd. On command, the dog had to open a door, grab a set of keys with his teeth, and give them to Clarabell. This worked like a charm in rehearsal, with Bobby Keeshan in civilian clothes. But later, on the air, the big dog took one look at Keeshan in the clown suit and went for Clarabell's throat. Keeshan had to hide in his dressing room until the animal's handler could call the creature off. So dogs and elephants were out; ponies were also notorious for peeing under TV lights.

One day in early 1953 Martin Stone, Bob Smith, and Judy Tyler were in New Orleans, where the Buffalo and the Princess were making personal appearances on behalf of Kellogg's. On their first evening in town, the three were walking in the French Quarter, searching for a restaurant, when Bob saw a marquee advertising a stripper who worked with a chimpanzee. Figuring they had to see this, Bob dragged Stone and Judy into the club, where they beheld a generously endowed ecdysiast doing an act with a moderately talented chimp named Zippy. This is great, the Buffalo thought, and he went backstage after the show, where he learned that Zippy was owned by the stripper's husband. Smith told Zippy's owner that he thought the chimp was terrific, but unfortunately they couldn't use the strip act on *Howdy*. Not one to be held back, Zippy left the Crescent City and migrated north to New York, where he soon joined the rest of the cast in Doodyville.

Until then there had been a certain amount of ill feeling in Doodyville whenever a new cast member showed up, but nothing to equal the venomous loathing the rest of the gang felt for the hard-to-get-to-know Zippy. There were problems: Zippy frequently liked to take a little nip out of someone's hand and would often freak out and start to scream in the studio. This drove the already high-strung *Howdy* cast bananas. Viewers often remarked that Zippy never seemed to look directly at the camera; this was because he was usually staring dumbly at his trainer, who was standing just off camera holding a cattle prod. Another of Zippy's adorable qualities was his love for the smell of fresh paint; occasionally he would escape and hoist himself up along the lighting fixtures at the top of the studio. Whenever this happened, the studio would have to be cleared and the actor who played Clarabell would have to put on his costume and climb up to retrieve Zippy, this being the only way anybody ever discovered to get the monkey down and working again.

"I *hated* Zippy," Eddie Kean says. "He was given a long-term contract and had about three tricks. It was ridiculous! The essence of Howdy's success in my perception was the miraculous way the puppets interacted with the live characters and the way the lunacy of the script blended with logic and common sense. What the hell was I supposed to have this chimp do? Foisting Zippy on a writer introduced a variety-show element that didn't belong on *Howdy Doody*. Remember," Kean adds cryptically, "that Tylenol had not been marketed yet."

Despite all these calamities, Howdy jes' grew. In April 1953 the show again topped the authoritative Trendex survey as the top day-time TV broadcast. That month Howdy himself made his debut on Mexican television in *La Hora de Jaudi Dudi,* licensed, as was a Canadian version of the show, by KAGRAN. In Canada, however, the show had different characters. Buffalo Bob was replaced up north by Timber Tom, who in one of his incarnations was played by a young singer named Robert Goulet.

In June 1953, NBC management decided that Howdy would be the guinea pig for the first experimental color broadcast of a regu-larly scheduled show. In 1950, the Federal Communications Com-mission had ruled that the new color television technology had to be "compatible" with the existing black-and-white technology. Until then, color TV was being designed for a slightly different type of receiver than the millions of black-and-white sets already in use. CBS's color system, then in development, was incompatible, and the network almost gave up in disgust. In 1953 the FCC reconsidered its decision and lowered the standards of acceptable compatibility. Since the color system being developed by RCA scientists met the FCC's new standards, NBC began experimental broadcasts as soon as it could. The network ran several "Compatible Color Spectacu-lars" early that year, but the system was so primitive that the shows had no black-and-white contrast at all, and millions tuned out. That June, *The Howdy Doody Show* was moved out of Studio 3A for a week and relocated in Billy Rose's Ziegfeld Theater at Fifty-fourth Street and Sixth Avenue. My father and his codirector, Bobby Hult-gren, studied the show and decided that while the puppets were colorful enough, the live characters' tan and brown costumes needed some tarting up. The Buffalo's dun-colored pioneer suit became light blue. Clarabell's bilious orange stripes became green. It was obvious to all that Howdy's sets were too drab for a color broadcast, so they were repainted in various semigarish hues. There were less than a hundred color receivers then in existence, almost none of them in private homes, so this show was seen in color only in offices and laboratories associated with NBC and RCA. The kids at home, watching on their ten-inch black-and-white sets, saw only a slightly washed-out and harshly lit version of their favorite show, but we Howdy insiders knew that a new era was about to begin.

Let's quickly run a kine from this era to scan the goings-on around Doodyville. Here's a show from June 16, 1953. We open on Captain Windy Scuttlebutt on the deck of his tug. "One of my escaped passengers is an imposter," he announces. "I gotta tell Howdy and the gang." Immediately we realize that we're somewhere in the middle of one of E. Kean's interminable story lines. We see the Peanuts wearing their Howdy beanies, and for a brief moment we get a glimpse of Princess Summerfall Winterspring. As Judy Tyler, who only does a short walk-on in this particular show, looks into the camera, I stop the old projector on "Still" and stare at her for a few minutes. There she is — pert, perky, vivacious, jumping with enthusiasm. Here I am, still in love more than thirty years later. After only a minute, the Princess is off the screen, replaced by Bill Lecornec as an Italian lyric tenor called Signore DoReMiFaSoLaTiDo. The Signore sings, accompanied by the Buff at the piano. Soon Clarabell comes in. It's Bob Nicholson's clown, more reasonable than Keeshan's. Clarabell squirts the Buffalo, and the Signore joins them in a chase around the piano as the Peanuts scream in true mirth. After the chase, Buffalo Bob is furious with the clown but is finally calmed by the Signore, who says that, after all, Clarabell is Pagliacco and should be allowed to get away with anything since he's just doing his job.

After a long segment for Colgate Ribbon Dental Cream, there's a subplot involving Howdy and Inspector John J. Fadoozle, who can't find his fedora because some malefactor has pinned it to his back. The Buffalo and Howdy then plug a TV magazine in Atlanta and welcome a station in Phoenix to the network. There follows a long absurdist dialogue between the Signore and Allen Swift's character Monsieur Fontainebleau, who is dressed in an artist's smock and carries a large prop palette. These two conduct a ridiculous discourse on identity; for minutes they stand there and insist on who they are before finally agreeing that they are not each other.

Clearly, Eddie Kean's legendary inkwell is beginning to run dry.

In quick order, Bob has the Peanuts sing the Colgate song again. The Inspector makes some kind of discovery aboard Scuttlebutt's tug, but what it is I don't know, because the story line continues to the next day and I don't have that kine.

As the show's credits run, I see my dad's picture and his listing as director. As I rewind the film in the projector, I realize with a slight flush that for some reason I'm still as proud of this now as I was back then as an incipient first-grader.

By 1953 Eddie Kean had been writing 250 Howdy scripts a year for six years, in addition to writing the first twenty Howdy Little Golden Books, ten of RCA's best-selling Howdy albums, hundreds of comic books and strips, and various Howdy radio shows and specials. Eddie hadn't taken a vacation since late 1947. A couple of times he had gone down to Miami for two weeks, lugging his big typewriter, and had written scripts between dog races, posting them back to Roger Muir via special delivery. But that hardly qualified as real time off, and during the fall of 1953, Eddie began to get a little . . . *out there*. He remembers, "I felt perverse one day and decided to try a story line that was completely at odds with TV's visual essence. So I had 'The Three Gonkletwerps' flying into Doodyville one day. What these things were, birds or insects, was never clear even to me, since the gonkletwerps were invisible. I didn't even have a plot, just the challenge of these invisible creatures.

"Howdy, whose idiotic acceptance of anybody as a prospective friend would have led him to invite Hitler in for a chat had they met, liked the gonkletwerps enormously, even though he didn't know who or what the hell they were. Mr. Bluster of course disliked the gonkletwerps merely because Howdy liked them. Meanwhile, these gonkletwerps did and said absolutely nothing.

"But after the first of these shows, the switchboard lit up. Frantic mothers were crying over long-distance lines to NBC: 'My children are scared. They're not eating. They can't sleep. Get rid of the gonkletwerps!' So the next day we substituted some riddle games and an endless Old-Time Movie that took up the whole show. That's show business.

"But I didn't consider myself really burned out," Kean insists. "By this time I felt that the enthusiasm of the cast for the show was expiring; they had become cynical, and for me the emotional involvement with *Howdy* was enormous. It was just too much for one writer, but my pride and professional jealousy had kept me at it alone." Eddie would continue to write the show for the rest of the year, but beginning in the late autumn of 1953 another writer began to suggest occasional story lines and subplots. Early in 1954 Eddie would stop writing *Howdy* altogether.

For me, the lights went off in Doodyville when Princess Summerfall Winterspring left town in November 1953. Judy Tyler's hasty exit from the *Howdy* show was good for her, bad for *Howdy,* and terrible for the children who had become attached to the teen siren. I didn't know it at the time, but the parting between the Princess and her masters at KAGRAN was not a particularly amicable one.

Judy Tyler was nineteen by then and had outgrown her ingenue role. By day she was ostensibly the sweet little Princess, but at night she and her husband still did their act at nightclubs around New York. Judy was getting a bad reputation around NBC for her dirty mouth and her various romantic liaisons, and several people close to the show say that if she hadn't left on her own, she would have been fired. And Martin Stone says he *did* fire her. He says he *had* to.

Judy's husband, Colin Romoff, is one of those who say that Judy left on her own. "Judy was a New York kid," Colin says. "She had street smarts and couldn't be intimidated. She was funny and laughed loud and infectiously. She knew how to say 'Fuck you, pal' and make it sound girlish and demure. She was a good cook, she didn't drink, and was a very funny dame.

"We were working outside a little bit, and she started to catch on. I wrote her an act for a club called the Blue Angel; she was a sensation and got a lot of publicity. At this point she realized she was growing up and it was time to move on from Howdy."

Other factors were at work as well. Martin Stone remembers that KAGRAN got complaints about Judy's behavior from sponsors. "Judy was problems, problems, problems," Stone declares. "But we loved her because she was tremendous! She had guts! She was sensational! But we'd have problems with her language in rehearsals, which would then get back to the agencies. Eventually there were several behavior factors which we felt would reflect negatively on the Princess and the show, and I had to fire her. We had to let her go.

"There were risqué incidents involving Judy," Stone continues, "and the Princess was our symbol of purity, beauty, loveliness, good behavior, and all that. After a while, the symbol wasn't matched by the person, and I felt it would be a catastrophe for the show if any of this was exposed. I had complaints about her behavior around the studios, particularly from the Colgate people. Then Judy was also involved [romantically] with a lot of people, and this got around on the floors and around NBC. At one point, it looked like it was going to blow up. I just remember Judy had to go, and fortunately it was coincident with her desire to move on anyway."

Most of Judy's colleagues confirm that she was a wild thing.

Bob Rippen: "She was a terribly sexy young gal thrown in with a bunch of guys. She was a sexed-up little thing and could turn your head. There are all sorts of stories about her because she was pretty free and easy. Most of these stories — drinking and stripping on nightclub tables — came from when they were out on the road opening supermarkets and shoe stores."

Bill Lecornec: "Judy! Judy was a real lovely sweet gal who slept with everybody. I loved Judy. She was a *sweet* gal, who was like all of us — she loved sex. As I said, she slept with everybody." Then Thunderthud corrects himself: "*I* never slept with her, though."

Bob Nicholson: "Judy was a delight to work with. After a while she got a little star-struck, however. When I became Clarabell, I would go out on weekend appearances with her, and while we got along fine, she would just as soon tell a store manager to go fuck himself as she would look at him. She had stars in her eyes and thought she was bigger than she was, but we had a lot of fun traveling."

Scott Brinker: "I went on personal appearances with Judy, some of which were embarrassing because of her attitude. She liked to shock people. We'd get to a hotel, and she would demand a room that adjoined mine. I was a married man! Once we went to Saint Louis. It was a very hot day, and she was wearing a suit and a sheer blouse with a net bra under it. When we got on the plane she took off her suit jacket and you could see her whole figure, which was very beautiful. There was a stampede to the front of the plane! The pilot came out and went nuts and we didn't know who was flying the plane. She was gorgeous, remember that. But she was rough and hard to handle."

As for the legends about Judy's prodigious romantic appetite, Brinker commented with finality: "Anybody who wanted to, could have. And did."

"What can I tell you about Judy?" asks Rhoda Mann. "She was not discreet. I wouldn't even repeat some of the stories she told me. That she was outrageous with her romantic escapades was undeniable. But what the hell did I care, anyway? I was a straight Polack."

But *I* care that Judy Tyler turns out to have been a love goddess in her private life. Perhaps she represented the same thing for the men in her life that she did for me — a living emblem of freshness, charm, beauty, and an ardent desire to please. Just knowing that she loved so deeply soothes the pain I still feel at having lost her.

And loss is what I felt that day late in 1953 when my mother and I boarded a train, changed in Jamaica, and arrived at Pennsylvania Station to witness Howdy's illumination of that year's Christmas tree in Rockefeller Center, a ceremony my father was directing. I remember huddling with my mom in the cold of the VIP section, gazing up at this immense blue spruce from the far woods of northern Maine, and then being thrilled when the thousands of multicolored bulbs winked on amid the glitter of lights from the windows of the surrounding skyscrapers. When we went upstairs to the studio, there was no Princess Summerfall Winterspring. She had left the previous month, and the rest of the cast felt decidedly blue without her. But my father assured me that Judy wasn't gone for good. He had watched her rehearse an upcoming Sid Caesar show, and he told me that if I was good I might be able to stay up on Saturday night and watch her in it.

Early in 1954, John F. Kennedy, the thirty-seven-year-old senator from Massachusetts, underwent major surgery on his ailing back at a New York hospital. Kennedy was a war hero, the scion of a well-known political family, and six years later would be elected President of the United States. During his convalescence he was visited by a reporter for a newspaper in his home state. The reporter duly made notes about the contents of Senator Kennedy's room. There was a tank of tropical fish, a large poster of Marilyn Monroe in blue shorts with her legs spread apart, and a Howdy Doody doll on the bed.

That Howdy Doody was John Kennedy's mascot in those days is an indication of the esteem and affection the American people felt for the little critter by 1954. But that year would bring important changes both for *The Howdy Doody Show* and for children's television in the United States. It was the year NBC began programming kids' shows on Saturday mornings, beginning with *Happy Felton's Spotlight Gang*. It was also the year that the legendary *Kukla, Fran & Ollie* was replaced by that unsophisticated vulgarian Soupy Sales, who went on to make television history when on one show he instructed his juvenile audience to empty their parents' wallets and send the little green pieces of paper with pictures of old men on them in to Soupy right away. Soupy flashed a box number on the screen, and within a week eighty thousand dollars in cash had flooded into NBC, along with bitter complaints from parents and the FCC.

There were big changes in Doodyville that year.

They started in January, when NBC sent the entire show to California for three weeks. NBC had built a new studio complex in Burbank, deep in the San Fernando Valley, and was beginning to phase out all its strip shows in New York to take advantage of cheaper production costs in California. As soon as he heard about this, Bob Smith told the network that he and *Howdy* would never leave New York, but NBC persuaded him to take the show out to the coast for a few weeks in the dead of winter just to give it a try.

Everyone at NBC and KAGRAN wanted a replacement for Judy Tyler as soon as possible. Sales of Princess paraphernalia had dropped off since Judy's departure, and there were fears that *Howdy* might lose the female half of its huge daily audience. So the KAGRAN people decided to hold auditions for the new Princess in Hollywood, where they were more likely to find a suitable young actress, someone more manipulable, it was hoped, than Judy.

So early in January the cast and crew — the whole show — set up in Burbank for three weeks. I remember when my father left home for the trip; I cried to think he would be gone for so long. He remembers the sense of luxury everyone felt in the spacious and spanking-new NBC television studios after having worked for so many years in the cramped and antiquated converted radio studios of the old RCA Building in New York. Bob Rippen remembers that they took along every prop in *Howdy*'s storeroom — the Supertalkascope, the Scopedoodle — but forgot the show's theme record, necessitating an emergency airlift by chartered plane in time for the first broadcast.

Another reason Doodyville was temporarily relocated to California was to give the rapidly expanding western audience a taste of a live *Howdy* show. Until then, West Coast stations had had to content themselves with broadcasting week-old *Howdy* kines. This was an opportunity to sell the show to new advertisers and to familiarize the western audience with the spontaneous glow of Howdy in all his bumbling glory.

The scripts, then, needed to be great, and they weren't. Eddie Kean was promoted to Program Supervisor, and KAGRAN began buying story lines from my father and other writers.

Meanwhile, everybody enjoyed the warm California sun in January. The show was a real curiosity, and stars like Red Skelton and Spike Jones would wander in to watch rehearsals. The directors had the run of NBC's extensive prop department, so Howdy improvised a lot of new chase routines. The show's management dealt with the problem of the new Princess by auditioning hundreds of young girls; the best of these were given second auditions during live *Howdy* broadcasts. Many people felt that the Buffalo didn't think Judy needed replacing. In his mind, the kids should have been happy enough with Buff, Howdy, Clarabell, and Dilly. But both NBC and KAGRAN insisted on a new girl, so the auditions went ahead.

Here are a couple of kines from those days. Let's watch *Howdy* trying to replace Princess Summerfall Winterspring. It's January 26, 1954. The main theme of this show, from the final week of the California series, is the search to find a "magic-power princess" before Mr. Bluster finds her. We see Chief Thunderchicken, identified as the medicine man of the Zulawuggawugga tribe, do a couple of magic tricks. He cuts a Peanut's tie off and then sticks it back together. "Remember, kids," the Buff admonishes, "that's a Howdy Doody don't!"

The Buffalo looks nervous. If they can't find a new Princess, he moans, they'll never make it back to Doodyville. NBC will collapse, and it'll be the end of television. No more Howdy, grieves Smith. No Martin and Lewis! Not even Pinky Lee, he says, in a jab at the aging clown (real name: Pincus Leff) who had begun a manic kids' show on NBC a few months earlier. Thunderchicken is horrified at this. "Kowa-No!" he explodes.

Cut to the puppet Windy Scuttlebutt, who's watching a small television on his tug. He spreads a rumor that Phineas T. Bluster has already found the new Princess.

Cut to Howdy Doody and Chief Thunderthud, who says he has come up with a young Indian maiden who tells fortunes. "Meet 'Papoose' Gina Runningwater," announces the Chief. After an epic Colgate ad featuring Happy Tooth, Papoose Gina (played by a sixteen-year-old actress named Gina Ginardi) goes into a trance, predicts that she will be the new Princess, and then launches into a dreadful circus ditty, accompanied by the Buffalo and Clarabell on two pianos.

After the song, Chief Thunderthud sidles up to the young but eager papoose and says, in his best sleazy-agent manner, "We'll call you later." It was an audition, right on camera.

After an Old-Time Movie and another Colgate ad in which the Buffalo suggests that using Colgate affords lifetime protection against tooth decay, the show mercifully runs out of time.

The Princess auditions continue two days later on a kine dated January 28. This time, Thunderthud and Thunderchicken discover the Buffalo sound asleep. They sympathize with the slumbering pioneer, they say, because he has spoken to 333 different papooses in the past few days. Howdy does an ad for Kellogg's Sugar Frosted Flakes. Then back to the plot: it turns out that Dilly Dally, Mr. Bluster, and Clarabell are in cahoots. It seems that there's another papoose named Hattaheela, a pretty blonde whom Bluster seduces into singing for him so she'll miss her scheduled audition with Howdy and the Buff. Here's another ad: Buffalo Bob sells a Sweetheart Doll premium with biblical fervor. One Kellogg's box top gets you a doll.

Finally Hattaheela auditions for Buffalo Bob. She's better than Gina Runningwater, and Smith even joins in with a little harmony. Clarabell plays the slide trombone. After another passionate pitch for Royal Pudding, Bob signs off for the week; anyone who wants to know the identity of Howdy's new girl has to wait until next week when they get back to Doodyville.

When the show got back to New York, Buffalo Bob let NBC know that there was no way he and Howdy were moving to the Coast. Bob told staff members that he didn't like the California life-style and wouldn't uproot his family from comfortably suburban New Rochelle. Why, the Buffalo fumed, California doesn't even have any baseball teams! Like everything else, this would eventually change.

So Howdy stayed in New York. Gina Ginardi was hired to replace Judy Tyler as the Princess, but she was ineffectual and was eventually let go. "She didn't last too long," one cast member recalls. "Why? Because you don't replace Bob Hope with Morty Putz."

Beginning in February 1954, after six unbroken years and more than fifteen hundred scripts, Eddie Kean stopped writing *The Howdy Doody Show*. Kean was relieved; for all that time there had never been any letup, mentally or physically. Eddie became the script supervisor for KAGRAN until he left the company the following year.

During that time he took the *Howdy* show to Cuba, where a station had licensed the show from KAGRAN. (Eddie was amused when an official of the Cuban TV channel informed him that they wanted the character of Clarabell changed from a clown to a police dog, explaining that Cubans would understand the humor more easily if it came from an actor dressed as a German shepherd.) One of Eddie's last acts on the show was to try to convince NBC to increase Howdy's budget to fight the coming challenge from Walt Disney. NBC refused, and Eddie Kean quit the business to become a stockbroker.

Howdy's writing chores were assumed by my father, so my house became a laboratory for Howdy's story lines and subplots. From the beginning Howard used other writers as well, including his old writing partner Steve deBaun and the comedy team of Jack Weinstock and Willie Gilbert, who earlier had worked on DuMont's *Captain Video*.

With Judy gone, new characters had to be invented, and over the next two years my father repopulated Doodyville. He came up with a Scotsman called Sandy McTavish and a pair of twin koala bears named Hyde and Zeke, as well as other major characters both live and on strings. Eddie Kean had written literally hundreds of songs and jingles for *Howdy,* and the Buffalo made it clear to Howard that he still wanted plenty of music on the show even though Eddie was gone. So Howard started buying songs from J. Fred Coots, a Broadway and Tin Pan Alley tunesmith. Bob didn't think much of Coots, but his songs were used on *Howdy* for several years.

The Howdy Doody Show sailed along on automatic pilot for the first six months of 1954. In February, it was again broadcast in color, this time for an entire week. I took note of my father spending his weekends bent over the typewriter, struggling to meet the assaultive and exhausting five-script-per-week schedule while maintaining a lead time of at least two weeks. It was a thrill to see elaborate plots and side trips hatched out of my dad's mischievous mind, and we grew very close during that year when I was six years old and he was trying out new skits and bits on me. The memory of him tapping away at his old Smith Corona still inspires me. I think it was sitting under his desk, hearing him mutter and work, that tripped the program that said I, too, would be a writer someday. And the handsome salary he earned during those times later helped to pay for my education. So I feel I owe a lot to Howdy Doody.

*　　　*　　　*

Meanwhile, Buffalo Bob Smith was getting restless. Since giving up his morning radio show he had time on his hands, and he was bored with appearing at shoe stores in the sticks. The insatiable urge to entertain was itching Bob like an insect bite.

Then, in the spring of 1954, rumor spread that CBS's Arthur Godfrey, America's premier radio morning man and a veritable TV institution as well, had cancer. Moreover, Godfrey had lost some of his popularity after firing his popular young crooner, Julius LaRosa, on the air. People hadn't liked that. So NBC decided to try to take advantage of his vulnerability by working up a "gang show" to compete with Godfrey and his troupe.

On June 2, 1954, *Howdy Doody* aired its sixteen hundredth telecast. Three weeks later, *The Bob Smith Show* premiered on the NBC radio network in the all-important 10:00–10:30 A.M. EDT time slot against Arthur Godfrey.

This was the Buffalo's run for the roses, his attempt to implant himself in the lives of the nation's mothers as he had in the hearts of their children. It was a typical morning variety show and used many members of the *Howdy* crew. Bob was the host/musician/raconteur, supported by vocalist Clark Dennis, a pop/jazz vocal quintet called the Honeydreamers, and a crack seventeen-piece NBC band led by Bobby Nicholson, who was relieved to get out of the clown suit and perform musically.

The radio show was an instant smash. Bob Smith let go of his Buffalo identity and charmed the brains out of his audience. The show was filled with light patter, jokes, big-band arrangements, and cunning vocal harmonies, all emceed by a honey-tongued smoothie who could sell anybody anything. After only a week, response to *The Bob Smith Show* was so positive that NBC executives decided to schedule the show to run a second time every day, Monday through Friday, ninety minutes after the radio broadcast, over the NBC television network. This meant that Bob and his crew would now be doing fifteen live shows per week — ten on TV, five on radio. They would have to begin rehearsing *The Bob Smith Show* at nine every morning. The radio show would air at ten, and then the crew would rehearse it again for its television broadcast at noon. After lunch, the day's routine for *Howdy* would begin, with more rehearsals until airtime at five-thirty.

The Bob Smith Show debuted on television on July 5, 1954. The show was directed by my father and Bob Hultgren and written by

Willie Gilbert and Jack Weinstock, the comedy team that occasionally wrote for *Howdy*. The show featured plenty of music, a "Memory Quiz" using members of a small studio audience, and a few comedy bits with a member of the Honeydreamers, Lew Anderson, who was good with one-liners and was planted in the audience to look like a civilian.

It turned out that the adults liked Bob Smith as much as the kids loved Buffalo Bob. *The Bob Smith Show* got surprise rave reviews, sold out its ad time immediately, and was proclaimed a hit in an NBC publicity release dated August 2, 1954: "BUFFALO BOB OF PEANUT GALLERY FAME SAYS 'HOWDY DOODY' TO ADULTS — AND RESPONSE IS BIG." Record amounts of fan mail poured in. The housewives loved the show.

But it was madness. After noting that Bob Smith was doing fifteen live network shows every week during the heat of the summer, the NBC release prophetically noted: "The thought of such frequent activity is enough to make a strong man wilt. But Bob grows strong on it, enjoying himself as much as his audience does."

Right from the beginning Bob had a feeling this breakneck pace might be a mistake. Although still somewhat weakened from a case of pneumonia eighteen months earlier, Smith nevertheless plunged right in. He was thirty-six years old and at the peak of his skill and charisma.

He used to get up at six, drive in to New York, rehearse the radio show, do the radio show, rehearse the TV show, do the TV show, and plunge right into the *Howdy* rehearsals. Suddenly he found himself on a suicide schedule. But the ratings were terrific, General Mills was going to buy all their time, and he was earning $25,000 a week, making him one of the best-paid men in America in those days.

Bob kept up this schedule for two months. I remember very well what happened on September 6, because it was the worst day of my life up to that time.

It was a Sunday morning. As usual, I went to Sunday school at the Cathedral of the Incarnation, the Episcopalian church where my family worshiped. As usual, I prayed for the Yankees to make me their batboy. Most of the children there were in my second-grade class. There was one girl I really liked: her name was Gail. I was playing with her when a nasty little shit named Georgie ran up and blindsided me right in the jaw, shouting at me never to bother Gail again. I was mortified, and I rubbed my jaw. Later that day, my parents held a party at our house to celebrate my seventh birthday. For some reason, probably overstimulation, I misbehaved and was told off and perhaps given a friendly whack. Not only that, but the Dinky Toys I received as presents were not the ones I had asked for. And that wasn't all: during the party someone called my father and told him that Buffalo Bob Smith had suffered a massive heart attack the previous night and would probably not live to do another Howdy Doody show.

As I said, it was the worst day of my life.

Pioneer Village, the set in Buffalo Bob's basement from which he broadcast parts of Howdy Doody *during convalescence from his heart attack in 1955. The camera is an Image Orthikon.* (BURT DUBROW COLLECTION)

Eight

The Mouse Kills Howdy

> Parents know the unease, even the bad conscience, that they feel when they use television to quiet their children, no matter how welcome the ensuing peace is. What television can do to children is turn them off. But what does it do to a whole people?
> — Eustace Tilley, 1986

BUFFALO BOB almost died that weekend.

At five o'clock on Sunday morning, the Buffalo had suffered a catastrophic heart attack, like his father before him. His condition was so critical that even though the ambulance arrived immediately, Bob couldn't be moved to the hospital until around 8:00 A.M. Later in the day, Mil got the diagnosis: coronary thrombosis, posterior, severe. The Buffalo would spend the next nine weeks in New Rochelle Hospital, extremely fortunate to be alive.

That afternoon, Mil called Roger Muir and told him the bad news. Muir called Stone and others, and by that evening many in the cast and crew knew what was going on. But not everyone. Monday morning, Bobby Nicholson arrived at NBC for the 8:00 A.M. rehearsal of the radio show. The Honeydreamers were there early to voice up, but Nick noted they looked forlorn. "How come you guys aren't singing?" Nick asked.

Lew Anderson, one of the Honeydreamers, answered quietly, "Bob's dying. He's had a heart attack. He's been comatose for twenty-four hours, and they don't think he's gonna pull through."

Nick was stunned. He called the hospital and was put through to Bob's cardiologist, who told him that Bob's condition was touch and go and, at best, he wouldn't be doing any shows for a long time. Ths news set off a general panic at NBC. Not only was *The Bob Smith Show* in big trouble without Smith; so was *Howdy Doody,* where, in addition to his emcee duties, Bob also did the supposedly irreplaceable voice of Howdy.

Somehow, they got through that first day. Skitch Henderson took over Bob's radio and noontime shows, followed the next day by NBC staff announcer Ed Herlihy. NBC broadcast the news of Bob's illness on *The Bob Smith Show* that day and issued a press release asking concerned fans not to phone the hospital with inquiries, since the switchboard there was already jammed with calls. That evening, *The Howdy Doody Show* was hosted by Bobby Nicholson in his role of Corny Cobb. Buffalo Bob, it was announced, was off on a secret mission. America's children did without Buffalo Bob, Howdy Doody, and Clarabell that week (Nick couldn't do the clown and host at the same time) while frantic auditions were held for someone to replace the Buffalo until he could make it back to Doodyville. While the auditions were going on *Howdy* was hosted by a rotation of Gabby Hayes, Nicholson, and Ed Herlihy. After a week, Skitch Henderson took over Bob's own TV show; NBC moved it to 4:00 P.M. and then quickly canceled it. The morning radio show was also canceled. Henderson was a talented bandleader, but the sponsors wanted Bob Smith to sell their products, not a substitute, however good.

Howdy Doody was the real problem, but from the beginning Howdy's management saw a ray of hope when the show's ratings remained steady. Even without the Buffalo, it seemed, the kids would watch Howdy, if only because there was nothing else on. Nevertheless, all those involved with the show were keenly aware that their livelihoods would be threatened if they couldn't come up with a voice for Howdy, who had, after all, grown out of Buffalo Bob's own character. It was at this point that Allen Swift, Man of a Thousand Voices, saved *The Howdy Doody Show* for the second time.

After he first came in and matched all the voices of the characters the show had lost after the Christmas Eve firing, Swift remembers, "Bob would look at me suspicously and say, 'Can *you* do Howdy?' and, sensing that his ego was involved with this, I'd say no. And he'd say, 'Damn! Nobody can do it. No one can do that character. They tried a lot of other voices, they had Paul Winchell in here, but nobody can do Howdy!'

"The truth was, I had never even tried Howdy, but that character was so broad that I knew I could handle it easily. When Bob had his heart attack, it was very traumatic for everybody, including me. First, I was very grateful to him, because *Howdy* was really the first good living I had ever had in the business. It was clean, it was fun, and I really dug it. When we heard about Bob, we all said, Oh, my God! But at some point I told Roger Muir that I could do the Howdy voice. He told me to go home and practice it over the weekend. So

I did Howdy's voice all weekend, and on Sunday I tried it out on a friend's child, who was blind. The kid thought that Howdy was in the room with him, and I knew it was going to be OK. So I went in on Monday. Stone and Muir were there, and I said [in Howdy's supposedly inimitable style], 'Ho ho, well howdy, boys and girls! Howdy, Buffalo Bob!' and Marty jumped up in the air and said, 'We got it!' "

Indeed, Allen Swift was such a skilled voice-man that some people in Doodyville thought he did Howdy even better than the Buffalo. So good was he that much later, after the Buff came back to the show, Swift continued to do Howdy's voice, and the cumbersome acetate recording system — for years the means by which Buff and Howdy had talked to each other — was eliminated.

Once they had Howdy Doody back, they knew everything was going to be all right. My father wrote Bob Smith out of the show, and while the auditions for a replacement continued, *Howdy* was hosted by a plethora of well-known crooners, actors, quiz-masters, ventriloquists, and announcers. Merv Griffin was considered and rejected. Ben Grauer, Ed Herlihy, Gene Rayburn, and Wright King all did shows. Other kiddie-show hosts, including Rex Marshall and Jimmy Blaine, were brought in and turned down. Gabby Hayes, whose show aired just before *Howdy* and was also owned by KAGRAN, was one of the most frequent substitutes. In October, Gabby emceed a gala Howdy show at the Center Theater, where he was visited by ventriloquist Paul Winchell, up to that point the most serious contender for the Buffalo's seat in the Peanut Gallery.

Meanwhile, the Buffalo was on his back. NBC had told him that he had only one job — to get better and get back to the show whenever his heart would permit. So for months Bob Smith watched his show from his hospital room and tried not to seethe with anger and frustration as he saw his creation butchered by his well-intentioned replacements. The problem was that none of these guys had the slightest idea how to talk to children, let alone sell them all the stuff that Howdy purveyed day after day.

Finally, in October 1954, KAGRAN's auditions hit paydirt. NBC announced with some jubilation that Howdy Doody had found a temporary but rock-solid replacement for Buffalo Bob.

His name was Bison Bill.

I remember him well. My father took me in to NBC for Bison Bill's opening night; he said he had developed this character and wanted to see what I thought of the Buffalo's replacement. I must admit I was dazzled from the beginning of the Bison's tenure. They brought him on that evening astride a big white horse. Bison Bill looked like a younger and handsomer version of Buffalo Bob and was dressed in an old-style cowboy blouse and a big white Stetson hat. Howard wrote Bison Bill as a more dashing and less slapstick version of the Buffalo, which was fine with me because by this time I wasn't laughing at the seltzer assaults anymore.

Like Buffalo Bob, Bison Bill was a local New York disc jockey. His real name was Ted Brown; born in New Jersey, he had broken into radio in Virginia after leaving Roanoke College. During his wartime service in the Army Air Corps he had been shot down in the famous raid over the Schweinfurt ball-bearing factory and had spent the rest of the war in a German stalag. In 1946 he went to work for WOR in New York. After three years he jumped to WNEW, and then spent the next twelve years as the morning man for WMGM, for four of them working with his wife. Their *Ted Brown & the Redhead* show was a New York radio staple in that era.

In September 1954, Ted Brown was emceeing a TV game show for Colgate on NBC, working with a troupe of cheerleaders called the Colgate Girls. "Taking our bows after the show," Brown says, "one of the Colgate Girls says out of the side of her mouth, 'Buffalo Bob had a heart attack and they're looking for someone to take over *Howdy Doody*. Go over and try to get it.' So my agent got me an audition, and I got the job as Bison Bill. But first I had to be OK'd by every sponsor. I got past Wonder Bread, Kellogg's, and Blue Bonnet Margarine." Then Brown did a closed-circuit Campbell's Soup commercial for the client in Chicago. Perching a kid on his knee, Bison Bill knocked him off balance by mistake, but recovered with, "And kids, *you'll* fall for Campbell's Soup, too!" The man from the sponsor was elated. "Did you write it that way?" he asked.

On his first day on *Howdy,* Bison Bill rode in to good reviews and was immediately accepted. He didn't even have much to do besides leading the Peanuts in the theme sing-along. Allen Swift was handling Howdy quite well, and Clarabell, Thunderthud, and Oil Well Willie carried the show, did most of the ads, and introduced the Old-Time Movie. Gradually, Brown learned the awful truth about life in the Peanut Gallery. "They had a rule," he recalls, "that if a kid cried during the warm-up or was disturbing the other kids, it couldn't be in the Peanut Gallery. Some of the mothers were monsters. They'd pick the kid up and — *wham!* 'You stop that! We drove five hundred miles for this!' But some kids couldn't handle it — the hot lights, the clown, the Chief! It was too much. One time a mother slapped her child, and during the show the poor kid was sick all over me. Other times, kids at the top [of the Gallery] would pee and it ran downhill onto me during the broadcast. Me and the other kids were soaked."

Interestingly, Brown had remarried right before he became Bison Bill, and he hoped that his new job would impress his wife's young son by her previous marriage. But the little boy, an avid Howdy fan, stopped watching the show the day after Bob Smith's heart attack. The child would *not* watch Bison Bill. Ted Brown pleaded with the boy to watch Howdy and even brought his Bison costume home and wore it around the house, to no avail whatsoever.

Let's have a look at one of Bison Bill's shows on a kinescope from late October 1954. The Bison — who seems rather inexperienced and wooden compared to the smooth-talking Buffalo Bob — is trying to mediate a bitterly fought campaign for Greatest Cowboy in America between Gabby Hayes and Phineas T. "Bronco" Bluster. Cut to Howdy, who does a Blue Bonnet commercial and whose voice sounds (to me) nothing like Smith's familiar tones. Then back to Gabby Hayes, who sings a duet called "Give Me a Wha-hoo" with Princess Gina. In short order, Princess Gina announces that she is homeless and needs a place to live. Enter "Wild Man" Bluster, who calls Gabby a make-believe cowboy. These two old geezers insult each other for five minutes. "You're afraid to feed fudge to a budgie!" Gabby tells Bluster.

Mercifully, Clarabell brings out some Blue Bonnet Margarine and the Bison does the commercial. Then the Supertalkascope is wheeled in for the Old-Time Movie. The narration is terrible (but interesting to me personally — it's peppered with arcane references to my family since Howard wrote the script). After the film there's a Royal Pudding commercial and then the mayhem starts again. Thunderthud and Gabby are at each other's throat. Gabby calls the Chief a televisionary Indian, and 'Thud retorts, "And Kowa-Moo to you." Then the Chief and the clown square off. Clarabell draws his seltzer bottle, but the conciliatory Bison Bill intervenes. There follows a long routine featuring Clarabell as a caveman and a large prop photo of a fierce gorilla. As the Chief gets down on one knee and sings "Hey There, You with the Stars in Your Eyes," Gabby Hayes brings out the dreaded Zippy, who proceeds to run amok.

Looking at this old kine, I could see how unfocused and chaotic

174

things had become in Doodyville without Buffalo Bob to hold it all together and make it flow. After a couple of months' worth of these confused and lackluster shows, the sponsors started to feel the same way.

At Christmastime the doctor told the Buffalo that he could work a little if he wanted, but fighting the traffic in and out of New York was strictly forbidden.

The sponsors wanted Bob back too. So a plan was hatched to bring the Buff back to Doodyville without his ever having to leave his own house. NBC had already built a small studio in Bob's New Rochelle basement in 1948 so Bob wouldn't have to quit his old drive-time show when *Howdy* started. The studio was equipped with news wires and turntables, and there was also a seven-foot grand piano and a Hammond organ and speaker. In short order, NBC turned this old radio studio into a one-camera TV studio that my father dubbed Pioneer Village. The premise, for the purpose of the show, was that Bob was still off on his secret mission, but could beam in from Pioneer Village when his good buddy Bison Bill needed a little help with a particularly tough commercial. The way it worked was this: cast and crew would rehearse the whole show in the afternoon, except for Bob's portion. During the break they would go remote to Bob's house, and he would rehearse the commercials, sitting at a desk or at his piano. Dress rehearsal was at four-fifteen, the broadcast at five-thirty. The Buffalo usually worked by himself, but occasionally he was joined by another character called Trapper John. This was the Honeydreamers' Lew Anderson, dressed as a Northwoodsman.

The Buffalo came back to Doodyville via live remote for the first time on January 17, 1955. Bison Bill and Princess Gina were very glad to see him, as were several million other kids and I. As Ted Brown says, "Nobody could talk to Howdy the way Bob did. He made it *real*. It was like Howdy was his child, his kid. The way he'd say, 'Awww, Howdy.' There was so much emotion there. Sometimes, watching Bob, I felt that he thought Howdy *was* real."

Shortly after the Buffalo's return, there was a change of clowns. "By then I had played Clarabell for two years," Bobby Nicholson says, "but I never liked it. I thought I was a lousy clown, and I hated being hidden behind all that makeup. After two years I begged Roger Muir: 'Get me out of the goddamned clown suit.' I just couldn't stand it anymore. I was a serious musician who practiced for hours every day, and I was spending my life in makeup and telling children to shut up."

So Nick was relieved of his heavy burden of seltzer and grease-paint. Yet this gave rise to another big problem, because a new Clarabell had to be found at once. My father came up with an answer. As director of the morning *Bob Smith Show,* he had been impressed by Lew Anderson of the Honeydreamers, who ad-libbed like a pro and often acted as Bob's stooge or as an audience plant. Why not try the clown suit on Lew Anderson?

It turned out that Lew was a natural, and so the third Clarabell was born early in 1955.

Like the second Clarabell, the third was a trained musician. Lew Anderson was born in Iowa in 1922. During the war he played clarinet and saxophone in Navy swing orchestras, entertaining thousands of sailors on carrier decks in the Pacific. After the war he worked with big bands in Chicago and then filled a vacancy in the Honeydreamers, a jazzy Chicago-based vocal quintet that had started out on staff at ABC in that city, where they appeared on *Garroway at Large.* When the Honeydreamers moved to New York, they started working on *The Bob Smith Show.* "The people that did that show were the same crew that produced *Howdy Doody,*" Lew says. "And I did audience plants and comedy skits. I was Lew J. Hayseed from Oklahoma. When Nicholson quit Clarabell, they came to me and said, 'Would you like to do it?' and I had never even seen *Howdy Doody!* They thought I'd be fool enough to fit into this other role. They said, here's this nut we might get to do this. So they put on the makeup and the clown suit and I walked into the studio and nobody knew the difference. Howard wrote Clarabell out of the script for a couple days so I'd have a chance to observe and adjust, but after that I went right into it. They told me not to worry if I made a mistake because that was Clarabell's thing anyway. The one thing I was afraid of was that I might accidentally talk. I was afraid to laugh."

Fortunately for Howdy Doody, Lew Anderson turned out to be a good mime, and soon his mild-mannered Clarabell was doing Colgate and Hostess ads by himself. Lew fit right in with the cast and crew, since he was a hip, somewhat bohemian musician with the appropriate tastes. Howdy legend even has Clarabell and Corny Cobb smoking a joint as they rode down some frigid Midwestern boulevard in a winter parade appearance that went along with their jobs.

Bison Bill and the gang maintained the Doodyville experience during most of 1955, while everyone waited for the Buffalo's return. As the year wore on, the Buff did more remotes from Pioneer Village. Howdy's two thousandth show was broadcast in January of that year. In just three broadcasts that March, Howdy collected more than three hundred thousand dimes for the March of Dimes antipolio campaign. In April a twenty-five-piece orchestra appeared in the studio to perform the "Howdy Doody Suite," written and conducted by Bob Nicholson.

In May, the Buffalo started to really get back to work. He and Howdy and Clarabell appeared in a forty-minute film that was made to be shown to hospitalized children. In September, after a restful summer in which he regained most of his strength, Buffalo Bob was told by his doctor that he could return to *Howdy Doody*. At last.

NBC decided that Buffalo Bob should come back with a real bang.

Until September 1955, there was no regularly scheduled color programming on American television, except for a ten-minute segment on NBC's midday *Home* show. The networks occasionally telecast special color "spectaculars," but that was all, since there weren't enough color receivers in American homes to justify the trouble and expense. But for years David Sarnoff had been saying that Howdy Doody and Milton Berle were responsible for selling more TV sets than anyone in history. Sometime in 1955, Sarnoff said to some aides, "Why don't we make Howdy sell RCA color sets the way he did with black-and-white?"

So they decided that when Buffalo Bob returned in September 1955 *Howdy Doody* would be the first television show to be broadcast in color every day.

The *Howdy* staff worked hard over the summer to get the show ready for the transition to color. First, after years in 3A, they moved into a brand-new studio: NBC knocked out a wall between 3G and 3F and called it 3K (for *Kolor*). A multihued new Doodyville set was designed for the new technology. RCA made a chart of Howdy's colors and sent a memo to RCA installers and repairmen, instructing them to deliver all new color sets to consumers' homes in the late afternoon so they could be fine-tuned to the *Howdy* colors at five-thirty.

Two important new elements were added as well. There had been no female presence on *The Howdy Doody Show* since the departure of Princess Gina many moons before. Now they added a character called the Story Princess, played by a mature actress instead of a coltish pixie. Her name was Alene Dalton, and she had originated the role a year or so earlier on KSL-TV in Salt Lake City, Utah.

Whereas Princess Summerfall Winterspring had been a singing member of Howdy's comedy troupe, the Story Princess was much more regal, dressed in a gorgeous gown, reading fables to the Peanuts instead of driving them bats with slapstick. "We thought we could have fun in color with the Story Princess," Buffalo Bob remembers. "She wore beautiful clothes and told fascinating stories, and we'd run color film behind her. She didn't last too long because it wasn't fast enough; Howdy was pretty much fast slapstick and comedy."

The other new feature was "Flight to Adventure," a series of short color films by Lowell Thomas, Jr., the son of the famed traveler and journalist. Thomas Jr. had a plane and made short documentaries about his travels, which ran in place of the now hopelessly passé Old-Time Movies and looked much better on the hazy and primitive color television broadcasts.

So the Buffalo returned to Doodyville full-time. His doctors told him they still didn't want him fighting traffic, since his heart remained fragile, so Bob Smith bought himself a limousine, hired a friend away from his police job to be his chauffeur, and learned to sip scotch and water on the way home from Doodyville. Since Nicholson lived almost next door in Pelham and Muir lived in Larchmont, they all used to ride home together in Bob's limo. It was such a cozy scene that soon Bob's chauffeur was hired to hold the cue-cards on *Howdy,* a show that was nothing if not a family operation.

At first there was some anxiety on the part of NBC and KAGRAN. Could the Buffalo take the pressure? The lights in Studio 3K were even hotter for the new color cameras, and the Buff had been a very sick man.

But from the very moment when Bob said, "Say kids, what time is it?" and the new set was illuminated in all its garish glory, my father knew it was going to be all right. Buffalo Bob was back.

Seeing Howdy in color every day was a revelation for the elite few who had the big RCA color screens, and children began to migrate to neighbors' homes just as they had in the old days, only this time to watch Howdy in color. A few weeks later, NBC began to broadcast *The Perry Como Show* in color on Saturday nights, and the American people began buying color receivers in droves.

The Buffalo's return meant that Bison Bill got the boot: there was room for only one pioneer/pitchman in Doodyville. So, not long after Bob Smith came back, there was a little on-air ceremony to say goodbye to Bison Bill. A white horse was brought in again, but a different one this time; this horse was so tall that Bison Bill's head was barely on camera. "Well, kids," the affable cowpoke said, "I guess it's time to say goodbye." At this moment, Ted Brown remembers, "I heard a sound like a fire hose. I looked at the kids in the Peanut Gallery, and their eyes were bugging out. But I still didn't know what it was until I saw the river of piss and a big pile of turds on the studio floor."

Much hilarity ensued. Almost all the *Howdy* veterans I polled could recall this happy incident. "Oh yeah," laughed Lew Anderson. "When Bison Bill left the show, his horse pissed and shat. Everyone was tiptoeing around."

Yes, the Buffalo came back from the dead that fall, and for a while — a deceptively short span in the autumn of 1955 — things were back to normal in Doodyville. But this was just an Indian summer, and soon the weather began to turn stormy for Howdy Doody. Howdy had virtually invented television and had survived the cast massacre and other debacles, but after Buffalo Bob's close call things would never be quite the same in Doodyville.

The changes began when Martin Stone, Howdy's commanding *eminence gris* since 1947, sold out his share of KAGRAN toward the end of 1955. By then, KAGRAN had marketed and merchandised every conceivable type of Howdy doodad and geegaw in existence. *Howdy Doody* had been milked for millions of dollars in merchandise and premiums, and as it finished its eighth year the show had begun to look as though it were being broadcast only for its ad content. Producer Roger Muir concedes that "eventually KAGRAN became too big, and the tail started to wag the dog. The sponsors and merchandisers took over the show, and at one point Ovaltine demanded that Clarabell speak his first-ever lines by doing a pitch for their chocolate drink."

So NBC decided to buy back Howdy's merchandising rights. Martin Stone sold his share of KAGRAN to the network and started his own merchandising company. When Stone left *Howdy,* Eddie Kean, who for a year had been working for KAGRAN on various projects, also left to be a stockbroker. The show lost two of its original members and found itself now wholly owned by the National Broadcasting Company. Doodyville had become a company town.

In October 1955 a tremor occurred in television that imperceptibly shook the secure domain of Howdy. This was the premiere of a new style of kids' show, a quieter and more instructive morning program for preschoolers called *Captain Kangaroo*. Over the years it would become the longest-running and most successful children's program in the history of television, but when it first went on the air over CBS, everyone at *Howdy* was surprised to find that Captain Kangaroo himself was played by their bumbling old pal Bobby Keeshan. After all, they reasoned, didn't the first Clarabell get fired because he supposedly had no talent?

Keeshan did have a hard time finding work after the cast was fired, back in December 1952, but in August 1953 he got back into television, through a tip from Roger Muir. Keeshan played Carny the Clown at the new ABC station in New York. Unlike Clarabell, Carny was a talking clown, who ate lunch on camera, joked with the audience about his backstage life, and showed cartoons. In mid-1954, Keeshan debuted a new show called *Tinker's Workshop* at 8:30 A.M. For months Keeshan had been trying to convince his bosses that there was a potentially huge preschool children's market for weekday-morning TV. The executives had laughed at him. But three weeks after Keeshan took *Tinker* (in which he played an elderly toymaker) onto the ABC network, the fall ratings sweeps revealed that the show had tied *Today* on NBC and beat Jack Paar's morning show on CBS. Bobby Keeshan was back in business.

During the summer of 1955, CBS decided to air a kids' show of its own in that 8:00 A.M. weekday time slot. Keeshan put *Captain Kangaroo* together to vie for the slot with show ideas entered by Martin Stone and comic Jerry Cologna. Keeshan won out and went on as the Kangaroo that October. Although it didn't compete directly with Howdy, the show was a distinct reaction against the fizzy mayhem Keeshan, as Clarabell, had once caused in Doodyville. Silenced for so long in his former role, Keeshan now spoke directly into the camera, softly and kindly, and there was none of Howdy's chases and mania. "I wasn't consciously going in the opposite direction from Howdy," Keeshan said much later, "because I thought Howdy Doody was fun. It followed traditional patterns like the Punch and Judy show. Maybe it [*Howdy*] was insane, but so what? It was still much better than what we see in children's TV today.

"When my son was born in 1951, I started looking at TV from a different perspective. There were so many facets of TV that we weren't even using. It was so intimate, and afforded us incredible opportunities [to do things] that we hadn't been able to do before in terms of talking to children. And that's where Kangaroo's 'soft' approach comes from." It was an approach that declared Howdy Doody passé, one that would keep Bobby Keeshan on the air in the same role for the next three decades, long after Howdy Doody was merely a nostalgic memory and an item in trivia quizzes.

But back in 1955, Howdy Doody had more pressing problems on his hands. Not only did Keeshan's show premiere in October, but on the third day of that month *The Mickey Mouse Club* broadcast its first hour-long show from 5:00 to 6:00 P.M. over the ABC network. This was direct competition, an obvious attempt by the upstart ABC and the all-powerful Walt Disney to grab Howdy Doody's loyal and extremely lucrative audience.

The grab worked. The Mouse killed Howdy.

It had all started back in 1953, when an antitrust decision had separated United Paramount Theaters from Paramount Pictures. The president of the theater chain, Leonard Goldenson, then acquired the starving thirteen-station ABC network, whose signals reached only about a third of American televisions and which had no real national coverage. Within a year both Goldenson and NBC's Pat Weaver were heavily courting Walt Disney, then (as now) regarded as "the only sure thing in show business." Eventually ABC, which needed Disney more than NBC did, put up some of the original investment capital for Disneyland. In return it got the hour-long hit series *Disneyland,* which it broadcast to a huge audience on Sunday nights, and later the daily *Mickey Mouse Club* variety show. Both shows devastated all the competition. In the two-station markets that had previously locked out ABC, the local NBC and CBS affiliates fell over each other scrambling to get "secondary affiliation" to ABC for access to the Disney shows. It was a landslide.

The Mickey Mouse Club was a big blow to *Howdy Doody*. By the time *Howdy* came on at five-thirty, America's children (me included) had already been watching the Mouse show for half an hour and were deeply hooked by its seductive and changeless rhythms. It was what Bob Smith called "a gang show." Hosted by two adults (the youngish Jimmy Dodd and an avuncular, goofy-looking Roy Williams), the *Club* boasted an adorable group of talented adolescents, the Mouseketeers. These legendary child stars of the fifties included Annette Funicello, Darlene Gillespie, Cubby O'Brien, Karen Pendleton, Bobby Burgess, Doreen Tracy, Sharon Baird, and Cheryl Holdridge. I was deeply involved with all of these attractive dancing kids in the unlimited mindscape of my eight-year-old fantasy life. Cubby and Karen were just a little older than me, and I was deeply in love at various times with both Darlene and Doreen. These kids were all great singers and tap dancers, but the real stars of the show were Mickey Mouse, Donald Duck, Pluto, Goofy, and the other animated characters. Timeless Disney cartoons alternated with clever skits and sketches by the Mouseketeers. Then, just as Howdy came on at five-thirty, the *Club* would run a fifteen-minute segment of one of its serials — "The Adventures of Spin and Marty," "Annette," "Corky and White Shadow," or "The Secret of Mystery Lake." I remember my mother one day telling me to switch to *Howdy Doody,* because my father wanted her to watch for something clever he had written; I threw a fit when she changed the channel because an episode of my beloved "Spin and Marty" was being shown on *Mickey Mouse.* (Marty was a rich boy from the east who arrived at a Wyoming dude ranch with his valet in tow, and had to prove himself to a bunch of tough teenage cowboys led by Spin. This serial made me almost drool with pleasure at the horseplay and fierce camaraderie depicted among the boys.) And my mother wanted me to watch the same old clown blasting the boring old Buffalo with the same old fizz. Who was she kidding? What did she think I was, a baby? I was in love with these kids on this new show, and no amount of familial pressure was going to keep me from watching *The Mickey Mouse Club.*

I didn't get in to the Peanut Gallery very often after the Mouse came on. Now the pressure was on the *Howdy* crew to come up with new and better stuff, in a futile attempt to compete with Disney. My father was expected to create material that would bring America's errant children back to Doodyville. Howard wanted Howdy to stick to his principles as an Innocent and eschewed violence and tension in the scripts. Increasingly, however, Buffalo Bob and Roger Muir were demanding more action in the story lines, because they were getting killed by the Mouse.

So new characters were born. Around Thanksgiving 1955 Howard wrote a story line about two tiny bears, Hyde and Zeke, who knew the answer to a puzzle whose solution would save Doodyville from foreclosure by the Bluster National Bank. My last visit to the Peanut Gallery took place about this time. My father had written one of Bob Smith's Welsh corgis, Happy Talk, into the plot of that night's show, and I remember that we drove to New Rochelle to pick up the little dog and take him in to the studio. At the end of the show, I hopped out of the Peanut Gallery to run to my father, who was standing just behind the cameras. A new NBC page, who didn't know me, grabbed me roughly by the arm, hurting my wrist. It was my first real introduction to the grim underside of the Peanut Gallery. Fortunately, Howard intervened. Later I felt better when I was allowed to walk Happy Talk back to the car in the Rockefeller Center garage, in front of that day's Peanuts and their parents. There were *ooh*s and *ahh*s, and I felt like a star.

Another new character was more controversial. Everyone felt that the Story Princess was too maternal, and that Howdy needed a girl. My father came up with a puppet called Heidi Doody, a long-lost relative of Howdy's. The Heidi puppet made by Margo Rose had flaxen-gold hair and wore an Austrian *dirndl* and peasant skirt. Howard and free-lance tunesmith J. Fred Coots wrote cute jingles for her, and NBC gave her November 1955 debut a big promotional push. Her voice was done quite nicely by Alene Dalton, and the little girls in the audience seemed to like her. The trouble was that the Buffalo didn't think much of Heidi Doody at all. He didn't like having to sing cutesy duets with a female puppet and never really got a feel for her character, even though Heidi Doody would be featured on the show for the next year. Howard sold Heidi to the Buffalo as hard as he could, but he knew the Buff was only buying her because he had nothing else on hand.

These were tough times for our divided family. My father was fighting to save Howdy from the Mouse, and I was sneaking over to my friend Alan's house at five-thirty to watch the second half of the Mousketeers' show. Adding to the confusion was the birth of my younger brother in October (announced by Buffalo Bob on TV) and the subsequent distraction of my heretofore doting parents and grandmother. No longer was I an only child, the star of the family. Now I was eight years old and officially an Older Brother, with a new set of reponsibilities and chores. It was no fun.

My last contact with Howdy Doody, as far as I can remember, occurred that November. Buffalo Bob was the host of the national telecast of Macy's Thanksgiving Parade (his guests were Danny Kaye, Pinky Lee, Buster Crabbe, and Hopalong Cassidy), and my father and I were to drive the *Howdy* cast down Broadway in Bob's Model T Ford. The car was ridiculous, flamingo red with canary-yellow wheels and a big picture of Howdy on each door. A New York state police officer had ordered us off the highway in New Rochelle because we were holding up traffic, and we had to thread our way into Manhattan on local roads through the Bronx and Harlem. Riding down the parade route with Chief Thunderthud, Clarabell, and

Sandy McTavish was a lot of fun, a blurred memory of ribald comments by the cast and of being under the gigantic balloons of cartoon characters — Mighty Mouse, Donald Duck, Woody Woodpecker — as they floated down Broadway. New York was beautiful and cold that day, and I remember wondering if the steam coming out of the bundled spectators' mouths was the same as the steam that floated up from the manholes in the streets.

I didn't see much of Howdy Doody after that. *Howdy* was always meant to play, according to Buffalo Bob's dictum, to children from three to eight. I was, therefore, past it. And I wasn't alone. This was the year that Kay Thompson's famous children's book, *Eloise,* came out, in which the dreadfully precocious six-year-old heroine says that the one thing she really hates is Howdy Doody. Stating this in a kids' book would have been commercial suicide a couple of years earlier. Now it was a sign of the times.

Looking back, I believe childhood ended for me then. Howdy Doody was the favorite pursuit and obsession of my early life; when I gave him up I think I let go of the blissful innocence of childhood as well. Thus began my slide into the years of what Dr. Freud called the Latency age.

Two significant events took place in December 1955. One of these occurred early in the month, when three large marionettes were dismembered and then burned in a lawyer's office somewhere in the RCA Building. This was part of the settlement of the lawsuit that Frank Paris had filed against NBC back in 1948, charging the network with breach of contract and defamation of character after Paris walked off the show with his original Howdy. It took Paris more than seven years, but NBC eventually settled out of court for a large cash payment and the right to destroy his three principal puppets — Howdy One, Mr. Huff, and Eustace. That December day, after seeing his puppets burned, Frank Paris pocketed a big check and then had to borrow his subway fare back to the Village from his lawyer. The greatest puppetmaster in America would struggle financially for the rest of his life.

The other notable occasion was Princess Summerfall Winterspring's Broadway debut, on December 1.

After leaving *Howdy Doody* two years earlier, Judy Tyler had worked on her nightclub act with her husband. She went to Hollywood to look for work in the movies and was offered another role as an Indian maiden, which she turned down. Judy was then twenty-one years old and a woman of the world. Coming back to the East, she went to work in summer stock, playing in *Annie Get Your Gun* in Warwick, Rhode Island, and in *Anything Goes* in Valley Forge, Pennsylvania. During the summer of 1955 she appeared on television again as part of the cast of *Sid Caesar Presents,* a summer replacement show on NBC, where she was seen by Arthur Hammerstein, the brother of the Broadway writer and lyricist Oscar Hammerstein II. For months Hammerstein and his partner Richard Rodgers had been searching for a young singer to play the role of Suzy (a girl of relaxed morality) in their upcoming production of *Pipe Dream,* a musical based on John Steinbeck's novel *Sweet Thursday.* Arthur called Oscar and said, "I found your girl." Judy auditioned and won the role with her booming contralto and fearless stage persona. The Princess was on Broadway, and she looked more beautiful than ever.

Pipe Dream starred William Johnson and opera singer Helen Traubel (who had left the Met because management deplored her second career as a nightclub performer), but the show was not really up to the Rodgers and Hammerstein standards. The critics panned the show but liked Judy Tyler, whose talent was simply too strong to be denied. Walter Kerr, writing in the *Herald Tribune,* said: "Judy Tyler is pretty and spirited as a girl who might have to spend a night in a boiler, and she makes a very nice thing out of 'Everybody's Got a Home But Me.'" *Pipe Dream* was seen by many influential people in the theater and in Hollywood. One of them, producer Howard W. Koch, summoned Judy to California for a screen test, and everyone in Doodyville assumed that Judy was on her way to becoming a very big star. They were right.

My father's tenure as head writer and script supervisor on *Howdy Doody* began to come to an end around Christmas 1955. For over a year he had been using Jack Weinstock and Willie Gilbert as principal suppliers of story lines and scripts aside from his own. Weinstock and Gilbert were a curious team. Willie was a Broadway type who lived in a hotel, hung around with showgirls and chorines, and had a *Guys and Dolls* look to him. Jack was a Manhattan urologist with a show-business clientele who used to tell stories about all his famous clients who couldn't get it up. Jack was the jokester and idea man, Willie the writer and typist. They had written for *Captain Video* and other kids' shows before coming to *Howdy,* and their work was fast, funny, and often tasteless. Their humor was pure borscht belt:

DILLY DALLY: Why does Mr. Bluster remind you of corned beef?
HOWDY: Gee, Dilly, I don't know.
DILLY: Because he runs to fat.

Howard would have to explain to Jack and Willie that jokes about corned beef wouldn't be understood in Kansas or Louisiana. Nevertheless, these two madmen wrote much of *Howdy* in those days and were genuinely talented. (Within a few years they would win a Pulitzer Prize for their work in the theater.)

A couple of weeks before Christmas, Jack and Willie proposed a *Howdy* story line in which Santa Claus would be kidnapped and held for ransom. The theory was that kids would be frightened into thinking that they might not get Christmas presents at all unless Howdy managed to set Santa free, which would happen, of course, on Christmas Eve. My father, who led the faction that wanted to keep Howdy Doody innocent and childlike, was opposed to this story idea and rejected it. But Jack and Willie went over Howard's head and pitched the concept to the Buffalo and Roger Muir, who bought it. There were a lot of meetings on this. Howard said that kidnapping Santa was a horrible idea that would genuinely frighten children. Others said, Damn the innocence, we've got to build our audience — the Mouse is killing us! In the end, Howard was backed up by the NBC Children's Advisory Group (headed by the dreaded Miss Frances of *Ding Dong School*), and the idea of kidnapping Santa was thrown out.

But Howard Davis could see that the handwriting was on the wall for Howdy Doody. The Mouse was murdering them in the ratings, Jack and Willie had the Buffalo's ear and that of the production people, and Howard's writing was almost tapped out anyway. One of his last projects was a wonderful good-behavior song, a collaboration with Bobby Nicholson called "Will My Dog Be Proud of Me?" that was used on the show for years and which I still sometimes find myself singing more than thirty years later.

So my father stopped writing *Howdy Doody* early in 1956. Roger Muir told him he could go back to just directing the show if he wanted, but the man who had since replaced Howard as codirector, Bob Hopkins, was a good friend, so Howard declined. Then my father heard over the NBC grapevine that the *Today* show was looking for a director to work with the difficult prima donna Dave Garroway. Since Howard had a reputation for "winging" shows that had to be broadcast with inadequate rehearsal, he was hired.

When any valued citizen of Doodyville left town for the last time, he or she was given a small inscribed silver plate. My father's says simply: "To Howard with thanks from Howdy Doody." There was a little goodbye party for him on the set. The Buffalo was cool, but Howard had many other friends on the show, among them Bill Lecornec, who almost cried. After that, my father began getting up at 2:00 A.M. to rehearse *Today,* and I didn't see that much of him for a while. (Dave Garroway's show was considered very hot back then and was broadcast live from the old RCA Exhibition Hall, where my father had started his career. One day Howard told one of his cameramen to pan the audience watching the show from the sidewalk, and the camera caught former President Harry Truman peering in along with the customary handful of tourists and commuters.) Occasionally I'd get up with Howard and visit the show. I got to meet Garroway's on-camera assistants — newscaster Frank Blair, sportscaster Jack Lescoulie, and the former chanteuse Helen O'Connell (who interviewed women and handled soft news). The *Today* show also had a resident chimp, J. Fred Muggs (named after J. Fred Coots). One morning when I was visiting the show, I was put in a chair with the chimp on my lap so my father could hold a shot of me at 8:59 as the credits rolled. Just at that moment, J. Fred Muggs bit me on my finger. I yelped with pain and dumped the monkey, coast to coast. That was my last appearance on national television for many years.

Howdy Doody went on without us, head to head against *The Mickey Mouse Club.* My father left the show in February 1956; four months later, NBC took *Howdy Doody* off the air on weekdays.

What happened?

During the late winter and spring of 1956, Doodyville had functioned normally. Jack Weinstock and Willie Gilbert wrote new characters, and Rufus and Margo Rose built marionettes to match. We're talking about such creations as Mambo the elephant, Tizzy the dinosaur, the Bloops, and a live character played by Allen Swift, the absentminded Professor Fitznoodle. Maybe you remember these, but *I* don't, because I was watching *Mickey Mouse.*

Here's a typical show from the era, on a kinescope dated April 13, 1956. The Buffalo, looking a little older now and somewhat portly in his pioneer suit, is still bellowing, "Say kids, what time is it?" Then he puts through a phone call to the "Do-er of the Day," a little girl in Saratoga Springs, New York, who is awarded the *Book of Knowledge,* an RCA portable radio, and a Columbia Fire Arrow bike. Then there's a promo for an RCA-sponsored Brooklyn Dodger Batboy contest. (Be still, my heart!) Now we see the Buffalo and Thunderthud in a circus setting, singing Eddie Kean's famous "Popcorn Song." After a dream sequence involving the Chief and a tightrope walker, Bob launches into an ad for Curad "Battle Ribbon" adhesive strips, which are camouflage-colored. Then follows a long rivalry sequence with Thunderthud, Lew Anderson's quite reasonable Clarabell, and Nicholson's Cornelius Cobb. There's not a drop of seltzer in sight. In the final ad, for Royal Pudding, the Buffalo gazes into the camera and asserts that one serving of Royal contains "seventy-four percent more food energy than a glass of milk." In the last minutes of the show we see an old friend, Inspector John J. Fadoozle, America's Number One *(BOOIINNGG!!)* Private Eye. Even eight years and several other writers later Eddie Kean's material always seemed to be the real *Howdy Doody.* This one is a Friday show; the last shot before the fade is of a church steeple. The Buffalo intones, "Boys and girls, ask your mom and dad to take you to church or Sunday school this Sunday."

In his day, my father had written the words "or synagogue or place of worship" into this part of the script, but the Buffalo had always changed it. He thought people should go to church.

Anyone with any memory of how fresh, dynamic, and plain sexy the *Mouse Club* seemed in 1956, compared to *Howdy Doody,* will remember what happened next.

The Buffalo remembers. "When the Mouse came on, we didn't know what was happening because we never could see it. We didn't have televisions at NBC. But I thought that if anybody could rip into *Howdy*'s ratings, it would be Walt Disney. I thought they'd be showing cartoons, but they had an attractive gang. It was a kids' talent show."

At NBC the executives were grumbling. Disney was getting the kids at five o'clock and holding on to them. *Howdy Doody* cost a fortune to produce, with a new script and a large live cast every day on a show that would never be repeated. It cost Walt Disney nothing to run his old cartoons, which comprised a good part of the Mouse hour. Pretty soon Howdy's advertisers started jumping to *The Mickey*

Mouse Club and ABC. By the time that April show we just saw was aired, Howdy was losing his grip. By May there were barely enough advertisers to sustain NBC's two shows for kids in the predinner hour. Gabby Hayes went off the air entirely. Burr Tillstrom and the Kuklapolitans were long gone. The era of live television was dying; the citizens of Doodyville constantly heard the sad refrain that cartoons were cheap to produce and could be broadcast to (and would be watched by) children over and over again.

By May NBC was firing people, and the entire cast, crew, and production staff feared that *Howdy Doody* would be canceled during the summer. But Roger Muir and his people knew they had enough loyal advertisers to maintain a successful commercial operation (if a much scaled-down one) if they broadcast *Howdy* weekly during the Saturday-morning kids' lineup. Robert Rippen, a *Howdy* exec since 1948, got his parting-gift silver ashtray around that time. So did Allen Swift, the man who had twice saved the day in Doodyville. "In 1956 my contract was up for renewal, after three years," Swift says. "Roger Muir called me into his office and said, 'Allen, we got the word from above that we've got to cut down on expenses, so — and we're all very grateful to you — we're letting you out of your contract.'

"It was a shock! I was only getting scale, so it made no sense to me at the time. Anyway, that was the end of my virginity. I became a businessman as well as an actor." Within six months after leaving Howdy, Swift had gone into business as a voice-man, the legendary Man of a Thousand Voices. Three months after that he became the host of *The Popeye Show with Captain Allen Swift* on WPIX-TV in New York, a program that ran for years.

But Howdy was doomed. The show had been hurt by NBC, which wouldn't buy cartoons and serials for Howdy because General Sarnoff didn't believe in showing old product — or film — on television. He passed on buying the extremely lucrative Popeye cartoon series for NBC for just that reason. "Television will drown in a sea of celluloid," Sarnoff would rant. "Television has got to be live!"

But the audience wasn't listening.

By the end of May, NBC was trying to figure out what to do with Howdy Doody. The network wanted the puppets off the air at five-thirty so they could put on *I Married Joan* reruns and make even more money by selling soap to the moms while they were cooking dinner. Yet NBC was having problems finding a slot for Howdy without disturbing any other popular show. Then Pinky Lee had his famous on-camera heart attack one Saturday morning, and suddenly there was a hole in the schedule.

Pinky Lee had been on NBC at ten o'clock on Saturday morning since January 1954. A manic and semicrazed baggy-pants comic of the old school, Pinky did sketches and alternated slapstick hysteria with poignant sad-sack routines. In 1956 he started a grueling schedule, commuting between New York and Los Angeles every week so he could appear on *Gumby* as well as his own show. After thirteen weeks of this, he collapsed during a live broadcast from New York, going down on camera to the horror of millions of kids. This was a traumatic event that I remember being discussed in my fourth-grade class that spring.

The Pinky Lee Show was canceled early in June 1956. On Friday, June 15, *Howdy Doody* was broadcast for the last time as a weekday strip show; at ten o'clock on June 16, Howdy began his run as a Saturday-morning weekly show. It was the end of an era.

Judy Tyler meets Elvis, from the filming of Jailhouse Rock, *June 1957.*
(COURTESY LORELEI HESS)

Nine

Goodbye, Kids

JUDY TYLER: Hey, you forgot something!
ELVIS PRESLEY: What?
JUDY TYLER: Me!
— *Jailhouse Rock*, 1957

I DON'T HAVE MANY MEMORIES of *The Howdy Doody Show* after it was relegated to the Saturday-morning kids' ghetto. At Howdy's 10:00 A.M. airtime on Saturdays, I was always either at choir practice or at a Little League game. Almost everything about *Howdy* changed drastically — the set, the characters, the very look and feel of the show — and now, when I review the old kinescopes of Howdy's 1956–1960 era, I find myself in a strange and unfamiliar Doodyville, a place that sometimes seems touched with the pathetic surrealism of a bad dream. Yet this version of *Howdy Doody* had a quite respectable four-year run, outlasting even *The Mickey Mouse Club*. Unlike his cartoon characters, Uncle Walt's Mousketeers eventually had to grow up.

At first Howdy's pared-down and slightly disgruntled cast and crew were dismayed at the schedule change. The Saturday show was broadcast live for its first year, which meant that everyone had to get up at 4:00 A.M. on the day of the broadcast. But in late 1957 or early 1958, with the advent of videotape, the routine changed. The Doodyville set was assembled only once a month, and five shows would be taped in a single day. This proved to be much cheaper for NBC, which needed Howdy's old studio for its newer shows. For the first time, the Buffalo and the whole gang could go home and watch Howdy with their children and laugh at their own mistakes.

Once they got over the initial shock of the cancellation of the daily show in June 1956, most of Howdy Doody's cast and crew were relieved to change pace after nine years. Many had seen it coming. "The show was old," says Bobby Nicholson. "The time salesmen were bored and didn't want to sell us the way they used to. The change was welcome, at least to the cast. Doing five shows a week is a tough chore. Now, with the new videotape that was coming in, we would take a week, tape five shows, and take four weeks off. It didn't eat into our income that much because it freed us to do other things."

"It was a well-deserved vacation," agrees the Buffalo. "They [NBC] renegotiated and gave me a contract at the same salary. The main difference now was that we had to have a complete half-hour show that began and ended in thirty minutes. We'd do five at a time because it was cheaper that way, and take the rest of the month off."

Soon cast members discovered that they much preferred life on the weekly show. Everyone was more relaxed, and the show was more fun. After Allen Swift was fired, Nicholson took over key puppet voices like Bluster, the Inspector, and the Flubadub. But voices were not Nick's main strength. "They were different," he admits, "but, you know, what the hell." Nick also took over all of *Howdy's* songwriting chores, while Jack Weinstock and Willie Gilbert wrote the scripts. Almost immediately *Howdy Doody* acquired an almost "put-on" quality that reflected both the hipness of musicians Nicholson and Lew Anderson and the wisecracking humor of Jack and Willie. There were many more ad-libs, double entendres, and on-camera crack-ups on the weekly show than ever would have been tolerated by the mass audience of Howdy's prime. Not everyone in Doodyville was thrilled by this. Some key people, among them Scott Brinker, felt that Jack and Willie wrote too "New York," catered to parents rather than kids with inside jokes, and sometimes got a little out of line. "The crew felt the show got very hammy," Brinker says.

But Nicholson remembers it differently. "It was a constant party. We worked like hell, we had great musicians like [guitarist] Tony Mottola and [trombonist] Will Bradley in our little studio band, and we made a lot of money. I personally loved the Saturday *Howdy Doody Show*."

And what was the old Buffalo going to do with himself now that he had so much free time on his hands? His chauffeur came up with an idea. Since Bob belonged to three country clubs in the area that were potential customers, why not open a liquor store? He could sell a lot of booze in New Rochelle. So Bob and his chauffeur opened a liquor store in New Rochelle's Wykagyl section. Then Bob's brother, Buffalo Vic, opened a shoe store across the street. The Buff liked to tell people, "Bob's in booze, Vic's in shoes."

Rehearsing Howdy *during the Saturday-morning era in the late 1950s. Producer Roger Muir (in coat and tie) goes over the script with Lew Anderson, at upper left. Bobby Nicholson appears in a kimono, with Buffalo Bob at lower left.* (BURT DUBROW COLLECTION)

Over the next few years, Doodyville was repopulated by Jack and Willie, puppeteers Rufus and Margo Rose, and Bobby Nicholson. The Roses made new puppets: Petey Bluster (the wimpy and loathsome nephew of Phineas T. Bluster), Tom Turtle, Paddle the Gnu, Bargaining Bill, and Detective Mike Hatchet. Comic actor Don Knotts played a short-lived and very nervous character called Tim Tremble. Zippy was fired after biting the Buffalo and was replaced by a slightly tamer chimp, Kokomo Junior.

After a year in the Howdy cast, Story Princess Alene Dalton left the show prior to its ninth-anniversary broadcast in December 1956. For a while Howdy relied on Heidi Doody, Sandra the witch, and Tizzy the dinosaur for the feminine touch, but eventually a blond actress from California, Marty Barris, was brought in to play a character that Jack and Willie called Peppy Mint. Again, the Buffalo didn't like her much. She was the daughter of Harry Barris, one of

Bing Crosby's original Rhythm Boys. "Somebody in Hollywood promoted her hard to NBC," Smith recalls, "and NBC said that we should find something for her to do." Peppy Mint was the last girl on *The Howdy Doody Show.*

And then there was Gumby, a stop-action clay animation character that made its network debut on *Howdy Doody* in March 1957. Soon Gumby had his own show right after *Howdy* on Saturday mornings, produced by Roger Muir and hosted by Bobby Nicholson in the role of Scotty McKee, proprietor of McKee's Fun Shop.

Later in that spring of 1957, there was a stir of excitement in Doodyville when cast and crew learned that their old girlfriend Princess Summerfall Winterspring was going to star in Elvis Presley's new movie, *Jailhouse Rock.* Judy Tyler and Elvis Presley, they marveled. What a concept!

Despite its lackluster reviews, the play *Pipe Dream* had indeed "discovered" Judy Tyler for the second time. She appeared on the cover of *Life* magazine as one of Broadway's shining young stars. The show had attracted all the important producers, directors, and agents of the day, and Judy was whisked off to Hollywood by agent Aubrey Schenck and producer Howard W. Koch, who quickly signed her to a five-picture deal after what is said to have been a spectacular screen test. In 1956 Judy made her first film, a cheap United Artists B-musical called *Bop Girl Goes Calypso,* and worked her nightclub act at joints like the Patio in Las Vegas and El Mocambo in Hollywood. By the end of the year Judy and her husband had drifted apart and were divorced. "As part of the divorce settlement," Colin Romoff remembers, "I didn't have to pay her anything. What Judy wanted me to do was write her a nightclub act, which I did."

At some point in early 1957, Judy's screen test and the rushes of *Bop Girl Goes Calypso* were seen by Elvis Presley and director Richard Thorpe, who were searching for an actress to play the female lead in Elvis's new film. Judy was perfect — tough, robust, a good singer with a great figure. Elvis told Metro-Goldwyn-Mayer that he wanted Judy Tyler for *Jailhouse Rock,* but MGM said it didn't want to sign a new star who had so many other commitments, including a five-picture deal with someone else. To help Judy clinch one of the most coveted Hollywood contracts of the year, Schenck and Koch reduced her commitment to two films instead of five, and Judy was signed to play opposite Elvis in one of the early blockbusters of the rock 'n' roll era. Judy celebrated by marrying her boyfriend, a handsome young television actor named Greg Lafayette, in Miami Beach in May 1957.

Elvis Presley, the gyrating former truck driver, had burst forth from Memphis, Tennessee, three years earlier. His 1955 appearances on Ed Sullivan's Sunday-night variety program had made him a national figure of rock and rebellion. Records like "Hound Dog" and "Love Me Tender" launched a music industry that has lasted for more than thirty years. His first two films established him as a major star all over the world; his third, *Jailhouse Rock,* was written as a serious adult movie in a rock 'n' roll context and was easily the best picture Presley ever made. It seems at once amazing and no accident at all that Judy Tyler was chosen to portray Elvis's first believable love interest.

Except for its production numbers (including the famous "Jailhouse Rock" sequence in a simulated vertical prison block), the film was relatively low-budget, and shooting went quickly. Judy and Elvis were very attracted to each other; their love scenes in the film are steamy, and they hold each other close in the production stills. Richard Thorpe overheard Elvis and Judy singing together between scenes and ordered a song written for them to do together in front of the camera. (The song, by Mike Stoller and Jerry Leiber, wasn't used in the film.) Judy plays a song-plugger (termed an "exploitation girl" in this contemporary music-biz exposé) who discovers sensitive ex-con Elvis singing in a bar, recently paroled after serving time for accidentally killing a man in a saloon fight. Judy books Elvis into a studio, cuts a demo, and tries to get him a record deal. But the slick record exec rips them off, so Judy and Elvis start their own record company. Their first release, "Treat Me Nice," is a big hit. Judy and Elvis kiss — so sweet a kiss! — but soon break up. After performing the great song "Jailhouse Rock" in an NBC spectacular, Elvis goes very Hollywood and loses contact with the people who helped him. Eventually his ex-con buddy punches him in the neck for being mean to Judy, and there are fears for Elvis's pipes. But Elvis recovers, embraces Judy, and sings another tune, and they sell their little indie record company for $750,000 and live happily ever after.

It didn't work out that way for Judy Tyler. On July 4, 1957, she and her husband were driving east from California, toward New York and their apartment on West Forty-fourth Street. Judy had finished shooting *Jailhouse Rock* just three days earlier, and the Lafayettes were eagerly heading home with their cat and dog in the car. It was nighttime, and Greg Lafayette had been at the wheel for hours. In Rock River, Wyoming, he apparently swung into a lane of oncoming traffic to avoid hitting a hay truck that was pulling onto U.S. Highway 30. Their car slammed into another. It was a terrible and bloody wreck. The driver of the other car was killed instantly, as were Judy's little dog and cat. Judy Tyler and her husband were taken, alive, to a hospital in Laramie, but Greg Lafayette died two hours later and Judy was dead by the following morning. She was twenty-three years old.

Judy's friends were devastated. There was a big funeral for Princess Summerfall Winterspring a few days later in Hartsdale, New York. All Doodyville, past and present, went. When a potentially tremendous career is nipped in the bud, everyone is miserable. People who were there say it was the saddest funeral they ever attended. I cried for several days after I heard the news of Judy's death, and I still feel the loss all these years later.

Elvis Presley felt it too. When the Associated Press reached him at home in Memphis, Elvis said: "Nothing has hurt me as bad in my life. All of us really loved that girl. I don't believe I can stand to see the movie that we made together, now." Indeed, when *Jailhouse Rock* was released in December 1957, Elvis refused to go to the premiere. *Jailhouse Rock* was undeniably the best movie Elvis Presley would ever make, and it remains a bitter irony that neither he nor Judy Tyler ever saw it.

During the autumn of 1957, Howdy Doody allayed his grief at the death of Princess Summerfall Winterspring by plunging into his work. In October, he and Buffalo Bob posted a hundred-dollar reward for information leading to the identification and location of the eight children who had served as Howdy's first studio audience back in December 1947. These young adults would then be invited to appear on Howdy's upcoming tenth-anniversary gala, to be broadcast on December 28. On November 2, Howdy announced a giant contest to find the American child with the most winning smile. This "Smile Contest" was billboarded on the next few shows and received massive promotion from NBC and much publicity. Five weeks later parents were told to send in pictures of their children; the winners would receive a thousand dollars and an encyclopedia, plus a trip to Doodyville and an appearance on the show. Within a month, more than two hundred thousand photographs filled Roger Muir's office, proof positive that ten years old or not, *The Howdy Doody Show* could still attract the under-eight crowd on Saturday mornings.

Howdy's tenth-anniversary show was a gala of sentiment and nostalgia. It was Howdy's twenty-two-hundredth show, a special hour-long live broadcast with a big band in Studio 8H, Toscanini's old lair. The theme was "This Is Your Life Howdy Doody," and, sure enough, the host of *This Is Your Life,* Ralph Edwards, appears on the show with a huge volume purporting to be Howdy's biography. The Buffalo sings "Happy Birthday" to Howdy and dives into the program. Three of the original Peanuts are introduced, now all college students in their late teens. There's an ad for Howdy Doody Modeling Compound, made by the Kid-O company, then a bit with Mr. Cobb and Clarabell, then a spot for Wonder Bread. Next we are introduced to an old friend, Pierre the Chef! It's the return of Dayton Allen! (For Dayton, this was a star turn — he had become one of the hottest comics in America on NBC's prime-time comedy hour, *The Steve Allen Show,* which ran on Sundays at eight opposite Ed Sullivan. In the role of "Man in the Street" — which he shared with comics Don Knotts, Tom Poston, and Louis Nye — Dayton was one of Steve Allen's funniest features. "Why not?" was Dayton's constant punchline, delivered in a tone of belligerent idiocy, and he convulsed the nation week after week.) As Pierre the Chef, Dayton decorates the face of a sleeping Chief Thunderthud with cake icing; Clarabell cleanses the Chief with a torrent of seltzer. A chase ensues, just like old times.

Then more looking back. Howdy's 1949 Peabody Award is trotted out, as is Billy Oltmann, who at age five had beaten out seventeen thousand other contestants in a Howdy lookalike contest back in 1950. The Buffalo reminisces about Howdy's campaign triumphs in '48 and '52, and sings "I'm for Howdy Doody." After ads for Hostess Cupcakes and Tootsie Rolls, there's a parade through Doodyville. We see Kokomo Junior, Dilly Dally, Windy Scuttlebutt, Heidi Doody, the Flubadub, Grampa Doody, and other characters float by. This proves to be a setup for the ten finalists of the big "Smile Contest," chosen from among the quarter-million entries that had poured in by airtime. At the end of the show, Bob holds up Lew Anderson's brand-new album, *Clarabell Clowns with Jazz,* and tells the kids to go out and buy it. Then the finale: "The Goodbye Song" and the peal of church bells, with the Buffalo now urging a visit to church "or place of worship." Stay tuned, he says as the old kine fills the take-up reel, for *Fury* and *Rough & Ready.*

*   *   *

198

The Howdy Doody Show began to get very tired and jaded in 1958, as if no one took it very seriously anymore. Many of Doodyville's citizens had branched out to new and lucrative ventures, leaving the Buffalo as the only permanent resident of the madhouse now televised from Studio 6B. Producer Roger Muir was also working with Pinky Lee (now recovered) and puppeteer Shari Lewis, while Nick was doing *Gumby* and other things. Bobby Keeshan was a smash as Captain Kangaroo and was on five mornings a week, totally eclipsing Howdy. Dayton Allen was a big star on Steve Allen's show. Lew Anderson had his own band, which played in clubs. After Dr. Jack Weinstock removed his partner Willie Gilbert's ruptured appendix in January, the pair began work on several outside projects. (Howdy's two writers would later go on to write the book of a Broadway musical based on Shepherd Mead's satiric book, *How to Succeed in Business Without Really Trying.* With the aid of composer Frank Loesser and the great play-doctor Abe Burrows, the show was an immense hit on Broadway in 1961, and won a Pulitzer Prize for Jack and Willie's collaborators.) Even Judy Tyler was a big star because of *Jailhouse Rock,* although she had been in her grave for almost a year.

All this success vexed Buffalo Bob Smith, who couldn't get arrested outside of Doodyville. That the Buffalo felt a certain resentment over this issue is evident from an extraordinary press release that NBC issued under Bob's name in June 1958. Titled "Why I'd Like to Do an Adult Eastern," the release is a three-page *cri de coeur* and plea for work. After explaining that he had begun his career as an "adult entertainer" on the radio and had been NBC's drive-time jock until Howdy had gotten too big for him to do both jobs, he chronicles his success with Howdy. Then, he writes, "a strange thing began to happen. As I became more and more identified with the character of Buffalo Bob it became increasingly difficult to sell just plain 'Bob Smith, adult entertainer.' Commercials, for instance, play a big part in augmenting a performer's income. But what sponsor of cigars would ever think of using 'Buffalo Bob' (the kid entertainer) to pitch his golden Havana filler? Somehow, parents frown on their kids smoking cigars. Not one sponsor in a hundred, not one casting director for a dramatic show, not one producer looking for a host-emcee or variety performer would think of 'Buffalo Bob' for a part. The fact that the adult entertainer, Bob Smith, probably sold a record amount of merchandise via TV, didn't sway them.

"Inasmuch as Howdy Doody, now in its 11th year, shows no sign of weakening, I'll probably stay in the role of Buffalo Bob forever . . . and love it! But sometime, just once more before I head for that great TV studio in the sky, I'd like to do a show as Bob Smith — for grown-up people — sort of an adult Eastern.

"Well [the Buff concludes, and you can almost hear the wistful sigh in this last 'graph], back to Doodyville!"

A tired and jaded Howdy Doody. What was he like?

Among Doody aficionados, one show of this era stands out. This is the notorious "Val Carny" episode from the fall of 1958, a show with so many on-camera crack-ups that parts of it are occasionally televised even now on "blooper" programs. "Val Carny" is also typical of a new Doodyville that rehashed and parodied the show's somewhat sordid past, in an unconscious effort to exorcize all the guilt over commercialization and exploitation that floated over Howdy's cast like an evil spirit.

Here's the "Val Carny" show, on a poor-quality videotape made available by a collector.

Enter Clarabell, carrying a sign announcing that the Val Carny Carnival is coming to Doodyville Park. Val Carny is played by Bobby Nicholson gotten up as a Buffalo Bill–style huckster with a cowboy hat and long flowing hair. Carny announces to Dilly Dally that his show is lacking something surefire that'll knock 'em dead. Enter Buffalo Bob, who invites Val to meet the Peanuts. "Do I have to?" Nicholson ad-libs, and both actors laugh involuntarily.

After a Thunderthud/Clarabell chase and concurrent Peanut pandemonium, Val Carny announces that he intends to sign Clarabell for his show and storms out. "I don't think he should have our Clarabell," the Buff says to the Peanuts. "We need Clarabell here in Doodyville. Kids, this could be serious. But Clarabell would *never* leave Doodyville," he reasons. "I'm sure of that."

Then Bob does an ad for a kids' swimming pool, which includes the line that the pool is "impervious to mildew and rot." Smith obviously thinks it's absurd to say this, and begins to break up at the line, laughing so hard that tears come out of his eyes. At this, the cameramen and floor people start to giggle. Still laughing, Bob does a scene with 'Thud and the clown. When Clarabell lets the Chief have it with the shpritz, Val Carny chortles with joy. In the next scene, Val offers Clarabell a huge contract to join his show. "Sign on the dotted line, young fella, and you'll be treated right."

Just then the Buffalo bursts in, still trying not to laugh and almost choking in the process. "Don't sign it, Clarabell! Do you know what this means? You'll have to leave Doodyville! You'll be leaving all your friends!" The Buffalo seizes the contract and accidentally rips it in two, thus further cracking himself up; he collapses into a purple-faced spasm of uncontrolled laughter. To get through the scene, he pretends to be crying. The other actors, Lew and Nick, are also trying to compose themselves as Lew grabs Val Carny's contract and signs it.

Clarabell leaving Doodyville and all his friends? Sound familiar? We're seeing a replay of Bobby Keeshan's supposed treason and disloyalty back in 1952. You can bet that poor Clarabell will be made to pay for this.

"Don't worry, Clarabell," Val Carny says to his new star. "You're working for me now. You'll have new friends. You'll have *me*. You'll meet Millie the tattooed lady and Phyllis the snake charmer!" Clarabell responds enthusiastically at this implied suggestion of sex, and Carny sneers, "I *knew* that'd get ya!" Clarabell packs his zebra-striped suitcase and disappears with Val.

Later in the show, Howdy and Buff and Thunderthud visit the Val Carny Carnival to see how Clarabell is getting along. But they are alarmed to see that Clarabell is being forced to walk a high wire without a net, even though he is terrified.

"You can't do that!" the Buffalo protests.

"He has to," Carny says. "He signed a contract. I don't care how scared he is."

With the help of early matte and chroma-key effects, the Buffalo goes up the wire and rescues Clarabell. "Steady . . . I'm coming after ya, buddy . . . careful, buddy . . . attaboy!"

Val: "Clarabell, you're fired! And Buffalo Bob, I'll never hire anyone from Doodyville again."

Buffalo: "That's right! No one would ever work for you. Poor clown, he can't even read."

The actors have managed to get through this part of the show without laughing too much, but at the end of this scene, Nicholson/Carny ad-libs to the Chief, "Get away from me, you Indian. What foolishness! Clowns and Indians, that's all I get around here." This slays the whole cast, and they fall apart again.

But now time is running out. The Buffalo announces that next week's show will feature Tizzy the dinosaur and tells the audience to stay tuned for Jimmy Blaine and *Rough & Ready*. As the credits roll, Clarabell appears and rips up his contract with Val Carny. The clown's tenure in Doodyville would last another two years.

The last two years of Howdy Doody's decline, 1959 and 1960, were sad ones for former Peanuts like myself. By then my father had left *Today* and the editorial side of the television business altogether. Rather than move his family all the way to California, where almost all network television was now being produced, he went to work for a large advertising agency, and we relocated to suburban Philadelphia to be near the company's headquarters. I remember those Saturday mornings when Howard and I would watch *Howdy* along with my younger brother, then four years old, whose interest wasn't much aroused by the spastic little marionette whose trials and tribulations our father had once concocted. Howard was unashamedly nostalgic for his days in relatively uncomplicated and cozy Doodyville, but none of us cared much for Howdy's now silly and sometimes violent plot lines. A show in 1959, for example, had a South American rebel leader named El Bandito coming to Doodyville to kill Buffalo Bob. It was up to Howdy and Clarabell to bring El Bandito to justice. In another show from that year a gunslinger came to Doodyville and vowed to drive Chief Thunderthud out of town. He brandished a gun at the Chief, something that would have been anathema in the days of Eddie Kean's strict prohibition of weapons. But by this time Jack and Willie were phoning the shows in, and *Howdy* was becoming more and more borscht belt. In early 1960 several shows concerned the kidnapping of Howdy Doody by a Turk called (get ready for the schmaltz) Prince Howlvah.

This was also the era in which sponsors got pushier. Again the client Ovaltine (Smith hated the stuff and called it Ovlatrine in rehearsal) demanded that, after twelve years of silence, Clarabell's first word be "Ovaltine." But the client was refused. Anything that wasn't nailed down in Doodyville could be sold (and by then over six hundred products had been merchandised), but not Clarabell's first word. Howdy still had *some* integrity.

But by 1960 all the old creative types had gotten out of network television, which had been taken over by the ad salesmen, the accountants, and the lawyers. During the summer of that important transitional year, the salesmen measured the attention span of their demographic targets on Saturday morning and made the fateful and irrevocable decision that low-budget cartoons were a better buy for the networks than live studio shows like — that's right — *Howdy Doody*. The networks realized they were paying thousands of dollars a week to kiddie hosts whose shows couldn't be repeated, when cartoons were cheap to begin with and their infinite number of reruns cost nothing. In September 1960, NBC announced that *Howdy Doody* (which had lost many longtime sponsors) would be canceled and replaced by an inexpensive taped show starring Shari Lewis, a precious and cloying ventriloquist sponsored by the National Biscuit Company who talked to sock-puppets with names like Lamb Chop and Hushpuppy.

NBC announced this sad news in a press release dated September 15, 1960. A special one-hour colorcast would mark the closing of *The Howdy Doody Show;* it would air Saturday, September 24, at 10:00 A.M., and would feature Howdy and the gang literally packing their bags and leaving Doodyville forever. If you read between the lines of this wistful release, it seems obvious that Jack and Willie were going to milk Howdy's swan song for every drop of maudlin sentimentality it was worth. As soon as the (generally expected) news of the cancellation had reached Doodyville, Jack and Willie had proposed that Clarabell finally speak on the last show. Everyone agreed that it was a touching idea and a great way to go out. Indeed, by 1960 it was Clarabell who lingered in the minds of the young American public as Howdy's biggest star. "Perhaps even more than they will miss Howdy and Bob," *Time* magazine reported on the last show, "U.S. kids will miss the mute clown Clarabell, who always sounded a sweet horn to indicate 'yes' and a sour one for 'no.' "

Howdy's swan song was taped in one of NBC's sixth-floor studios sometime in the third week of September in front of a Gallery composed of the children of NBC and Howdy employees. "It was very sad," Bob Nicholson remembers. "We were putting an institution to rest. But it wasn't too maudlin. Jack and Willie wrote the script, and there was some argument over whether Clarabell should talk. We all sobbed a little bit; after all, you can't work with people for years and years under all circumstances and not feel sad about wrapping."

Let's go to the videotape. Howdy's last show (Bill Lecornec's whiskey voice announces that it is the two thousand, three hundred and forty-third) opens with the Buffalo standing in front of an empty Peanut Gallery, silent and poignant. There follows a sequence with Sandra the witch (voiced by Rufus Rose), during which the Peanuts are led in. Then Clarabell mimes to the Buffalo that he has a big surprise for everyone. "Later, Clarabell," says the Buff, brushing off the poor clown.

Cut to an ad for Nabisco Rice and Wheat Honeys. Then back to Chief Thunderthud; he's packing his trunk. Clarabell comes in, ties the Chief to the trunk, and then cools him off with a spurt of seltzer.

Out comes Howdy's memorabilia. They trot out the old Peabody Award from 1949, but it has lost any meaning by this point. Here's the 1948 Howdy for President poster, and the Buff does a chorus of "I'm for Howdy Doody."

Then it's goodbye to the Doodyville animals — the legendary Flubadub, my father's bears, Hyde and Zeke, Mambo the elephant, Tommy Turtle, and other grotesques.

Sob.

Then Clarabell comes in with a sign that says CLARABELL'S BIG SURPRISE, but the clown soon loses control, soaks Mr. Cobb, and is banished off camera before the surprise can be revealed.

It goes on like this for a while, nostalgia amid spasms of seltzer. All the while, Clarabell's surprise is put off, heightening the suspense in a vain attempt to stay Howdy's inevitable end at 10:59:50 EDT. Longtime sponsors Marx Toys and Colgate with Gardol are lauded. Mr. Bluster announces his deep depression and regret because he won't be mayor of Doodyville anymore. Corny Cobb brings out a scrapbook, and there's more groveling: the "Howdy Daddy" show in '49; the Howdy lookalike kid in '50; the cast freezing their behinds riding in an open car at the Saint Paul Winter Carnival in '53. The Buff, Corny, and Clarabell perform the surefire Three Phonebooth Routine, a chase invented by Eddie Kean thirteen years earlier.

As the end of the hour approaches, *The Howdy Doody Show* begins to get very sad. The camera lingers on the hard-core Doodyville gang — Buffalo Bob, Dilly Dally, the Flubadub — as Howdy says goodbye for the last time. One final time, the Buffalo sings "The Goodbye Song," but the lyrics have been changed because he won't, after all, be seeing us next Saturday.

When the song is over, in *The Howdy Doody Show*'s last seconds after thirteen years, the camera dollies in close, *very close,* to Clarabell. There is a little drumroll, and Clarabell's face completely fills the screen. The drumroll stops, and Lew Anderson, fighting back the tears, manages to croak out, in a cross between a sob and a whisper . . .

"Goodbye, kids."

Fade to black. The Peanuts are stunned and silent. There is a tinkling of the celesta to break the spell. Roll credits.

Like millions of other Americans who had been alerted to the end of *Howdy* by a media blitz that September, my father and I watched Clarabell say goodbye on that last show, he with fascination and regret, and I with an Attitude. At that point I was thirteen years old and above it all, too embarrassed about my childhood association with Howdy to crow about my too-recent Peanuthood. My father had tears in his eyes as I switched off the set and went out to play ball in the brave sunshine of autumn.

Buffalo Bob Smith was also watching at home, thanks to the miracle of videotape, with his five-year-old son, Chris. When the show was over at last, the Buffalo later told a reporter, "I ran out of the house and quietly went to the golf course. I didn't play very well that day."

Bob Smith with a fan during the Howdy Doody *revival in 1970.* (EDDIE KEAN COLLECTION)

Ten

The Revival Shows

To-night has seen me assume the motley for a short time — it clung to my skin as I took it off, and the old cap and bells rang mournfully as I quitted them forever . . .

— Joseph Grimaldi, 1828

THE GOOD CITIZENS of Doodyville were distraught over the cancellation of Howdy Doody. Hadn't Howdy himself almost single-handedly invented television? Wasn't *The Howdy Doody Show* the longest-running show on the air? Hadn't the little feller earned his masters at NBC an estimated two hundred million dollars over the past thirteen years?

"The crew was very broken up," Lew Anderson remembers. "They had been together a very long time. The sadness at the end was very emotional and very sincere. Most people never saw each other again."

And so scattered the citizens of Doodyville. Buffalo Bob left show business. For a while he stayed in New Rochelle, playing golf and hanging out at his liquor store. Then he bought an apartment house in Fort Lauderdale, Florida, and moved south. For years he had been taking summer vacations at a cabin he had built on a remote lake in northern Maine; now, in his retirement, the Buffalo bought a radio station in nearby Calais, Maine, and then two more in the area. The man who had done more than anyone else to introduce television into the American home was really a radio buff at heart. Bob loved to take a shift at the microphone at one of his stations and do six hours of small-town radio on some big local occasion like Rotary Day.

And the others?

Bobby Keeshan was still on the air as Captain Kangaroo — low-key, medium cool, the antithesis of his role on *Howdy* — and would remain at CBS for two more decades. Roger Muir and Bobby Nicholson stayed in touch and formed a TV production company that had its biggest success when Nick came up with *The Newlywed Game*

208

in the mid-1960s. Bill Lecornec disappeared into southern California. Lew Anderson continued to work in New York as an arranger and musician. Puppetmaster Rufus Rose took almost all of the puppets in the cast home to his studio in Connecticut and stored them in a barrel, expecting (like many Howdy oldtimers) that they would somehow be on the air again soon. In 1961 fire broke out in Rose's workshop, gutting the area where Howdy, Bluster, and the others were stored. In his anguish over the damage, Rose told the press that Howdy had burned up, and this was front-page news all over America the following day. NBC then sued Rufus Rose and his insurance company for neglect.

It turned out, however, that Rufus had in fact stored Howdy and the gang in a steel barrel, and that the puppets had only been scorched and soaked. Rufus Rose countersued NBC. When the lawyers were finished, there was a settlement: NBC retained ownership of the characters, but the court awarded physical possession of the puppets to Rufus to use as he saw fit, provided he didn't try to put them on the air.

It also turned out that the real Howdy had never been in any danger, because the original puppet, the one made by Velma Dawson back in 1948, had gone home with Bob Smith. Rufus had Double Doody. Photo Doody, the still-life doll with ball sockets for joints, had stayed with Roger Muir.

Howdy Doody was forgotten during the sixties, although he was subliminally remembered by elements of the emergent youth culture, surfer division, who kept Thunderthud's war cry, "Kowabonga," au courant throughout that dangerous and exhilarating decade. During the sixties the generation for which *The Howdy Doody Show* was created and broadcast participated in cultural and political upheavals unprecedented in American history. There was a mass protest movement, spawned by the civil rights marches and sit-ins, that (with a little help from the folk-song people) evolved into a broad-based peace movement during the escalation of the Vietnam war late in the decade. The Peanuts grew up with the assassinations of the Kennedy brothers and Martin Luther King. They became college students, hippies, peaceniks, draftees, and ordinary kids worried about their jobs, the ecology, and the Bomb. The Peanuts — many of them, at least — experienced Alienation. Buffalo Bob was replaced as generational father-figure by media-wise gurus like Professor Timothy Leary, who advised the Peanuts to eat mind-bending hallucinogens and Tune In, Turn On, and Drop Out. Other gurus told the Peanuts to meditate and Be Here Now. The Beatles told the Peanuts to Let It Be. The Rolling Stones told them to Let It Rock. Lyndon Johnson and Richard Nixon told the Peanuts to go to Southeast Asia and fight communism.

By the end of the sixties, Howdy's old Peanuts were a pretty confused bunch. In 1970 they decided they needed another fix of Howdy Doody Time. And so commenced the Howdy revivals.

The first Howdy revival began as part of the trivia craze that swept American campuses in the late sixties. Already nostalgic for the cozy innocence of the secure fifties, students began asking each other arcane questions about the Flubadub's animal lineage and the number of brothers in Phineas T. Bluster's family.

In 1970 Buffalo Bob Smith was living in Florida half the year and in Maine the other half. Except for his local notoriety in Lauderdale and his radio personality in Maine, Bob had spent the decade that followed the last *Howdy* broadcast in obscurity, "irrelevant," in the terminology of those ideologically charged times.

In January 1970 the Buffalo got the first call of the Howdy revival. It was from a senior at the University of Pennsylvania who wanted Bob to come up to Philadelphia and do a Howdy Doody show. "We wanna relive our carefree childhood days," the kid is supposed to have said. Bob said that he had a kinescope of Howdy's tenth-anniversary show he could show to the students, and maybe he could do a couple of tunes if they put a piano on the stage. The problem is, the always canny Buffalo told the kid, you can't afford me. But this was 1970, and the Penn students wanted their Howdy. The kid offered the Buffalo a thousand dollars. Bob said OK, asked for a percentage of the gate, and got it.

A few weeks later, police had to be called to the Irvine Auditorium at the University of Pennsylvania to control the crowds that had turned out to see the old Buffalo. The place was packed. Kids were hanging in through the windows. Buffalo Bob was greeted by the collegiate ex-Peanuts as if he were a lost god from their childhood. They screamed and stomped and whistled as they beheld their old pals Clarabell and Thunderthud on the kinescope Bob showed. Then Bob played a few numbers on the piano, and there was a question-and-answer session that got noticeably downbeat when the Peanuts asked about the Princess and the Buffalo told them her story and her fate.

Bob's performance got rave notices in the Philadelphia papers;

the wire services picked up the story and sent photos of Buffalo Bob — graying and a little heavy, maybe, but undeniably him — to papers all over America. Then nearby Temple and Villanova universities invited Bob to do shows, and the old Buffalo knew he was back in business. He got a booking agent, printed a brochure, had Willie Gilbert write some updated naughty lyrics that turned "The Rhyming Song" into a reefer gag, and toured on the college lecture circuit for two years.

Bob's young road manager on those tours was a college-age ex-Peanut from New Rochelle named Burt Dubrow. Burt had been one of those children who grew up knowing that Buffalo Bob ran a liquor store over in Wykagyl, and one day as a ten-year-old he took the M bus down North Avenue and walked into the store. Behind the counter was a man in dark glasses and a checked shirt. Burt asked the man if this was Buffalo Bob's store, and the man took off his shades, leaned down, and said, "I'm Buffalo Bob."

So Burt began to pester the Buffalo, in a nice kind of way. At first the Buffalo gave Burt a signed photo of himself and Howdy. Then Burt wheedled sixteen tickets to a Saturday Howdy show for his Cub Scout pack. The Buffalo took to sending Burt over to see Buffalo Vic in his shoe store across the street to get rid of him. Finally, Buffalo Bob started hiding in the back of the store when young Burt showed up. Burt then discovered that Clarabell lived in nearby White Plains, so he started bothering Lew Anderson as well. Eventually he clocked a lot of hours in the Peanut Gallery on the Saturday show and got to know many of the cast and crew.

Burt was a student at Graham Junior College in Boston when the Buffalo started doing his Howdy revival shows in 1970. He had stayed in touch with Bob and Lew Anderson during the sixties, and now organized a benefit show in Boston that would feature the return of Clarabell the clown. Lew came up to Boston with his original clown suit, but it had been ten years since he had put on the makeup, and in the end Burt had to remind him how to do it.

Soon after that, the Buffalo asked Burt Dubrow to be his road manager and master of ceremonies. Their first gig was two shows in Sanders Theater at Harvard University. I was also a student in Boston at that time, and I was in Harvard's Peanut Gallery for both of those shows.

The Harvard audience was rabid. Students packed the century-old wooden theater and began to chant the names of *Howdy*'s sponsors while waiting for the Buffalo. "TWINKIES, TWINKIES," they yelled. "WONDER BREAD, WONDER BREAD, WONDER BREAD!!!" Burt warmed up the crowd before showing the tenth-anniversary kine, and as he listed the Howdy characters the kids would see on the film, the audience got up and cheered. The loudest cheers, then and always, seemed to be for Clarabell. When the forty-eight-minute kine was over, Burt came back out and did his line: "And now, here's the man that every little girl wanted to marry and every little boy wanted to be — BUFFALO BOB SMITH!"

Pandemonium. Mania at Harvard, and at every other school they visited.

"Buff would walk out in his mustard-colored suit from the old days," Burt says, "and you'd have thought this audience had seen a ghost. Bob looked great, told the kids they were back in the Peanut Gallery, and from that moment on he was completely in command. You have to remember that this was in the middle of all the tension of the Vietnam war, and we saw Bob and felt . . . *He's come back for us.* The feeling in those halls was tremendous. You'd see college girls weeping. They were all smoking pot, and every night you could go out in the audiences and get a contact high.

"It was pure escapism. Everybody forgot about the war and rebellion. If Bob sang, *'Who's the funniest clown you know?'* they'd all sing back, *'Clarabell!'* like they were supposed to." Bob went out of his way to make it hip. He flashed the peace sign, sang about ending the Vietnam war in "The Rhyming Song," and did marijuana humor. The first of these jokes came early in the show. The Buffalo would hit a flat note on his piano and then lean over it and pull out a packet of Zig-Zags from inside. "That Clarabell," he moaned. "You never know where he's going to leave his rolling papers."

Pandemonium. The ex-Peanuts would go wild. *The Buffalo is with us.*

Bob kept the shows simple. There would be a couple of sing-alongs, and then the Buff would reminisce about the elections and other *Howdy* highlights and answer questions from the audience — mostly about Princess Summerfall Winterspring. Bob would somberly describe Judy Tyler's tragic demise, and the kids would gasp in shock — *Ahhh!* He would tell the kids about Bobby Keeshan and Dayton Allen and an embarrassing moment when a five-year-old Peanut with bladder urgency peed into a jack-o-lantern just off camera while Bob tried to do a commercial and the whole show cracked up. He'd tell the kids about the time a Peanut said "fart" on the old Howdy radio show. If things were really loose, he'd do some hokey old jokes.

He'd do piano humor, like playing "Chopsticks" in the style of Beethoven and Bach. He would try to get the kids to sing along with Eddie Kean's classic "Do Do a Howdy Doody Do (But Don't Do a Howdy Doody Don't)," but the kids usually didn't remember it. What they did remember were the words to the immortal "Brush Your Teeth with Colgate, Colgate Dental Cream."

This first series of Howdy revivals stretched over a couple of years in the early 1970s. Bob Smith did about five hundred shows and got a lot of publicity. Sensing a fad and a bonanza, NBC renewed copyright on Howdy Doody in 1972 and authorized a fresh line of Howdy merchandise for the trivia kids and the nostalgia market.

Not all the publicity surrounding the revival was so great. Bob's act was sometimes derided in the press as "second-rate" and "corny," and some critics deplored the marijuana jokes and general stonedness that seemed to surround the shows. The *New York Daily News* of April 1, 1971, said: "Buffalo Bob discounted talk that many college students are stoned on marijuana and view his antics as another way of enhancing their drug euphoria. The collegians simply wanted to be kids again, he insisted."

The first revival of Howdy reached an apex of sorts when Buffalo Bob did two shows at that Lower East Side temple of American counterculture, the Fillmore East. At first Bob hadn't wanted to play the infamous rock palace, but he relented after Burt Dubrow assured him that the Fillmore audience would be made up of the same kids who came to the college shows. It was the only time Burt ever saw Buffalo Bob Smith nervous backstage.

The two shows sold out in two hours, and the Fillmore kids cheered and shouted. "The whole audience was stoned," Burt says. "You couldn't see out there, it was so smoky." They sang along with "I'm for Howdy Doody" and laughed at the Buffalo's gags about Spiro Agnew, Vietnam, the Pill, and, as he put it, fags. The Fillmore shows were recorded for an album that Bob wanted to put out. Pianist Dick Hyman came out and accompanied him on a song Bobby Nicholson had composed especially for these two dates. Called "Ride On Through," it was intended as an affirmation of the Buffalo's ultimate faith in the generation whose early evenings and Saturday mornings he had occupied for so many years. "Ride On Through" was Buffalo Bob's way of telling us that times might be tough, but that he had faith in us and knew we would somehow carry on, tackle the world's problems, and solve them. *"You know, I once owned you kids,"* the song began. It was true.

At the end of every show, the Buffalo would yell "Right on" once or twice. His exit line almost every night was "Goodnight, sweet kids, I love you."

Eventually, the Buffalo's Howdy revival exhausted the college lecture circuit. Beginning around 1973, he and Lew Anderson teamed up to tour American shopping malls as Buffalo Bob and Clarabell, cutting ribbons and opening stores, spraying seltzer and giving away balloons just as they had in the old days.

Several years passed. In 1976 there was a second Howdy Doody revival when Roger Muir and Buffalo Bob got the show back on the air, this time in syndication. The effort was called *The New Howdy Doody Show,* and it bombed.

Serious discussions about a comeback for Howdy had begun in 1974, after the Buffalo and Clarabell had been doing the shopping-mall circuit for a couple of years. The genuine outpouring of emotion that Bob Smith and Lew Anderson experienced, all of it coming from adults (alumni, Smith called them), convinced the Buffalo that he and Howdy could pull off the hardest and most elusive trick in show business — the Comeback.

"The Mouse Club came back as reruns [in late 1974]," Smith remembers, "and we said, 'Why can't *Howdy* come back?'" So the Buffalo got together with the successful production firm of Nicholson & Muir, which found a bankroller, the giant Metromedia communications conglomerate, to finance a one-hour pilot to be presented to the networks and independent stations for syndication. The new show was written by Nicholson and Willie Gilbert (Jack Weinstock had died in the late 1960s) and featured a changed and crowded Doodyville plus a new Howdy Doody puppet with — incredibly — long hair.

The new-look *Howdy* was at least good enough for Metromedia to back a twenty-six-week daily series, or 130 episodes, a half hour every weekday, just like the old show.

The New Howdy Doody Show was taped in Miami and syndicated on stations all across America. The shows were taped in color in front of an expanded Peanut Gallery that included the whole family, not just the Peanuts themselves. Metromedia had insisted that the new *Howdy* have plenty of adult appeal as well as kid stuff, expecting to reach a market that included now-grown *Howdy* alumni as well as a new generation of video kids. The cast included a gray-haired Buffalo; a still-mischievous Clarabell Hornblow, played by Lew Anderson (the original, Bobby Keeshan, was in his *twenty-first* year as Captain Kangaroo); Cornelius Cobb, now designated a prop man instead of a storekeeper and played by Bobby Nicholson; "Nicholson Muir," a mythical producer played by Bill Lecornec (whom Muir had found working as a theater manager in Los Angeles); and Happy Harmony, Doodyville school teacher and Princess clone, played by actress Marilyn Patch. Also featured was a black singer and musician named Jackie Davis, the first cast member of color to perform in previously segregated Doodyville.

Since Rufus Rose had died in 1975, the marionettes on *The New Howdy Doody Show* were worked by New York puppeteer Paddy Blackwood. Roger Muir had overruled the Buffalo and insisted that the new Howdy have long hair, so the new puppet sported a brown bouffant "do" that swept down over his shoulders. Of the original puppets only Dilly, Bluster, and the immortal Flubadub made the comeback shows. They were joined by a new puppet, a flying saucer called Outer Orbit voiced by Bobby Nicholson.

Buffalo Bob and the rest of the gang had extremely high hopes for Howdy's comeback. Once they had all been stars on the biggest show in America. With this new show — featuring more music, a bigger studio audience, better color — they had a chance to ride the rainbow all over again. Veterans of the Comeback recall a poignant moment: in the final seconds before the beginning of taping for the first of the new shows, Buffalo Bob was standing in front of the puppet bridge, hidden from the audience by a curtain. Just before going out, Bob turned and took both of the new Howdy's hands in his, looked the puppet in the eye, and said, "Good luck, little buddy."

At that moment the curtain opened, the four hundred Peanuts and parents began to holler and whistle, and Buffalo Bob Smith stepped back into the brilliant glare of the white-hot studio lights.

But *The New Howdy Doody Show* was a flop in syndication. The networks ignored it, it failed to reach many major markets, and, since it was syndicated and not on a network, *New Howdy* aired at a different time in every city and never reached the massive unified audience of the old days. There were other mistakes as well. The larger Peanut Gallery of four hundred kids and adults destroyed the sense of intimacy the old show had, and with adults in the audience, the writers had no one on whom to focus the jokes. Eddie Kean had come up with some material, at Roger Muir's request, but Muir had rejected it. Kean's postmortem analysis applied to the whole effort:

"I couldn't write a gag that would appeal to both a four-year-old and a forty-year-old." No one else could either, and the long-haired Howdy marionette looked silly.

There were also some problems with continuity in the shows. Ten shows were taped every six days, with studio audiences never seeing a whole show. So the rhythm and spontaneity that had served the original Howdy so well in the wild and woolly days of live television was never allowed to build and careen as it once had. Instead, the shows seemed patched together and somewhat forced. In the end, the ratings told the story. The new *Howdy* had some small success in the Midwest and the South, but died on both coasts. When the time came for Metromedia to renew *The New Howdy Doody Show* for another twenty-six weeks, it declined. Howdy Doody had reached the end of the road.

The new Doodyville gang was disappointed but not really surprised. Everyone knew at heart that the old days were gone, and with them the era when doing a television show had actually been fun. There were a lot of recriminations and regrets. "I have mixed emotions," the Buffalo still says. "I don't think we should have changed Howdy. And we had too many in the Peanut Gallery. Instead of forty kids we had the alumni and their kids and it was too much. Most of all," he sighs, as if this were the one poison barb that had killed everything, "I wish they hadn't changed the original Howdy."

Lew Anderson, Clarabell from 1954 to 1960. (BURT DUBROW COLLECTION)

Eleven

Dangling in Time

It was a rousing good adventure! Let's not worry about whether it
was a dream or not!
— Phineas T. Bluster

I NEVER SAW *The New Howdy Doody Show* back in 1976, and
it's a good thing, too, because when I eventually watched some
episodes on videotape as part of the research for this book, I didn't
like what I saw. The old *Howdy* show and its vibrant young cast
had provided the iconography of my childhood. My family's association with Howdy Doody and my visits behind the scenes of the
Peanut Gallery had taught me the perspective of fantasy and reality
necessary to comprehend the craft of writing. Seeing *Howdy Doody*
created on a workmanlike, day-to-day basis gave me a sense of the
empowerment and confidence it takes to write for a living. In my
mind, Howdy deserved a treasured corner in the dim memory of his
generation, not a new haircut and a bunch of grandfathers running
around in makeup.

Beginning in the early 1980s, my father and I began to toy with
the idea of writing a book about *The Howdy Doody Show*. Over the
years we sent each other clippings from newspapers and magazines,
enough to amass a huge file, since by now Howdy Doody has become
a treasured symbol and paradigm for the Baby Boom generation,
most of whom, like Howdy himself, turn forty sometime during the
mid- to late 1980s.

The most interesting clippings so far seem to cluster around 1983.
In April of that year, I was walking down East Eighty-sixth Street
in New York when I looked at a newsstand and saw the headline
CLARABELL FIGHTING FOR LIFE screaming from the front page of the
New York Post. The jump to page 3 revealed that Lew Anderson
was in guarded but stable condition after undergoing double-bypass
heart surgery in Rochester. Around the same time, the Associated

Press reported (in a story picked up by almost every paper in the country) that a vandal had broken into Roger Muir's office and destroyed Howdy Doody. "They decapitated him and tore off an arm," Muir was quoted as saying. "We'll have to see if he can be fixed up. He's pretty badly hurt, though." The wire services sent out a gruesome photo of a dismembered Photo Doody, the stringless doll that had reposed under a glass case in Muir's office. (The doll was eventually restored by Paddy Blackwood; the murder remains unsolved, with no leads.)

In November 1983, an extraordinary article appeared in *TV Guide* under the title "Howdy Doody: the First Hippie." Written by journalist Jeff Greenfield with tongue stuck firmly in cheek, the article maintained that Howdy Doody was responsible for all the upheaval and rebellion of the 1960s. Howdy, Greenfield wrote, was "one of the most authentically subversive TV shows in American history."

He continues: "Consider what the real lessons of *Howdy Doody* were. In the moral universe of that program, *the grown-ups were the bad guys* [italics his]. The only more-or-less normal adult was Buffalo Bob himself, and he was often the butt of practical jokes. Almost every other memorable grown-up was either a manipulative, evil schemer, such as the Inspector, or an unbelievably pompous bore, such as Phineas T. Bluster.

"And who were the good guys? Howdy, of course, a kid; other marionettes, such as Dilly Dally and Flubadub; native Americans, such as Chief Thunderthud and Princess Summerfall Winterspring, automatically distanced from middle-class suburban grown-ups; and, of course, Clarabell the clown.

"Now does this moral universe remind you of anything? It should. It was, almost precisely, the good-guy-bad-guy lineup offered by the youth of the 1960s — *the same folks who had been nurtured at the knees of Howdy Doody and Company* [italics his]."

Greenfield went on to tie every issue from antimilitarism to environmentalism to the sayings of Chairman Doody, and declared that those typically sixties media of political expression, the be-in and the guerrilla theater movement, "came from a show that featured a fellow in garish makeup and dress spritzing seltzer or hurling pies at outraged grown-ups. It was that cultural mole, Clarabell the clown, who bears the dubious distinction of being the very first Yippie."

Clarabell? A cultural mole?

Dead on.

Greenfield's theory was of course picked up immediately by the wire services and duly disseminated to the nation's press. Down in Florida, the Buffalo was outraged. He called up Eddie Kean, after three decades, and asked him to write a rebuttal to be published under the Buff's name. Eddie wrote it, but *TV Guide* wouldn't print it. *USA Today,* in its front-page coverage of this burning controversy, quoted Jeff Greenfield as saying that it would be the worst day of his life if he offended Buffalo Bob.

The last word in this affair came from Abbie Hoffman a short time later, when the founder of the Yippies issued a ringing denial that Howdy Doody had been any sort of radical inspiration. Hoffman maintained that the show he had watched and been inspired by was the much more subtle and subversive *Kukla, Fran & Ollie.*

Those of us who watched both shows understand what Abbie was saying. Yet the Greenfield theory was given extra reinforcement in 1985 when the brilliant anarchomic Andy Kaufman died of cancer. Kaufman had gone further out than anyone to develop the bleak but hilarious *comedie noir* of the *Saturday Night Live* era in the 1970s. He often invited whole audiences out for milk and cookies after a show and reveled in the generally loathsome characters and personas his talent assumed. His many fans were shocked (but not really surprised) when, at Kaufman's death, the picture distributed with his obituary showed him holding a Howdy Doody doll close to his cheek.

In the mid-1980s, Howdy's generation, since childhood the mainstay of the American consumer state, attained maturity. By the time their immense population bulge hit the end of its first forty years, the Baby Boomers had become their country's buyers and sellers, and consequently the chief target of Madison Avenue's national advertising campaigns. By 1985 advertisers had discovered that a surefire way to get a Boomer's attention while he or she was leafing through a mag or watching the tube was to flash a picture of Howdy. That year Howdy returned to the airwaves, not as an entertainer but as a salesman. General Telephone & Electric (GT&E) flashed old black-and-white *Howdy* footage on the screen to remind us of the good old days. The Florida Tourist Board had a white-haired Buffalo Bob and Howdy beckoning inhabitants of the frigid North to come on down to Florida, the subtext aimed at the Boomers being *Say kids, what time is it? Look where Howdy is!* Metropolitan Life used Howdy in print campaigns, as did the Sony Corporation with not a trace of irony. The character that had once sold millions of RCA TV sets was now being used to move a better product from Japan.

Not that it mattered that much. By 1986, when Sony ran its Howdy campaign, the puppet was lucky to get any work at all. The TV universe that Howdy Doody had dominated no longer existed. Network television itself was declining in audience with every rating period, its programming eclipsed by cable TV, video cassette recorders, and independent stations. In 1986 the General Electric Company bought RCA, sixty years after the two companies were separated by court order. When, later that year, NBC announced that it would leave its studios in the RCA Building in New York after more than half a century, my father and I decided that we'd better get over to Doodyville for one last look at the site before it was lost to us forever.

NBC guards its studio complex in the RCA Building quite tightly, and normally the only way civilians like ourselves can gain access is through the official studio tours, guided by NBC pages and restricted to star attractions like the sets for *Today* and *NBC Nightl News*. But Howard and I wanted to go to Doodyville on a nostalgic visit to the place where both of our careers had begun, so we had to pull some strings. Fortunately, after leaving NBC thirty years earlier, Howard had chosen to go into the advertising business, and by this time he was an officer in one of the largest ad agencies in the world, N. W. Ayer. It took only a call or two to get us our own private NBC junior ad exec for a jaunt through the RCA Building.

The past washed over us as we entered the giant art deco lobby. It was my first visit to the building in many years, and I recalled my childhood awe at the monumental 1930s murals and the black marble floor inlaid with great bronze rectangles. We took the elevator to the forty-seventh floor to pick up our guide (and his all-important building pass) and then descended again to the third floor. At first we were confused, since it has been extensively remodeled over the years. The old "green room" area where Grace Kelly used to shmooze with other NBC contract players is now an office and storage area. After a few wrong turns we finally found Studio 3A.

Doodyville. At last.

On the day of our visit in January 1986, Studio 3A was set up for an NBC kids' show called *Main Street,* whose simple stage occupied the same corner of the studio where I had once sat in the Peanut Gallery. My father found the old studio basically unchanged, except for advanced technology and the absence of a window for the control room. We stood there for a minute. The day's show had already been taped, and Doodyville was dark and quiet. We looked at each other and heard the faintest of echoes — the splash of seltzer, the wild laughter of excited children.

We pressed on to the control room, confident that we would run into some of Howard's old NBC colleagues, since many of the young war-vet technicians who began their NBC careers in the late 1940s when they were in their twenties are now reaching retirement age and have been with the network as seasoned and very unionized pros for all these years. Indeed, one of the first people we encountered was an audio man who had been at NBC since 1950. He told us he had worked on *Howdy Doody* and almost choked when I asked if he had any memories of that one-time terror of NBC, Dayton Allen. One day, he said, he had made the mistake of getting on an elevator with Dayton, who predictably displayed himself to a woman passenger. Content to find that Dayton Allen legends still circulated around the network after all this time, we began to say our goodbyes to Doodyville, but the audio man ran after us and caught us at the elevator. In 1952, the man wanted to tell us, he had been showing a girlfriend a darkened Studio 8H, Arturo Toscanini's old haunt. When he turned the studio light on, a furious Dayton had raised his head from a tryst on the studio sofa and told them to get the bleep out.

We continued our tour, visiting other studios, now occupied by the news department's morning and evening shows. Up on the sixth floor, the studio *Howdy* had moved to after it began colorcasting in 1955 is now occupied by WNBC's local news operation. As we watched the crew rehearsing for the evening's broadcast, my father recognized the operator of Howdy Doody's number two camera, B. J. Bjornson, who had worked on *Howdy* from the show's earliest days. Bjornson looked frail and elderly to me, but then I watched him manhandle a big video camera around the floor toward the news desk and felt the respect due a master artisan who had dedicated an entire career to perfecting his craft. Howard and B.J. had a nice reunion, and we stole up to the eighth floor to get a quick peek at Studio 8H.

Since 1975, the studio that NBC built for its great symphony orchestra has been the home of *Saturday Night Live*. Here frolicked the Coneheads and the Killer Bees. The team of Aykroyd and Belushi used this studio to project the spirit of guerrilla theater into

America's living rooms. We talked to some of the show's crew, idling between rehearsals for that weekend's live show. The lighting director had worked on *Howdy* and vaguely remembered my father, and I asked him what he recalled about life in Doodyville. He said that all he could really remember was Dayton Allen bumping and grinding against Rhoda Mann on the puppet bridge. "I'm a married woman!" Rhoda would shout. "I can't work like this," she would cry.

The lighting director asked me if Dayton was a millionaire now. I replied that Dayton was reputed to be very well off, and the man said that in the old days Dayton had always told everybody to buy gold stocks, which sold for pennies then and today are worth zillions. "Tell Dayton to come see us," the man said as we left. "He's got a lot of friends at NBC."

On the way down on the elevator, I thought of Proust's assertion that memories cannot be summoned by conscious processes, but only by the involuntary sensations of smell and taste. In the musty smell of that old deco elevator was some of the secret of my youth, and the acrid scent of Studio 3A meant as much to me as a dozen old *Howdy* kines. I'm sure that if I could but taste again the miniature loaves of Wonder Bread that were handed out to the Peanuts after every show, my astral self would leave my body and fly back into the past.

In a sense, the year I spent researching this book was a journey into the past. I located and visited and interviewed dozens of people who had worked on *The Howdy Doody Show* — cast members, crew members, NBC employees, and agency people, as well as dozens of Howdy's victims, all Baby Boom kids like myself, many of whom had actually sat in the Peanut Gallery or glumly remained at home while older siblings got to go. (This happened to my wife, and she still hasn't forgiven her older brother thirty-five years later!)

At first, my father and I thought it would be easy to track down the Doodyville gang. Almost everybody was in their late sixties and either still in the business or only recently retired from it. We knew that puppeteer Rufus Rose had died in Connecticut in 1975, after serving five terms in that state's legislature. Frank Paris, who built the original Howdy, had died in 1984 in southern California, his puppets and memorabilia maintained now by his colleague Alan Cook. While working on the book, we also learned that Alene Dalton, *Howdy*'s Story Princess, passed away in Salt Lake City in 1986.

Eventually, we found everyone whose words appear in this book, although some were easier to locate than others.

Roger Muir, Howdy's longtime producer, still runs Nicholson & Muir Productions in Larchmont, New York. His company produces TV game shows all over the world, and when last I spoke with him he was still trying to get Howdy Doody back on the air in time for his fortieth anniversary in late 1987.

Martin Stone, the pioneer behind-the-scenes showman who originated the *Howdy* show in 1947, is now a partner of Whitney Communications in New York. He sits on the board of the *International Herald Tribune* and operates from an art-filled office on the top of the Time-Life building in Rockefeller Center. This urbane, hard-nosed, and still powerful lawyer told me that not a day goes by without him missing the risky glamour of doing a live kids' show five nights a week, and I believed him. I knew the way he felt.

Bob Rippen, Howdy's first director, retired recently after a long career in communications at Rutgers University and still lives in the pretty town in central New Jersey where he grew up.

It was easy to find Dayton Allen, because he has a real-estate business in Ardsley, New York. Mostly retired from show biz, he occasionally deigns to take cameo roles in prestige films like *The Cotton Club,* a movie whose best scene the irrepressible Dayton walked away with.

Our interview was a scream. It began in his office in the old graystone gatehouse he inhabits with his wife, Elvi, a beautiful actress who once auditioned for the Princess role on *Howdy* after Judy Tyler left. (She was rejected when KAGRAN discovered she was Dayton's girlfriend.) Dayton shpritzed and fibbed at every turn. He peeled a banana and ostentatiously tossed the peel on the floor near where I was sitting. It turned out he didn't like interviews, and he claimed he couldn't recall Howdy Doody very well. Soon we moved into the living room so Dayton could more easily debate the fine points of their mutual history with Elvi. When things calmed down, I asked about the legendary "blue" Howdy rehearsals. After some hemming and a soupçon of hawing, Dayton allowed that, yes, "Sometimes we'd do some blue material in rehearsal. I say 'blue,' but today you could do that stuff in church." Most of the gags, Dayton said, involved conversations between Howdy and Mr. Bluster on the remarkable aspects of the Princess's figure.

"Dayton," I ventured in a mock-conspiratorial tone when Elvi had left the room, "what about all these stories of beautiful hookers visiting the dressing rooms of certain Howdy cast members?"

The distinguished senior comedian blushed slightly and snorted away a laugh. "Oh yeah, sure," he said, "there were a couple of nuns we used to entertain. We used to shake their hands and lead them on studio tours. Then we'd always go back to the dressing rooms so they could sit down and rest."

Rhoda Mann, Howdy's original puppeteer, lives right down the road from Dayton in Westchester County. She's still one of the first-call voiceover people working in commercials. So is Allen Swift, the Man of a Thousand Voices, who also paints in his sumptuous north-lit studio on West Fifty-seventh Street near Carnegie Hall. Ted Brown, the New York deejay who became Bison Bill after Bob Smith's heart attack, is the ever-suave morning man on New York's WNEW and keeps a Howdy doll displayed in his apartment on Central Park West. "Howdy was such a great opportunity for me," he says in tones similar to those of all Howdy's people. "All of a sudden, I was on the number-one show in television. Back in 1954, I led Macy's Thanksgiving parade, and that was definitely one of the biggest thrills of my life."

Scott Brinker, the Staten Island cabinetmaker who built all of *Howdy*'s props and most of the major marionettes, divides his time in retirement between homes in Florida and New Jersey. His wife, Edith, held *Howdy*'s cue-cards until the last show in 1960. In the basement of Brinker's lakeside house in western New Jersey are hundreds of ancient Howdy Doody kinescopes, by far the most complete collection anywhere, including at NBC.

The young NBC staff makeup artist who designed Clarabell, Dick Smith, is still in the business. In 1985 he won an Academy Award for his brilliant work on *Amadeus*. When I contacted him, Dick Smith protested that he didn't want to be known for his work on *Howdy Doody* because he thought Clarabell's was the worst makeup job in the history of clowning.

Lew Anderson, the third and final Clarabell, is a working arranger and bandleader in Manhattan; he also releases albums of his jazz and pop arrangements and leads a monthly lunchtime band at the Women's Republican Club in midtown. He makes occasional appearances as Clarabell with Buffalo Bob, steadfastly maintaining the clown's mute integrity since his one sanctioned slip-up on September 24, 1960. Anderson's only other real lapse as Clarabell's human incarnation was in a cable-TV special for teenagers, where Lew took off his clown makeup and costume.

The first Clarabell, the klutzy ex-page who everyone thought had no talent, went on to become a television legend. *Captain Kangaroo,* which began in 1955, stayed on daily television until 1982, when CBS expanded its morning news show and ate up the Captain's twenty-seven-year-old time slot. CBS moved the Kangaroo to weekends and canceled the show in 1984, twenty-nine years after its premiere, the longest run in network television history. The kid who supposedly had no talent outlasted Howdy by nearly a quarter of a century. There never had to be a *Captain Kangaroo* revival.

I met with Bobby Keeshan in his old office at CBS. Portly and prosperous (he is reputed to own part of the huge ICM agency), he was happy to talk about his days as Clarabell, but his remarks hinted at a lingering sadness over the way his tenure as America's favorite clown had ended. It's no secret that Buffalo Bob Smith never forgave Bobby Keeshan for leaving Howdy and then becoming a bigger success than the Buffalo. Smith even insulted Keeshan when he was interviewed for a *People* magazine tribute to Captain Kangaroo, saying that the two people who followed Bobby in the role of Clarabell had more talent in their little fingers than Bobby had in all his two hundred pounds.

I asked Bobby Keeshan what his reaction was to the Buffalo's sour grapes. Looking out his window over the graying Hudson River, the old clown said, "I feel I have to say this. I was a young kid, nineteen years of age, with no experience or background whatsoever. Bob Smith gave me an opportunity. *He* didn't think it was an opportunity; if he had thought it was an opportunity he probably would have given it to one of his friends. But at that time you still couldn't get anybody to work in television.

"But he did show enough faith and confidence in me to give me this opportunity. And he also taught me. I learned so much from Bob Smith. His sense of timing was awesome; I have that sense of timing now. He taught me things about timing, about putting a show together, back-timing a show — everything I used on *Captain Kangaroo*. One of the reasons that *Captain Kangaroo* was such a success is that it ran so smoothly, and that happened because I ran that show with all the talents that Bob Smith taught me. He is my father in the business. I give him one-hundred-percent credit for my success, because I would not be here today if I hadn't learned all the technical aspects of the medium from him. I put what he taught me to work on *Captain Kangaroo,* and we ran for thirty years.

"And to this day," Keeshan concluded, shaking his head in exhausted wonderment, "he won't acknowledge that *Captain Kangaroo* was any kind of success."

Anyone looking for the scattered citizenry of Doodyville should be prepared to spend some time in southern Florida. The Buffalo is in Lauderdale for six months of the year, not far from his old friend Bob Nicholson, who has retired from a long career in television and music (he was conductor of the well-regarded Westchester Symphony for many years after leaving Howdy). Eddie Kean, Howdy's protean creator from 1947 to 1954, lives in Miami's Coconut Grove section and works as a writer. He also enjoys playing piano in various Miami hotels and clubs. He often starts his sets with "You Make Me Feel So Young" and still feels protective of Howdy's integrity as a symbol of innocence. Bill Lecornec — nasty Chief Thunderthud — also lives in Miami. He moved there when *The New Howdy Doody Show* brought him in from California. Bill liked the weather and stayed.

My search for my childhood in Howdy Doody had begun during the summer of 1984, when I dreamed that dream about Princess Summerfall Winterspring. I found the Princess, all right, incarnate in the memories of those who had worked with and loved her, animate in the old Howdy kinescopes and cavorting with that other vanished godling, Elvis, in *Jailhouse Rock.* To learn more about Judy Tyler, I found her first husband, Colin Romoff, who is still one of the premier vocal coaches in New York. Colin put me onto Judy's mother, Mrs. Lorelei Hess, who lives near Chicago. Mrs. Hess eventually told me how to find Judy. So, two years after my quest for the Princess had begun, I found myself at the entrance to the Ferncliff Mausoleum in Hartsdale, New York. Judy Tyler's remains are interred with those of her second husband in the mausoleum's Nizanger Room. I thought very hard about Howdy Doody's supernaturally beautiful goddess of love as my footsteps sounded loud on the stone floor and I laid a bouquet of forget-me-nots against the cold wall by her tomb. Driving home afterward, I recalled the jumble of things I had heard about Judy Tyler. Keeshan had called her an enigma, a wild creature who had suffered the abuses of life as a child star. Colin Romoff's words kept coming back to me. "What I remember of her now," he had said, "she probably would have been a major star on Broadway, dominating the late nineteen-fifties and the sixties. She had wonderful presence, terrific ears, she would have sung better as she went along, she was a good actress. She would have made a major mark."

As I thought about Judy Tyler that night, my eyes stayed wet for a hundred and fifty miles.

Of course, I found the old Buffalo as well. After some arduous detective work (Roger Muir gave me his phone number), I tracked down the veteran pioneer at his hideout deep in the cold lake forests of northern Maine. To get there, I left my home near Boston at three in the afternoon on the eve of the summer solstice in late June. Heading northeast on the Maine Turnpike, I threaded through Portland and Augusta and Bangor and then turned east toward Canada on the famous "Airline Highway," Route 9 — a hundred miles of woods, lakes, logging trucks, and mountainous grandeur. The sun set in my rearview mirror about an hour before I hit the end of the line — Calais, Maine, hard by the New Brunswick border, so far east that when the sun rose again it was four in the morning, Atlantic time. I awoke at seven in the International Motel, to which I had been directed by the Buffalo, who lives another hour north of Calais. (I knew I had arrived in Buffalo Country when the motel clerk the night before volunteered that Bob Smith had told him to expect me.) After breakfast with some Micmac and Penobscot Indians at the local McDonald's, I headed north on mighty U.S. 1, in this territory a two-lane blacktop logging road that connects Indian reservations and picturesque Colonial (read Tory) Maine villages. To find Buffalo Bob, you have to turn off the main road in whiteclapboard Princeton and head toward Grand Lake Stream. It's a one-lane road that crosses solitary wooden bridges over roaring lakefeeder streams in the middle of luxurious nowhere. It's total Moose Country. After some convoluted turns I found the Buffalo's driveway and then paused halfway down it, letting the motor idle for a minute. Grand Lake is so quiet that later the sharp-eared Buffalo would ask me why I had stopped in the road on the way in.

Buffalo Bob and Buffalo Mil Smith live here next to Grand Lake six months of the year. The house is a Mainesque Bavarian chalet, very comfortable and tasteful, whose walls display a collection of local antique farm and craft tools. A Sony Betamax cassette recorder sits atop the television. Bob's big Mercedes waits in the garage. The only sign of Bob's long rule in Doodyville is an inscribed blue coffee mug that rests on a table. It says "Buffalo Bob" and was given to him, coincidentally, by my father for Christmas in 1954.

The Buffalo and I talked for several hours on his roomy screened-in porch, protected from the strong solstitial sun by the shade of tall oak trees. The porch overlooks the huge, serene, unbroken lake, which melds with the ice-blue sky and a distant green island to compose the Big Picture, a northern wilderness vista whose foreground contains a beautiful motorized guide canoe that Bob moors at a little jetty in front of the house. The local birds sang and called to each other in counterpoint to our conversation. The Buffalo is an expert storyteller, and his memories of his show are generally accurate, with the usual biases and opinions thrown in. After all these years, some slightly tall tales have been invented to stretch through parts of the story that are messy, embarrassing, or best forgotten. Bob wiped tears from his eyes as he talked about his father, but then sprung to the attack whenever we spoke of Bobby Keeshan. Old rivalries die hard, and later that year when Keeshan's big comeback special on CBS was rudely panned by the TV critics, the naughty Buffalo sent copies of *Variety*'s devastating review to a few of his friends.

The Buffalo sold his radio stations a few years ago and now spends his time fishing, swimming, golfing, and cooking. Ever the choirmaster, he plays the organ both at his Lutheran church in Pompano Beach and at the Congregational church in nearby Princeton, Maine. He told me that he and Lew Anderson still do appearances at malls, and from time to time Bob and Howdy can be seen on commercials and TV specials, such as the NBC fiftieth-anniversary broadcast in June 1986. (Bob and Howdy appeared on this program in a tribute to Kukla's puppeteer, Burr Tillstrom, who had died earlier that year. But Buffalo Bob never thought much of the Kuklapolitans, and he made this clear in the ditty he and Howdy sang on the show. This NBC special also replayed Clarabell's final "Goodbye, kids," which the network had to obtain from a collector.)

Buffalo Bob Smith is still a natural ham and an uninhibited showman, and the thing that emerges most clearly from our conversation is that the Buffalo wants back into show business. He's seventy years old, with white hair, a place in Florida, millions in the bank, a Benz in the garage, three strong sons — everything most people spend their entire careers working for. But the Buffalo wants *more* career! How, though? *The Howdy Doody Show* is gone forever. NBC told Howdy's old producers that it wasn't even interested in putting a fortieth-anniversary special on the air when Howdy turned forty in December 1987. NBC told Howdy to get lost. And Bob Smith *knows* the old days are gone forever. "You can't afford to do a show like *Howdy* anymore," he said. "This is why even *Captain Kangaroo* went off the air. The numbers just aren't there. How are you going to get the ratings your sponsors need when your audience is two to twelve? When we make appearances, people ask me why Howdy isn't on today. I point out that even shows like *Sesame Street* need corporate sponsors like IBM to keep going."

Bob Smith has mellowed with age. His manner and his pitch are softer now, and his act, once corny and a little forced, is more subdued. Most of all, Buffalo Bob still has that magic, that ability to step right through a TV screen and talk to children. This was demonstrated to me when Bob Smith and Clarabell appeared on *Sally Jessy Raphael,* a nationally syndicated talk show produced by the Buff's old road manager, Burt Dubrow. Bob was sitting at the piano, talking to the audience, and he looked into the camera and asked a rhetorical question. My seven-year-old daughter, watching with me at home, gazed back at the Buffalo and answered him. All this time off the air, I thought to myself, and he still has *it.* I won't be surprised if this snow-haired septuagenarian makes a big comeback one day.

As my research for this book started to wind down, my father retired after a forty-year career in television and advertising. When he left NBC in 1958, Howard Davis joined the old-line agency N. W. Ayer and stayed there for the rest of his career. Ayer has handled AT&T's advertising since the nineteenth century, and it was this account that Howard occupied himself with, in most of its many aspects. Ayer is a world-class agency, and my father was evidently much loved there, since his colleagues threw him a moving retirement party in their fortieth-floor offices overlooking Rockefeller Center. The company is now located in Burlington House, an immense slab of steel and glass at Fifty-fourth Street and Sixth Avenue. As I walked toward the building to go to Howard's party, I remembered that on this site had once stood the old Ziegfeld Theater, where chorines had danced and where my father had broadcast Howdy in color back in 1953. Outside Howdy's studio at 30 Rockefeller Center, the Sixth Avenue of my childhood had been composed of old New York blocks of brownstones and shops. Now media-owned monoliths seem to march down both sides of the avenue like a regiment of mammoth soldiers. I looked around and realized that the New York of my childhood — lunch at Schrafft's, Checker cabs, theater matinees, Howdy at 5:30 — was a thing of the past, irrevocable and far away.

Up in the executive suite, we had drinks overlooking the great metropolis at twilight, then a cordon bleu dinner and a round of affectionate toasts. Then the party retired to a comfortable lounge whose soft lighting emphasized the twinkling of other midtown towers that hovered near our own aerie. There was a piano player, and we harmonized on the songs of my father's generation: "A Nightingale Sang in Berkeley Square"; "Comin' In on a Wing and a Prayer"; "We'll Meet Again." I felt very proud as I watched my handsome father bask in the praise and esteem of his friends that night. He had always seemed to me emblematic of his generation, those young people who had conquered fascism and returned to invent a new world. I had a bittersweet taste in my mouth the night of his retirement party, as if I were attending a changing of the guard.

After I interviewed everyone my father and I could find who had been connected to *Howdy Doody,* I started to think about the puppets. Where was the Doodyville gang?

Buffalo Bob has Velma Dawson's original Howdy Doody. Howdy, happily retired in Florida, lives in a glass case in the Buffalo's pad. His twin brother, Double Doody, having narrowly escaped a flaming demise in Rufus Rose's workshop, is unfortunately now institutionalized in Washington, D.C., where he resides within the walls of the Smithsonian Institution. Occasionally, Double Doody is put on display, incorrectly identified as Howdy. Their brother, Photo Doody, rebuilt after his mugging, stays at home with Roger Muir in Westchester.

The fate of some of the other puppets is uncertain. Many were lost in the same 1961 fire that almost took the life of Double Doody, and some of those in the Rose collection today may be reconstructions. The Flubadub and several other key marionettes are missing.

I drove down to Margo Rose's house in Connecticut one winter day to visit the surviving Howdy Doody puppets. It was a sentimental journey, since Rufus Rose and my father had been friendly, and I had come to the Roses' house on the shore of Long Island Sound thirty years before with my parents. The Rose family has been on this land since the seventeenth century, and I remembered the house and puppet theater Rufus had built, with its little stage that gave onto the large living room whose walls were and are bedecked with an impressive collection of old clocks.

Rufus died in 1975, but his wife, Margo, an expert craftswoman who built many of the later *Howdy* marionettes, still lives in their house. She is in her eighties and continues to be active in puppetry, teaching at the nearby Eugene O'Neill Center for the Arts. After we talked for a little while about Rufus and about her life on *Howdy Doody*, Margo asked me if I wanted to see the puppets. Yes, I gushed in spite of myself, and a strange feeling came over me as she led the way out a back door to the garage.

Margo keeps the survivors of the 1961 fire in a trunk in her garage. As I stood and gaped, she took Phineas T. Bluster out of his storage bag and hung him up on a rack. Bluster swayed before me, perfect in every detail, from monocle to waistcoat. Then she brought out Heidi Doody, the little blond sister my father wrote in for Howdy. Margo hung up Heidi and brought out Dilly Dally in his glasses and red sweater. In swift succession, Captain Windy Scuttlebutt, Grampa Doody, Inspector John J. Fadoozle (in exquisite tweed cape and deerstalker hat), Buzz Beaver, and Mambo the elephant were in turn suspended from Margo's rack. Then she reached into another trunk and hung up the copy of Howdy that she had built late in the show, as well as Tom Turtle and an Indian princess puppet that dates from about 1959, Howdy's penultimate year.

I stood there for a long moment, gazing at the dangling cast of *The Howdy Doody Show* as they hung there in the garage, swaying gently in late-afternoon light, completely suspended in time.

Acknowledgments

Thanks and love to Judith Arons for her wisdom and her grace.

Most humble thanks to all the citizens of Doodyville who helped with memories and archives for this book, especially Howard and Hana Davis, Eddie Kean, Robert Keeshan, Burt Dubrow, Lorelei Hess, Martin Stone, Scott Brinker, Bob and Mil Smith, Roger Muir, Dayton Allen, Bill Lecornec, Allen Swift, Rhoda Mann, Margo Rose, Bob Rippen, Bob Nicholson, Lew Anderson, Ted Brown, and Colin Romoff.

For supporting this mad endeavor with assistance both material and spiritual, thanks to Ron Bernstein, Christina Coffin, Beth Rashbaum, David and Anne Doubilet, Fritz Jacobi, Peter Smith, Joe Dine, NBC, Alan Cook, Velma Dawson, Alan Greenberg, Stephen Arons, James Isaacs, Bill Glasser, Barbara Beardslee, the David Beiber Archives, Lily Aisha Arons Davis, the Nelsons, Ruth and Andy Dean, Rob Friedlander, Lee Trombetta, Roy Pace, and N. W. Ayer, Inc. (Louis T. Hagopian, chairman). Thanks also to Chris Davis and Dorothy Straight.

The best published information on *The Howdy Doody Show* appears in a monthly newsletter, *The Howdy Doody Times,* which is the official journal of the Doodyville Historical Society. This book must acknowledge a debt to the newsletter's two editors, Tom Johnson and Jeff Judson, who have been publishing it since 1978. (For subscription information write HDT, 12 Everitts Hill Road, Flemington NJ 08822.)

Other sources used in preparing this book include *Saturday Morning TV,* by Gary Grossman (Dell, 1981); *About Television,* by Martin Mayer (Harper & Row, 1972); *Kids' TV: The First 25 Years,* by Stuart Fischer (Facts on File, 1983); and *The Golden Age of Television,* by Max Wilk (Delacorte, 1976).